ASGARDIANS OF THE GALAXY

THE WAR OF THE REALMS

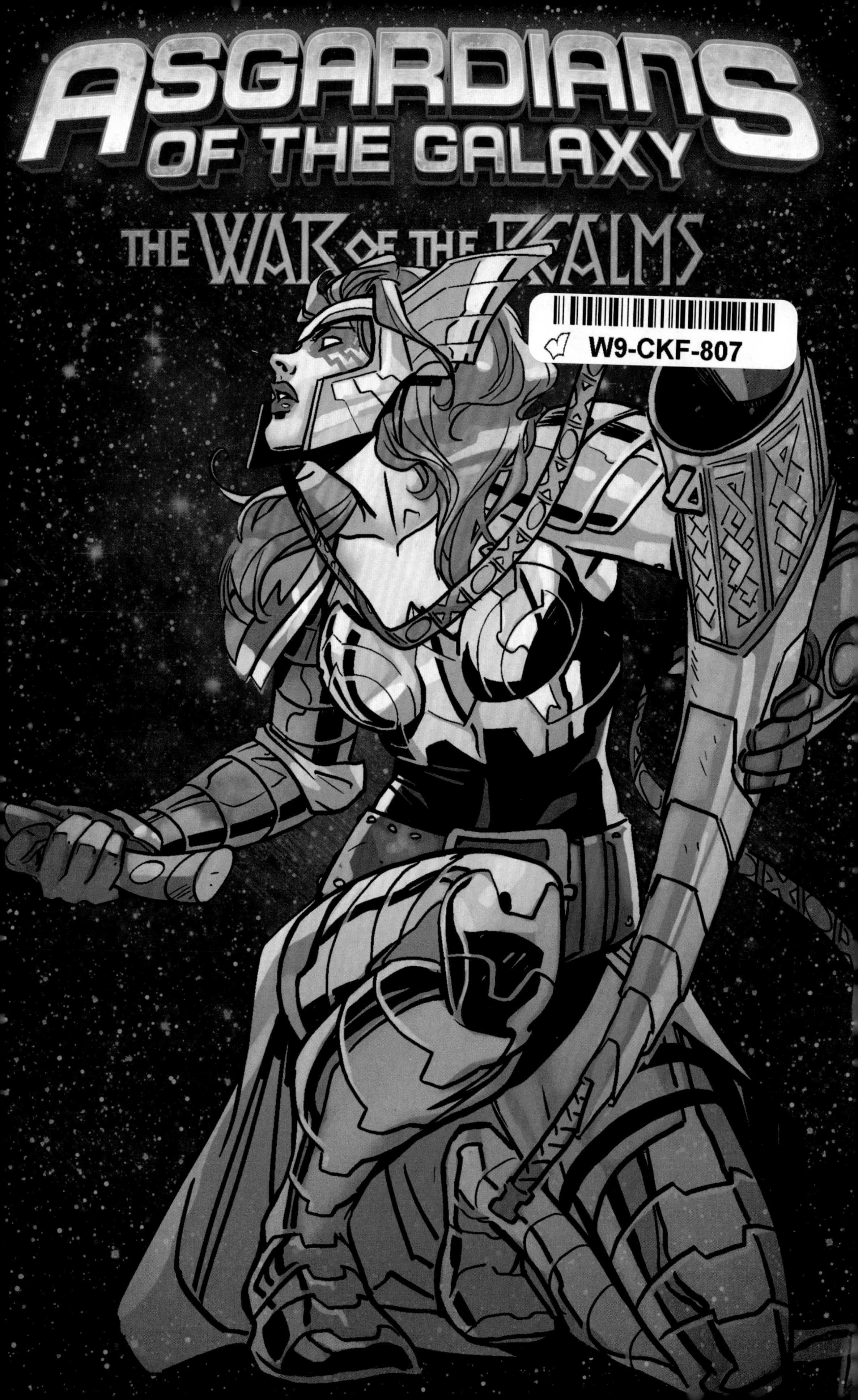

Intending to bring about Ragnarok, space pirate Nebula kidnapped a dwarf and forced him to lead her to an ancient horn that calls forth the **NAGLFAR**, an armada manned by now-soulless corpses of gods who have since been reborn into new bodies. To steal back the beacon, **KID LOKI**—a shadow of the "true" Loki—made a bargain with Thor's sister **ANGELA**: For her help recruiting and leading a team of Asgardians against Nebula, Loki promised to help her find her ex-girlfriend **SERA**, who mysteriously disappeared months ago.

With a little trickster magic, the Asgardians were successful, and Thor entrusted Angela with the Naglfar Beacon. Loki has a plan to hide the beacon for safekeeping and make good on his bargain with Angela. But can the god of lies be trusted this time?

ANGELA

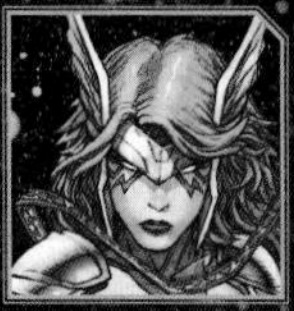

The firstborn child of Odin and Freyja, Angela was kidnapped and believed slain by the Queen of Angels, but a handmaiden rescued her. When Heven was reopened to the other realms years later, Angela's heritage was revealed. Branded a traitor by both Asgard and Heven, she now lives by her own code: Nothing for nothing—everything has its price.

VALKYRIE

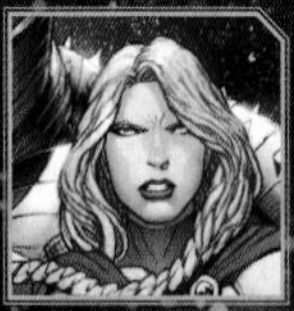

Brunnhilde served Asgard for centuries as the leader of the Valkyrior, warrior goddesses who usher the worthy fallen to Valhalla. More recently, she led the Fearless Defenders, a group of women selected to be the shield maidens of Midgard.

ANNABELLE RIGGS

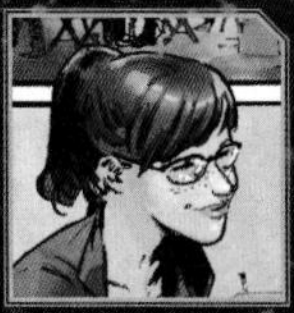

Archaeologist Annabelle Riggs joined the Fearless Defenders and died saving Valkyrie from the power of the Doom Maidens. Unwilling to accept Annabelle's sacrifice, Brunnhilde journeyed to Valhalla and brought her back by merging their life forces so they now share one body.

SKURGE THE EXECUTIONER

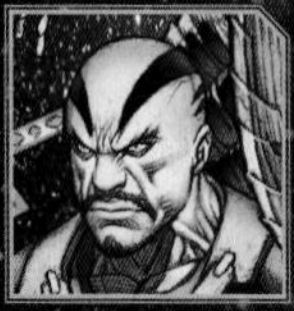

One of Asgard's greatest warriors, Skurge fell in love with Amora the Enchantress and has often fought fellow Asgardians in her name. He was redeemed when he died holding the bridge Gjallerbru against Hela with nothing but a pair of Midgardian M16s. Since then, he has wandered Hel in search of a purpose.

THUNDERSTRIKE

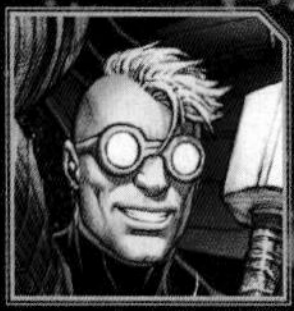

When Eric Masterson proved himself a true hero, he was granted the enchanted mace Thunderstrike by Odin. After Eric died in battle, Captain America gave the mace to Eric's son, Kevin, who soon proved himself worthy of the title and the weapon.

THROG

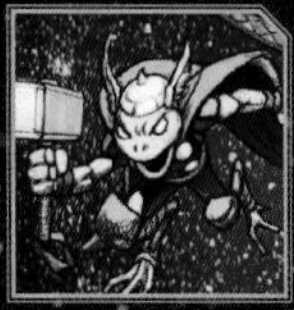

After his wife's death, Simon Walterson sought help from a witch, who turned him into a frog. When Loki turned his brother Thor into a frog, the two human-amphibians found themselves allies. Thor was soon restored, but Simon grabbed a fragment of Mjolnir and was transformed into Throg, the Frog of Thunder.

URZUUL

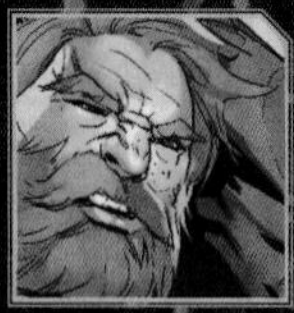

Desperate to prove herself stronger than Thanos' daughter Gamora, who recently kidnapped a dwarf to forge powerful armor for her, Nebula captured and murdered an entire clan of dwarves, leaving only Urzuul alive to build her a weapon. Determined to redeem himself, Urzuul has joined the Asgardians to help protect the beacon.

ASGARDIANS OF THE GALAXY

THE WAR OF THE REALMS

CULLEN BUNN
WRITER

MATTEO BUFFAGNI (#6-7),
STEFANO LANDINI (#7), **MATTEO LOLLI** (#8),
PAOLO VILLANELLI (#9) & **LUCA MARESCA** (#10)
ARTISTS

FEDERICO BLEE
COLOR ARTIST

VC's CORY PETIT
LETTERER

JAMAL CAMPBELL (#6-7) AND
GERARDO SANDOVAL & **ANTONIO FABELA** (#8-10)
COVER ART

WIL MOSS
SUPERVISING EDITOR

SARAH BRUNSTAD
EDITOR

TOM BREVOORT
EXECUTIVE EDITOR

ANGELA CO-CREATED BY
TODD McFARLANE & **NEIL GAIMAN**

SPECIAL THANKS TO **SILVIA MONTUORI**

COLLECTION EDITOR **JENNIFER GRÜNWALD**
ASSISTANT EDITOR **CAITLIN O'CONNELL**
ASSOCIATE MANAGING EDITOR **KATERI WOODY**
EDITOR, SPECIAL PROJECTS **MARK D. BEAZLEY**
VP PRODUCTION & SPECIAL PROJECTS **JEFF YOUNGQUIST**
SVP PRINT, SALES & MARKETING **DAVID GABRIEL**

BOOK DESIGN **SALENA MAHINA, ADAM DEL RE & MANNY MEDEROS**

EDITOR IN CHIEF **C.B. CEBULSKI**
CHIEF CREATIVE OFFICER **JOE QUESADA**
PRESIDENT **DAN BUCKLEY**
EXECUTIVE PRODUCER **ALAN FINE**

ASGARDIANS OF THE GALAXY VOL. 2: WAR OF THE REALMS. Contains material originally published in magazine form as ASGARDIANS OF THE GALAXY #6-10. First printing 2019. ISBN 978-1-302-91692-3. Published by MARVEL WORLDWIDE, INC., a subsidiary of MARVEL ENTERTAINMENT, LLC. OFFICE OF PUBLICATION: 135 West 50th Street, New York, NY 10020. © 2019 MARVEL No similarity between any of the names, characters, persons, and/or institutions in this magazine with those of any living or dead person or institution is intended, and any such similarity which may exist is purely coincidental. **Printed in Canada.** DAN BUCKLEY, President, Marvel Entertainment; JOHN NEE, Publisher; JOE QUESADA, Chief Creative Officer; TOM BREVOORT, SVP of Publishing; DAVID BOGART, Associate Publisher & SVP of Talent Affairs; DAVID GABRIEL, SVP of Sales & Marketing, Publishing; JEFF YOUNGQUIST, VP of Production & Special Projects; DAN CARR, Executive Director of Publishing Technology; ALEX MORALES, Director of Publishing Operations; DAN EDINGTON, Managing Editor; SUSAN CRESPI, Production Manager; STAN LEE, Chairman Emeritus. For information regarding advertising in Marvel Comics or on Marvel.com, please contact Vit DeBellis, Custom Solutions & Integrated Advertising Manager, at vdebellis@marvel.com. For Marvel subscription inquiries, please call 888-511-5480. **Manufactured between 6/21/2019 and 7/23/2019 by SOLISCO PRINTERS, SCOTT, QC, CANADA.**

10 9 8 7 6 5 4 3 2 1

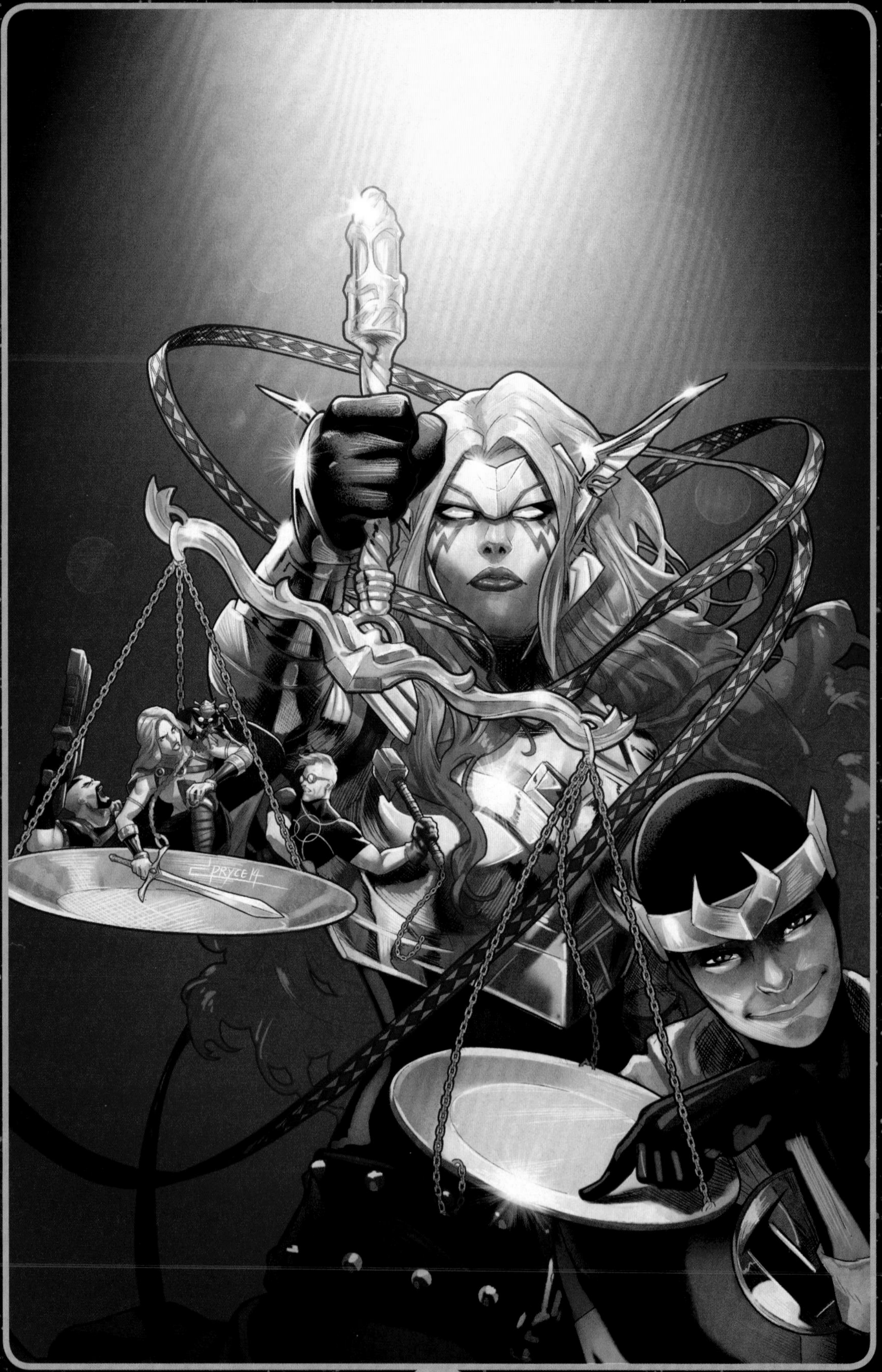

6

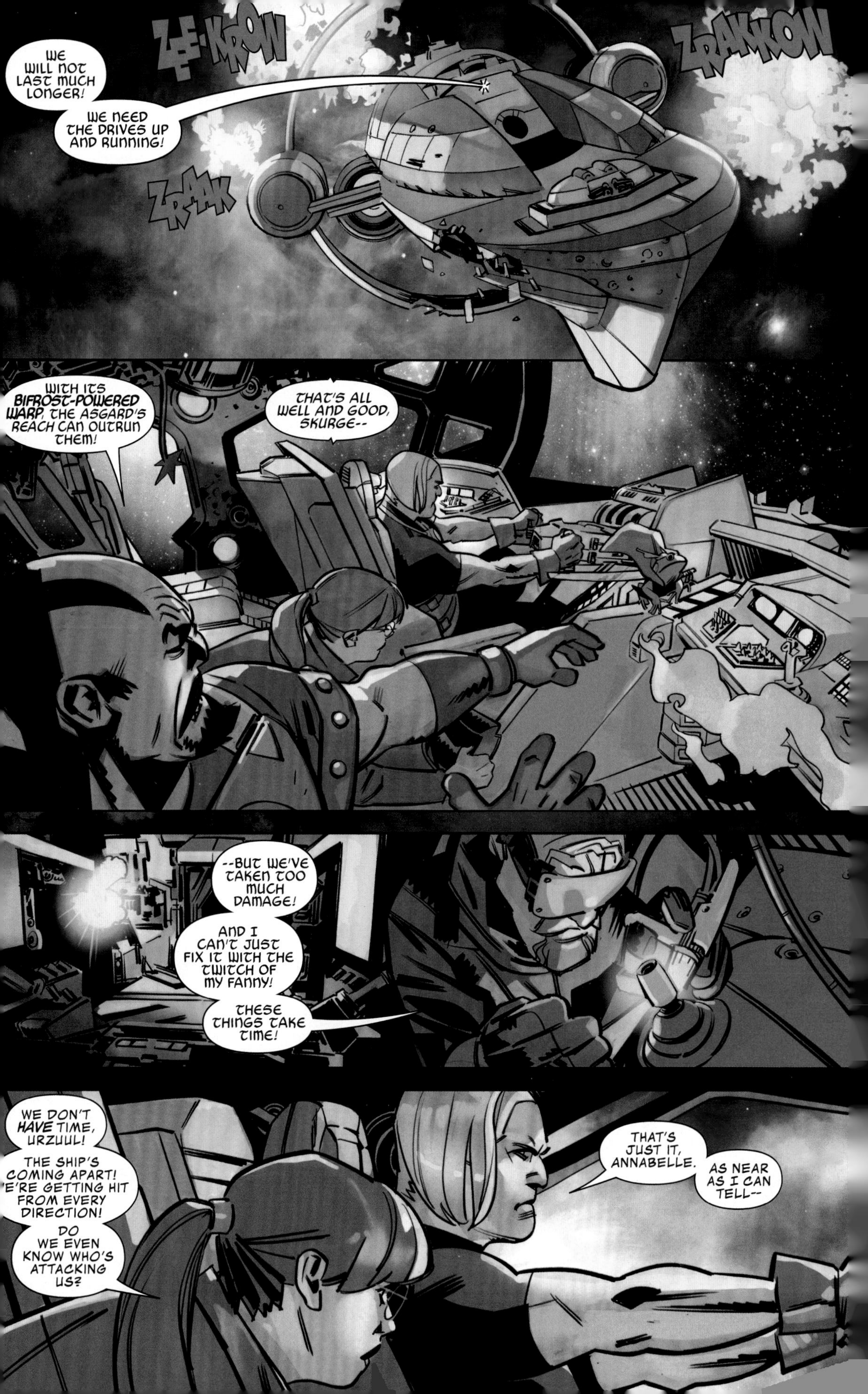
ZEE-KROW
WE WILL NOT LAST MUCH LONGER!
WE NEED THE DRIVES UP AND RUNNING!
ZRAKKOW
ZRAAK
WITH ITS BIFROST-POWERED WARP, THE ASGARD'S REACH CAN OUTRUN THEM!
THAT'S ALL WELL AND GOOD, SKURGE--
--BUT WE'VE TAKEN TOO MUCH DAMAGE!
AND I CAN'T JUST FIX IT WITH THE TWITCH OF MY FANNY!
THESE THINGS TAKE TIME!
WE DON'T HAVE TIME, URZUUL!
THE SHIP'S COMING APART!
'E'RE GETTING HIT FROM EVERY DIRECTION!
DO WE EVEN KNOW WHO'S ATTACKING US?
THAT'S JUST IT, ANNABELLE.
AS NEAR AS I CAN TELL--

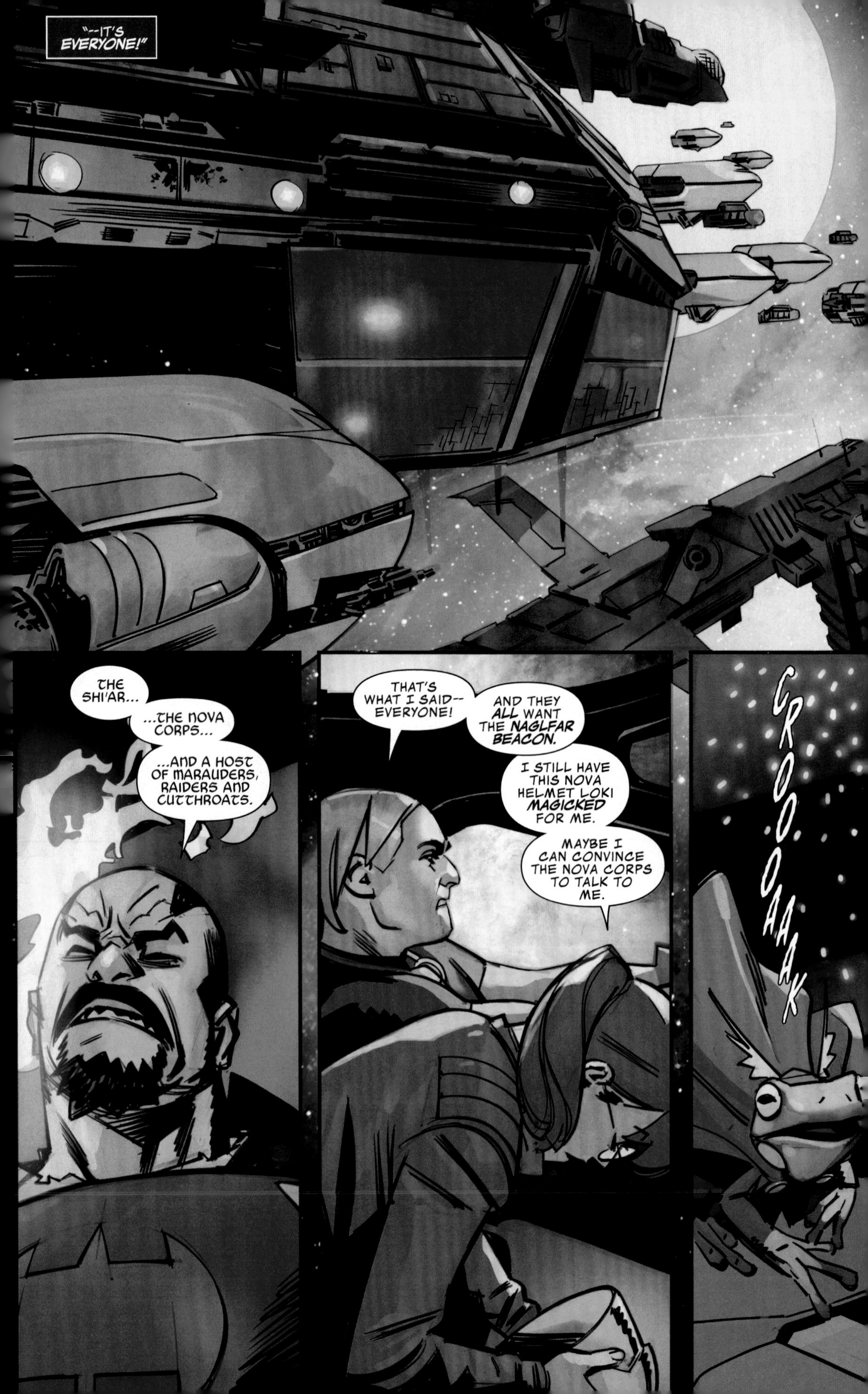
"--IT'S EVERYONE!"
THE SHI'AR...
...THE NOVA CORPS...
...AND A HOST OF MARAUDERS, RAIDERS AND CUTTHROATS.
THAT'S WHAT I SAID-- EVERYONE!
AND THEY ALL WANT THE NAGLFAR BEACON.
I STILL HAVE THIS NOVA HELMET LOKI MAGICKED FOR ME.
MAYBE I CAN CONVINCE THE NOVA CORPS TO TALK TO ME.
CROOOAAAK

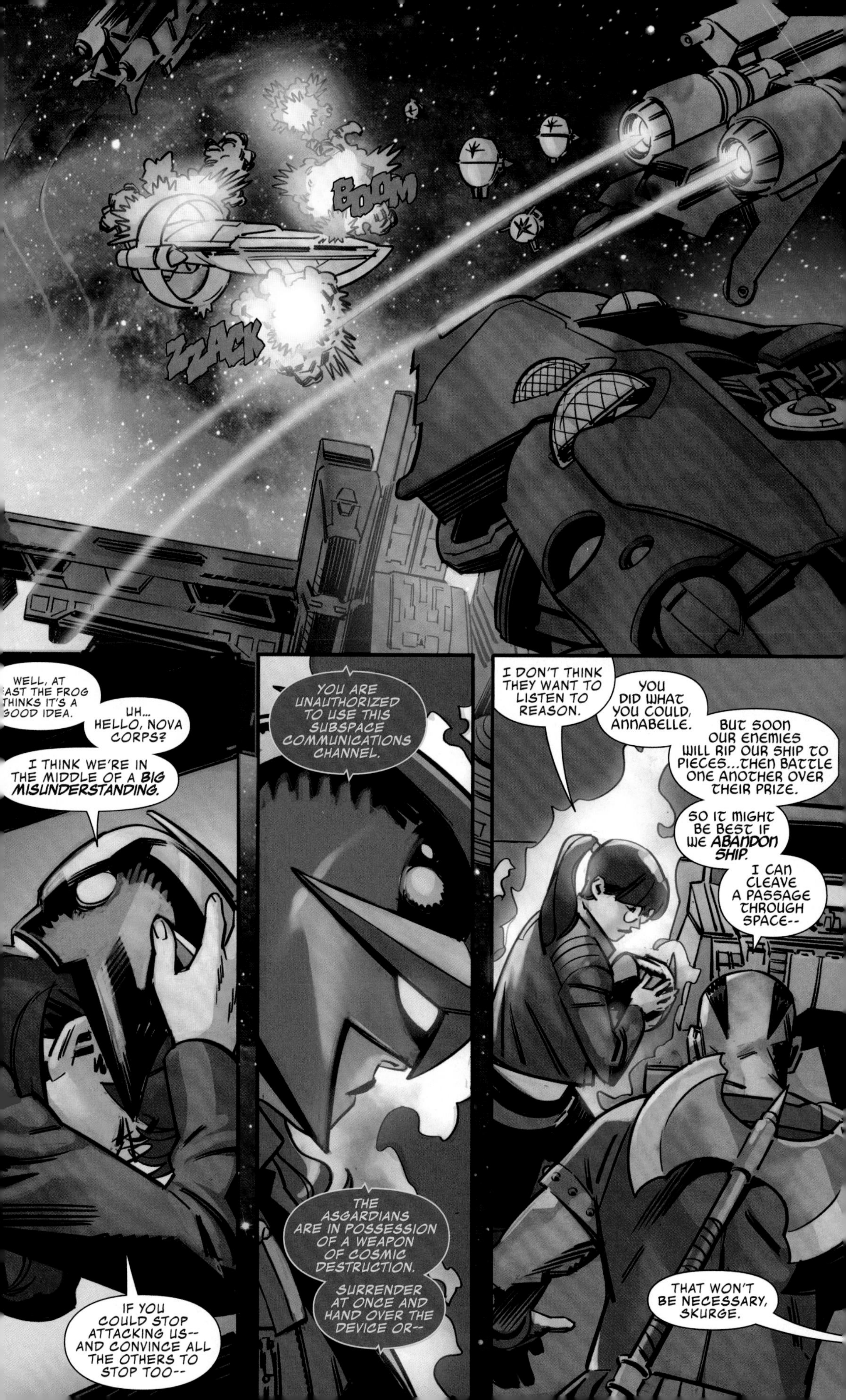
BOOM
ZZACK
WELL, AT LEAST THE FROG THINKS IT'S A GOOD IDEA.
UH... HELLO, NOVA CORPS?
I THINK WE'RE IN THE MIDDLE OF A BIG MISUNDERSTANDING.
IF YOU COULD STOP ATTACKING US-- AND CONVINCE ALL THE OTHERS TO STOP TOO--
YOU ARE UNAUTHORIZED TO USE THIS SUBSPACE COMMUNICATIONS CHANNEL.
THE ASGARDIANS ARE IN POSSESSION OF A WEAPON OF COSMIC DESTRUCTION.
SURRENDER AT ONCE AND HAND OVER THE DEVICE OR--
I DON'T THINK THEY WANT TO LISTEN TO REASON.
YOU DID WHAT YOU COULD, ANNABELLE.
BUT SOON OUR ENEMIES WILL RIP OUR SHIP TO PIECES...THEN BATTLE ONE ANOTHER OVER THEIR PRIZE.
SO IT MIGHT BE BEST IF WE ABANDON SHIP.
I CAN CLEAVE A PASSAGE THROUGH SPACE--
THAT WON'T BE NECESSARY, SKURGE.

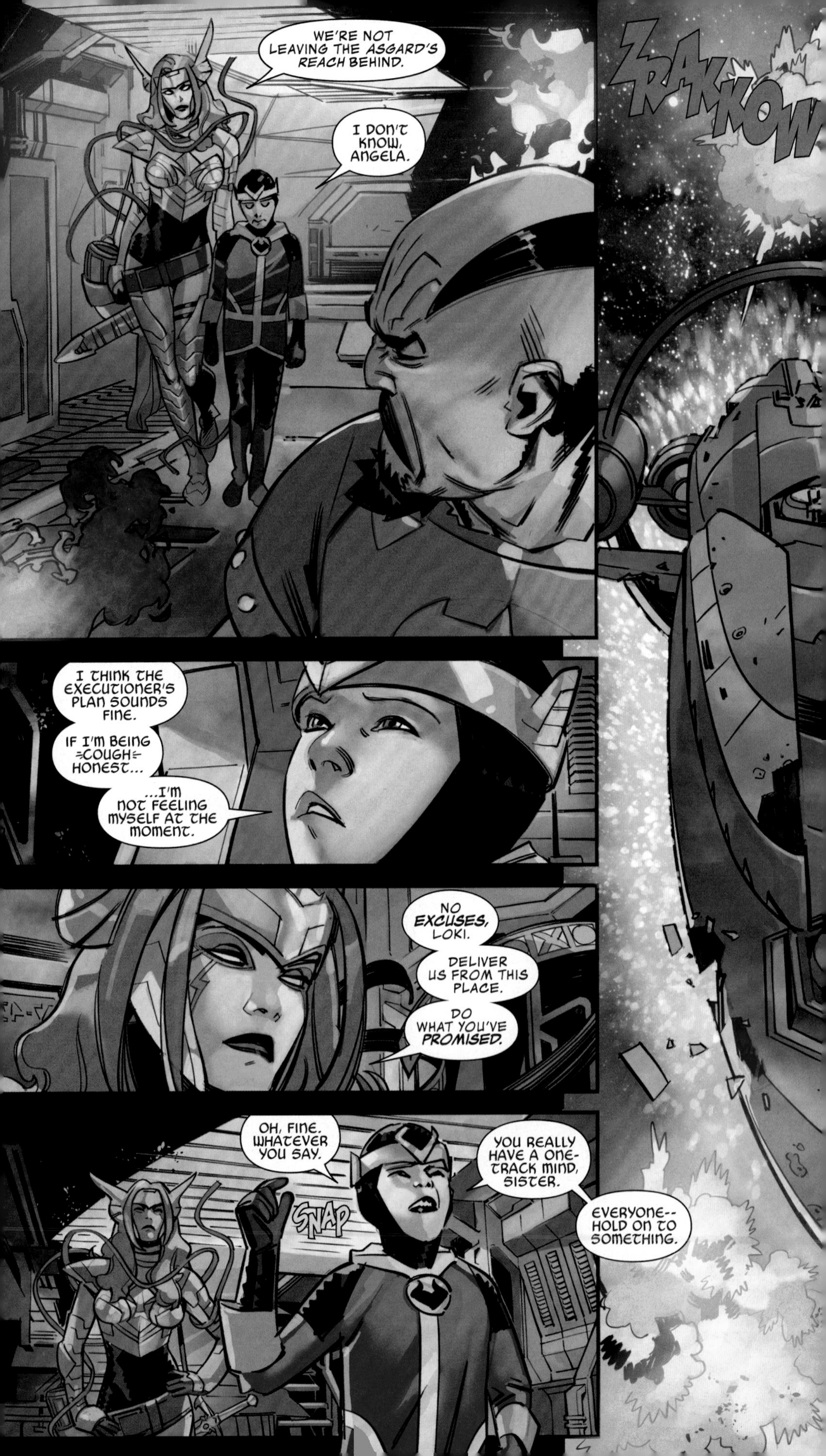
WE'RE NOT LEAVING THE ASGARD'S REACH BEHIND.
I DON'T KNOW, ANGELA.
ZRAKKOW
I THINK THE EXECUTIONER'S PLAN SOUNDS FINE.
IF I'M BEING =COUGH= HONEST...
...I'M NOT FEELING MYSELF AT THE MOMENT.
NO EXCUSES, LOKI.
DELIVER US FROM THIS PLACE.
DO WHAT YOU'VE PROMISED.
OH, FINE. WHATEVER YOU SAY.
SNAP
YOU REALLY HAVE A ONE-TRACK MIND, SISTER.
EVERYONE-- HOLD ON TO SOMETHING.

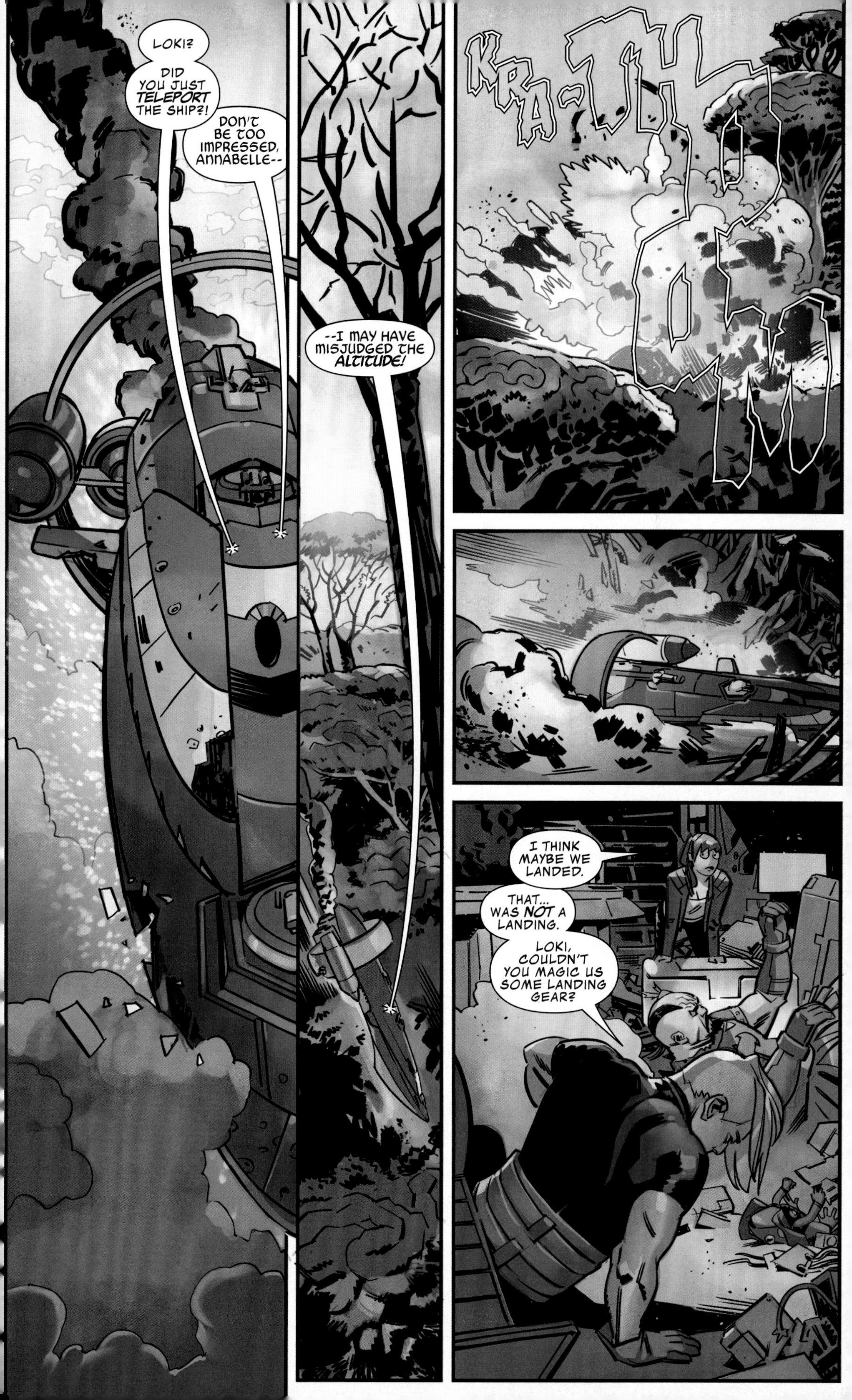
LOKI?
DID YOU JUST TELEPORT THE SHIP?!
DON'T BE TOO IMPRESSED, ANNABELLE--
--I MAY HAVE MISJUDGED THE ALTITUDE!
KRA-THOOM
I THINK MAYBE WE LANDED.
THAT... WAS NOT A LANDING.
LOKI, COULDN'T YOU MAGIC US SOME LANDING GEAR?

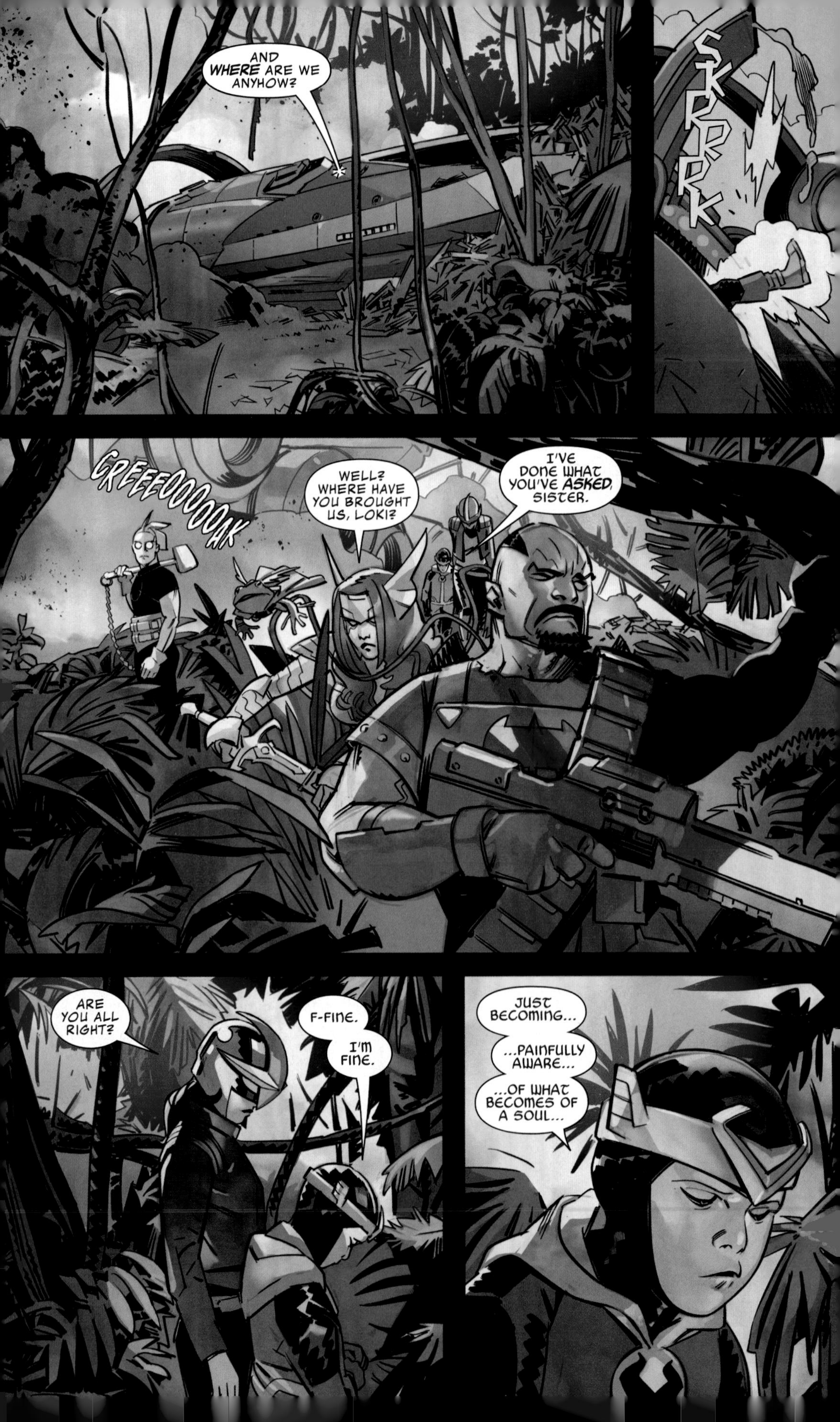
AND WHERE ARE WE ANYHOW?
SKRRK
CREEEOOOOOAK
WELL? WHERE HAVE YOU BROUGHT US, LOKI?
I'VE DONE WHAT YOU'VE ASKED, SISTER.
ARE YOU ALL RIGHT?
F-FINE.
I'M FINE.
JUST BECOMING...
...PAINFULLY AWARE...
...OF WHAT BECOMES OF A SOUL...

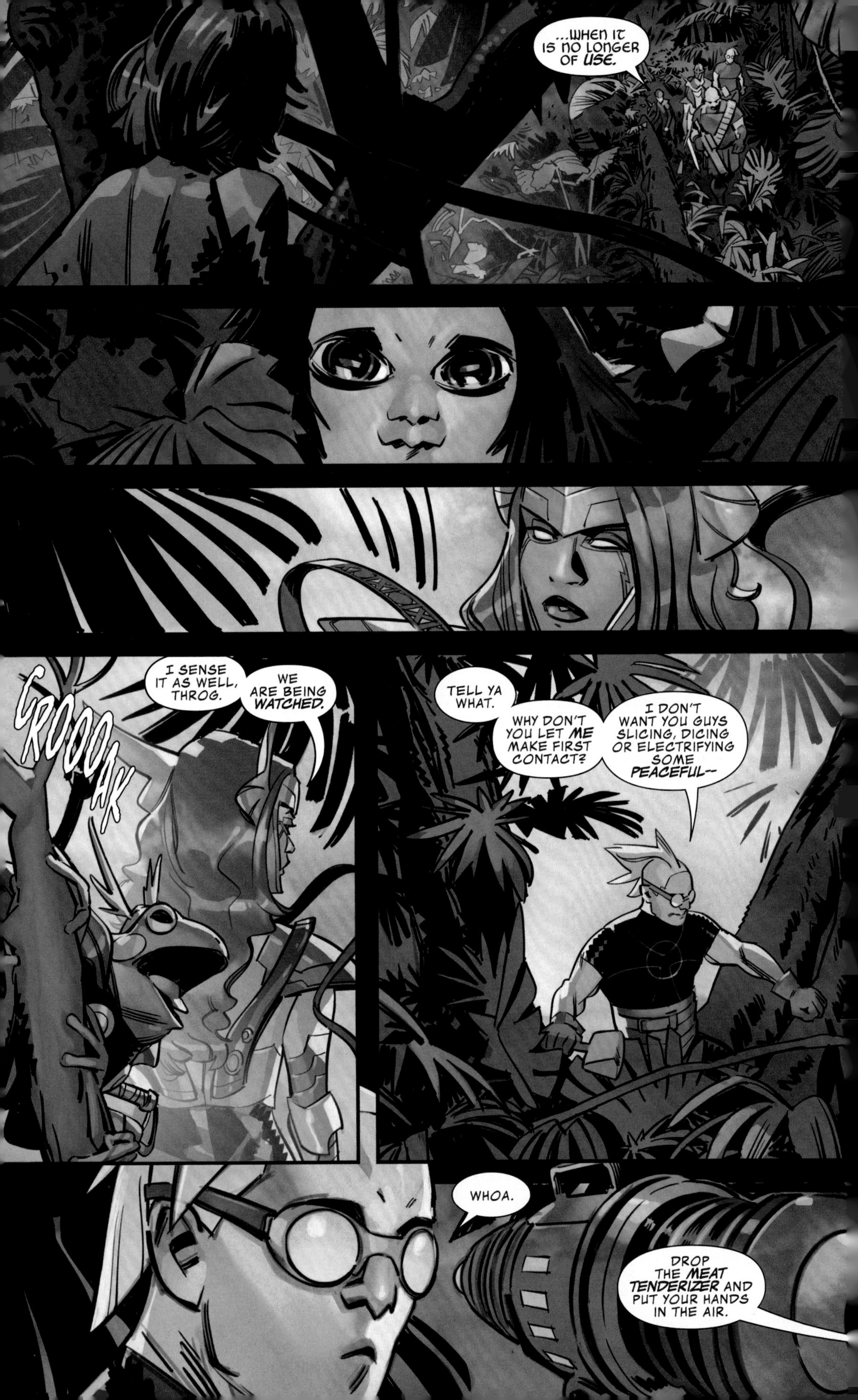
...WHEN IT IS NO LONGER OF USE.
GROOOOAK
I SENSE IT AS WELL, THROG.
WE ARE BEING WATCHED.
TELL YA WHAT.
WHY DON'T YOU LET ME MAKE FIRST CONTACT?
I DON'T WANT YOU GUYS SLICING, DICING OR ELECTRIFYING SOME PEACEFUL--
WHOA.
DROP THE MEAT TENDERIZER AND PUT YOUR HANDS IN THE AIR.

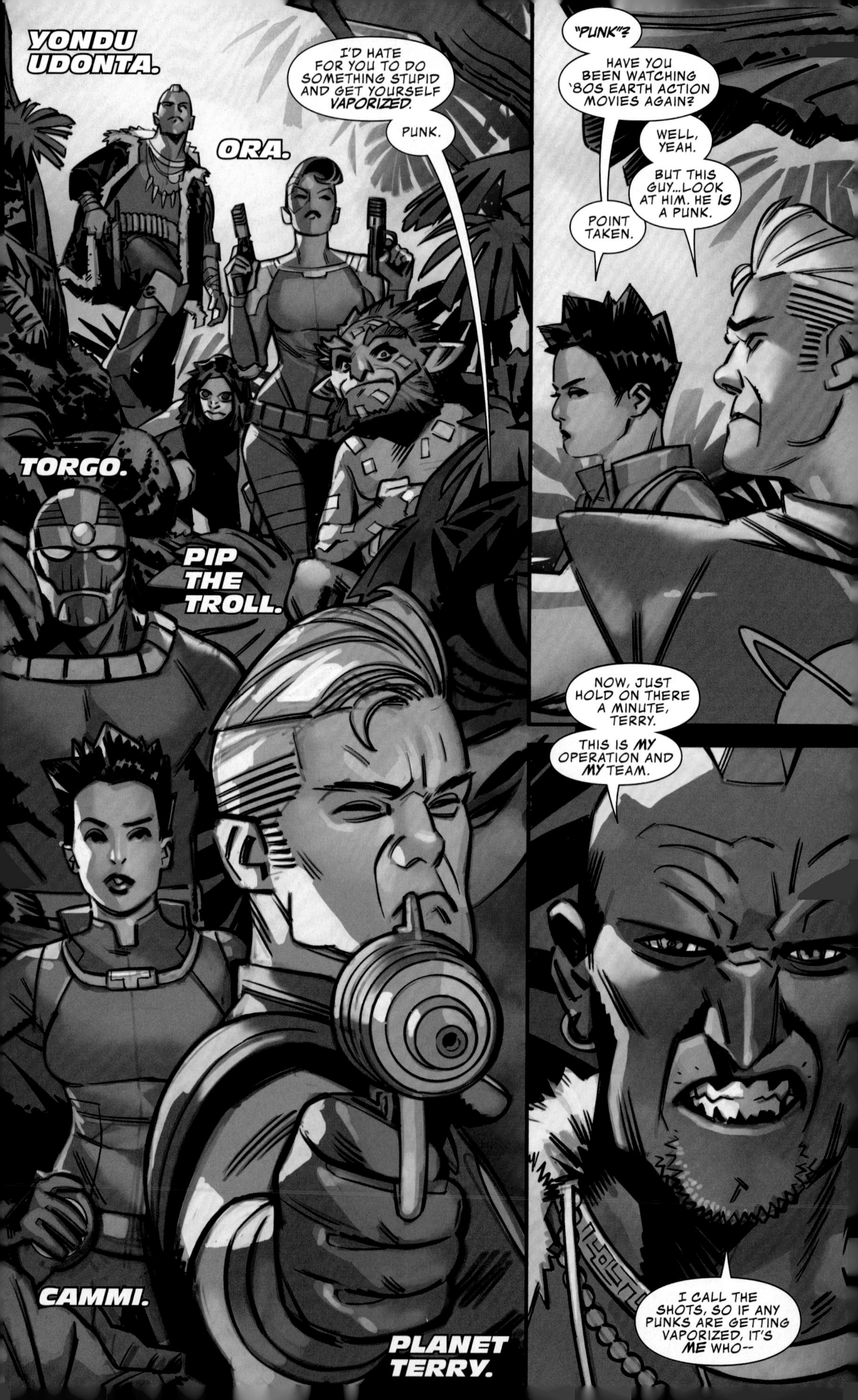
YONDU UDONTA.
ORA.
I'D HATE FOR YOU TO DO SOMETHING STUPID AND GET YOURSELF VAPORIZED.
PUNK.
TORGO.
PIP THE TROLL.
CAMMI.
PLANET TERRY.
"PUNK"?
HAVE YOU BEEN WATCHING '80S EARTH ACTION MOVIES AGAIN?
WELL, YEAH.
BUT THIS GUY...LOOK AT HIM. HE IS A PUNK.
POINT TAKEN.
NOW, JUST HOLD ON THERE A MINUTE, TERRY.
THIS IS MY OPERATION AND MY TEAM.
I CALL THE SHOTS, SO IF ANY PUNKS ARE GETTING VAPORIZED, IT'S ME WHO--

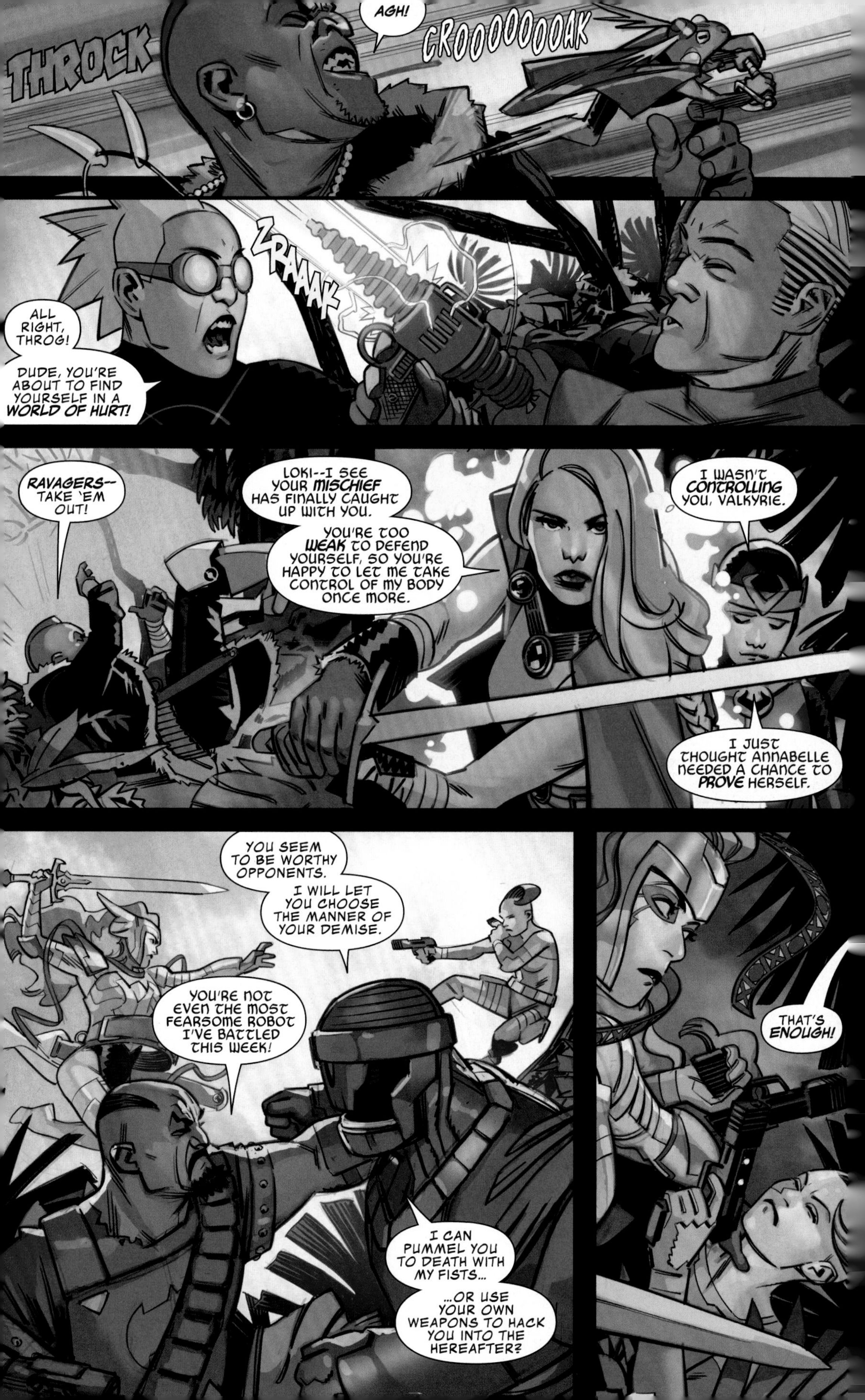

AGH!
THROCK
CROOOOOOOOAK
ZRAAAAK
ALL RIGHT, THROG!
DUDE, YOU'RE ABOUT TO FIND YOURSELF IN A WORLD OF HURT!
RAVAGERS-- TAKE 'EM OUT!
LOKI--I SEE YOUR MISCHIEF HAS FINALLY CAUGHT UP WITH YOU.
YOU'RE TOO WEAK TO DEFEND YOURSELF, SO YOU'RE HAPPY TO LET ME TAKE CONTROL OF MY BODY ONCE MORE.
I WASN'T CONTROLLING YOU, VALKYRIE.
I JUST THOUGHT ANNABELLE NEEDED A CHANCE TO PROVE HERSELF.
YOU SEEM TO BE WORTHY OPPONENTS.
I WILL LET YOU CHOOSE THE MANNER OF YOUR DEMISE.
YOU'RE NOT EVEN THE MOST FEARSOME ROBOT I'VE BATTLED THIS WEEK!
I CAN PUMMEL YOU TO DEATH WITH MY FISTS...
...OR USE YOUR OWN WEAPONS TO HACK YOU INTO THE HEREAFTER?
THAT'S ENOUGH!

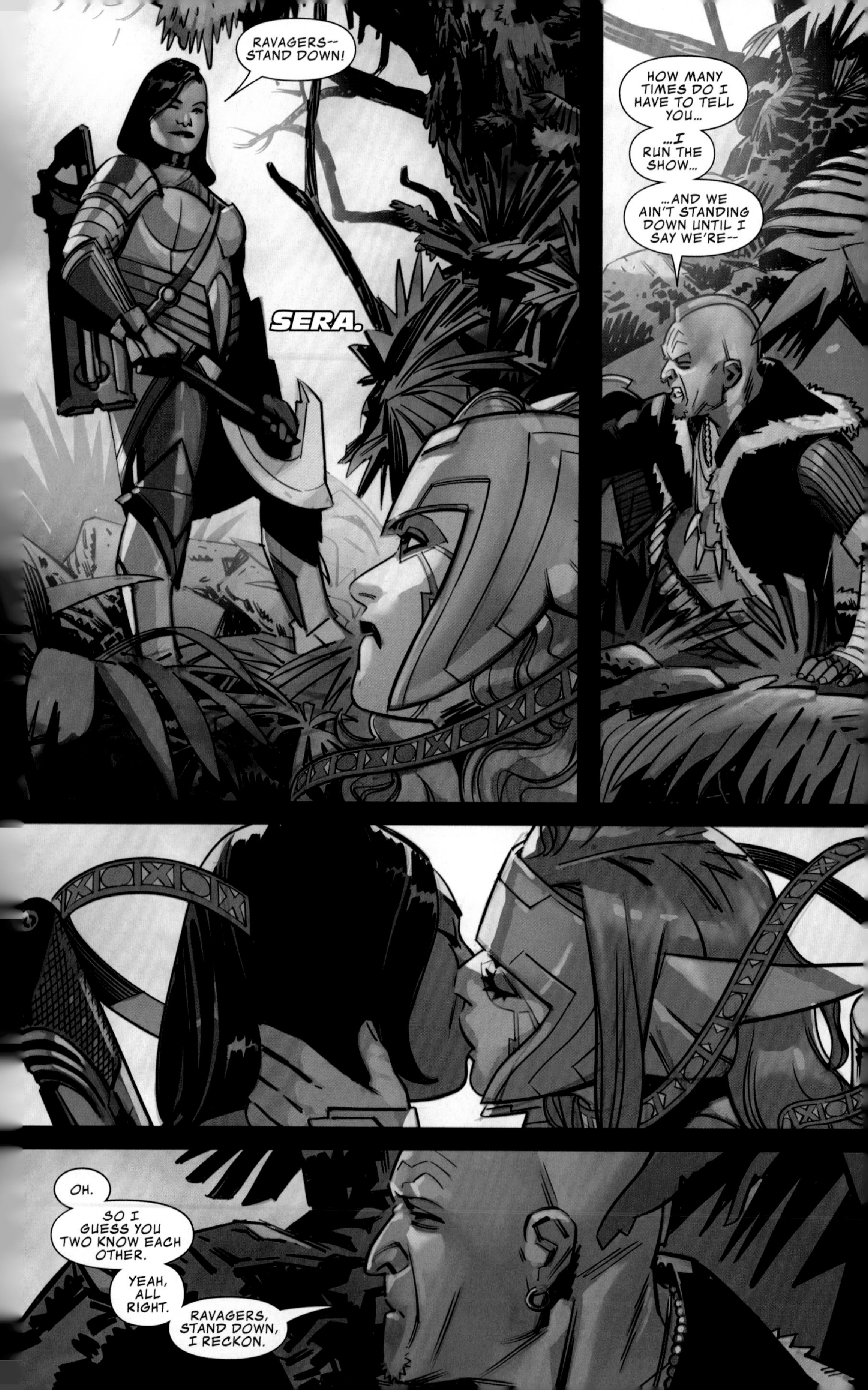
RAVAGERS-- STAND DOWN!
SERA.
HOW MANY TIMES DO I HAVE TO TELL YOU...
...I RUN THE SHOW...
...AND WE AIN'T STANDING DOWN UNTIL I SAY WE'RE--
OH.
SO I GUESS YOU TWO KNOW EACH OTHER.
YEAH, ALL RIGHT.
RAVAGERS, STAND DOWN, I RECKON.

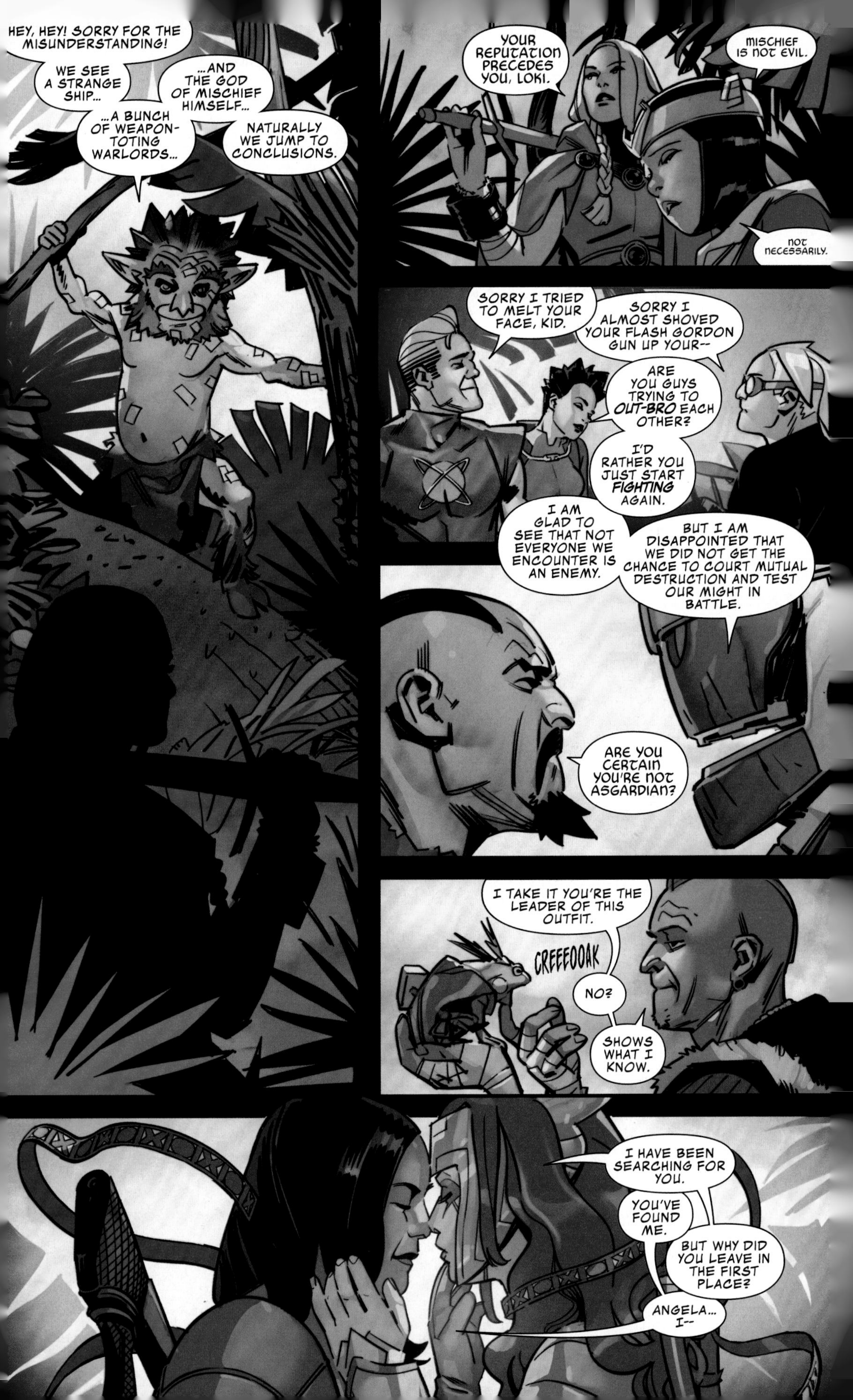
HEY, HEY! SORRY FOR THE MISUNDERSTANDING!
WE SEE A STRANGE SHIP...
...AND THE GOD OF MISCHIEF HIMSELF...
...A BUNCH OF WEAPON-TOTING WARLORDS...
NATURALLY WE JUMP TO CONCLUSIONS.
YOUR REPUTATION PRECEDES YOU, LOKI.
MISCHIEF IS NOT EVIL.
NOT NECESSARILY.
SORRY I TRIED TO MELT YOUR FACE, KID.
SORRY I ALMOST SHOVED YOUR FLASH GORDON GUN UP YOUR--
ARE YOU GUYS TRYING TO OUT-BRO EACH OTHER?
I'D RATHER YOU JUST START FIGHTING AGAIN.
I AM GLAD TO SEE THAT NOT EVERYONE WE ENCOUNTER IS AN ENEMY.
BUT I AM DISAPPOINTED THAT WE DID NOT GET THE CHANCE TO COURT MUTUAL DESTRUCTION AND TEST OUR MIGHT IN BATTLE.
ARE YOU CERTAIN YOU'RE NOT ASGARDIAN?
I TAKE IT YOU'RE THE LEADER OF THIS OUTFIT.
CREEEOOAK
NO?
SHOWS WHAT I KNOW.
I HAVE BEEN SEARCHING FOR YOU.
YOU'VE FOUND ME.
BUT WHY DID YOU LEAVE IN THE FIRST PLACE?
ANGELA... I--

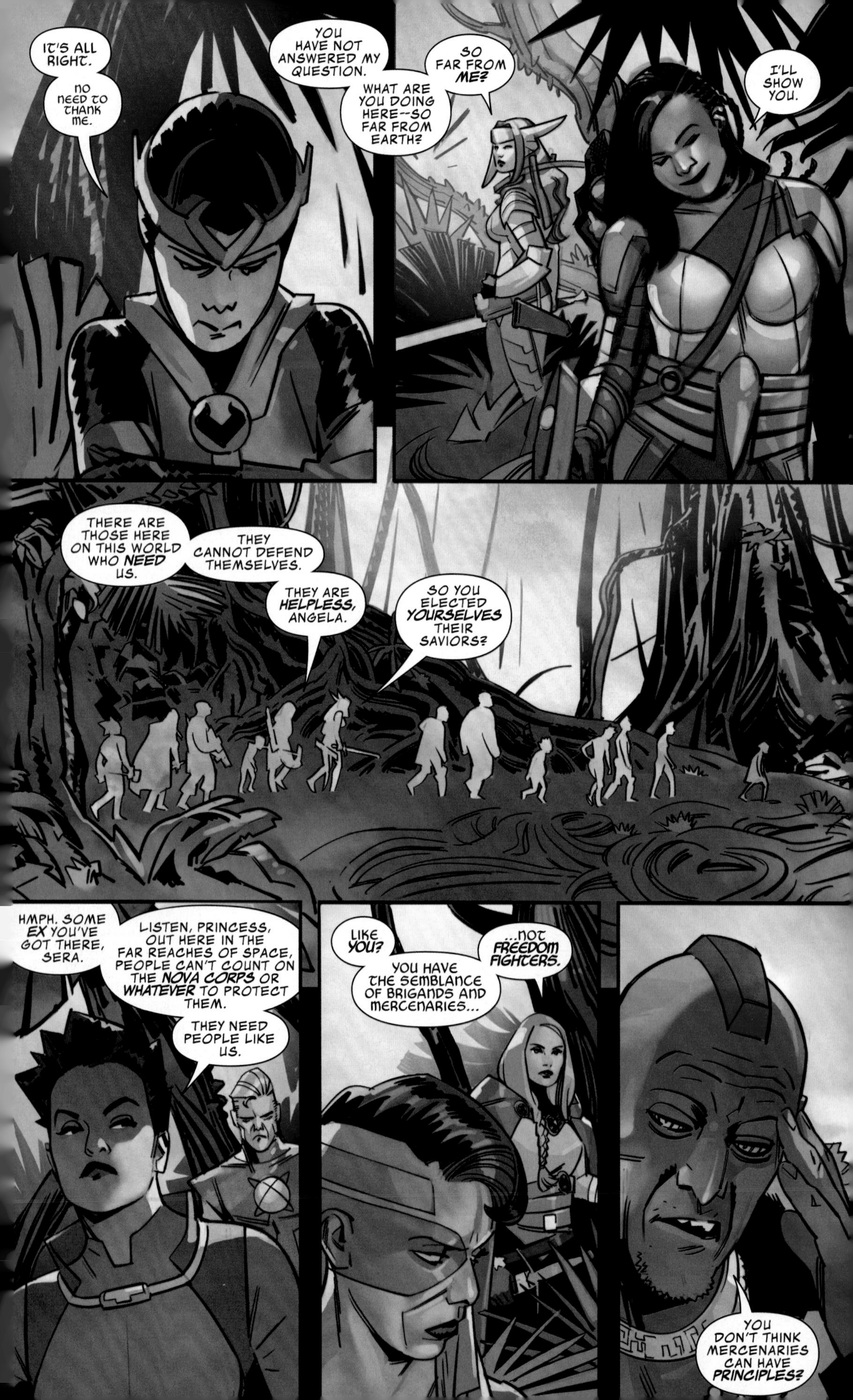
IT'S ALL RIGHT.
NO NEED TO THANK ME.
YOU HAVE NOT ANSWERED MY QUESTION.
WHAT ARE YOU DOING HERE--SO FAR FROM EARTH?
SO FAR FROM ME?
I'LL SHOW YOU.
THERE ARE THOSE HERE ON THIS WORLD WHO NEED US.
THEY CANNOT DEFEND THEMSELVES.
THEY ARE HELPLESS, ANGELA.
SO YOU ELECTED YOURSELVES THEIR SAVIORS?
HMPH. SOME EX YOU'VE GOT THERE, SERA.
LISTEN, PRINCESS, OUT HERE IN THE FAR REACHES OF SPACE, PEOPLE CAN'T COUNT ON THE NOVA CORPS OR WHATEVER TO PROTECT THEM.
THEY NEED PEOPLE LIKE US.
LIKE YOU?
YOU HAVE THE SEMBLANCE OF BRIGANDS AND MERCENARIES...
...NOT FREEDOM FIGHTERS.
YOU DON'T THINK MERCENARIES CAN HAVE PRINCIPLES?

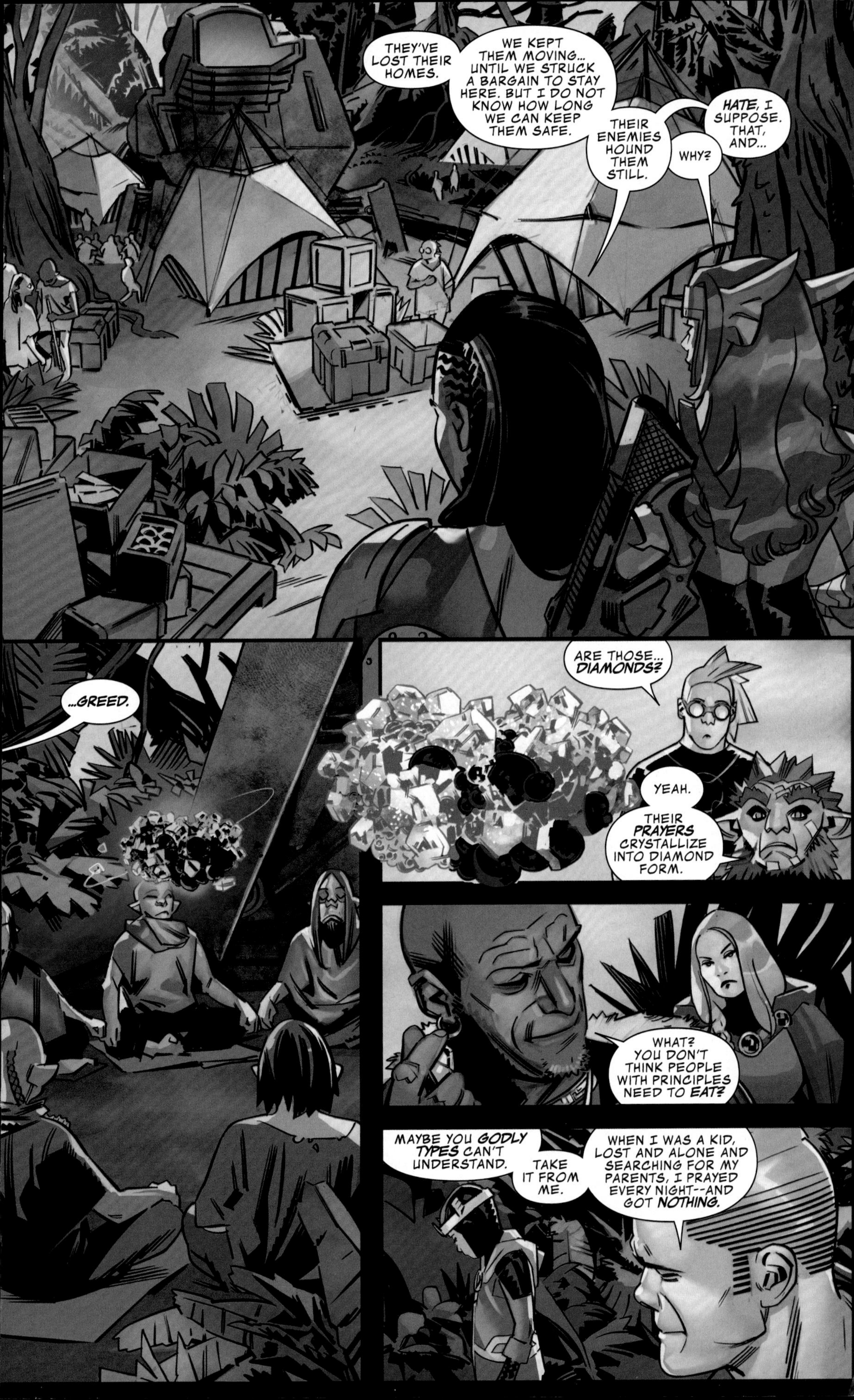
THEY'VE LOST THEIR HOMES.
WE KEPT THEM MOVING... UNTIL WE STRUCK A BARGAIN TO STAY HERE. BUT I DO NOT KNOW HOW LONG WE CAN KEEP THEM SAFE.
THEIR ENEMIES HOUND THEM STILL.
WHY?
HATE, I SUPPOSE. THAT, AND...
...GREED.
ARE THOSE... DIAMONDS?
YEAH.
THEIR PRAYERS CRYSTALLIZE INTO DIAMOND FORM.
WHAT? YOU DON'T THINK PEOPLE WITH PRINCIPLES NEED TO EAT?
MAYBE YOU GODLY TYPES CAN'T UNDERSTAND.
TAKE IT FROM ME.
WHEN I WAS A KID, LOST AND ALONE AND SEARCHING FOR MY PARENTS, I PRAYED EVERY NIGHT--AND GOT NOTHING.

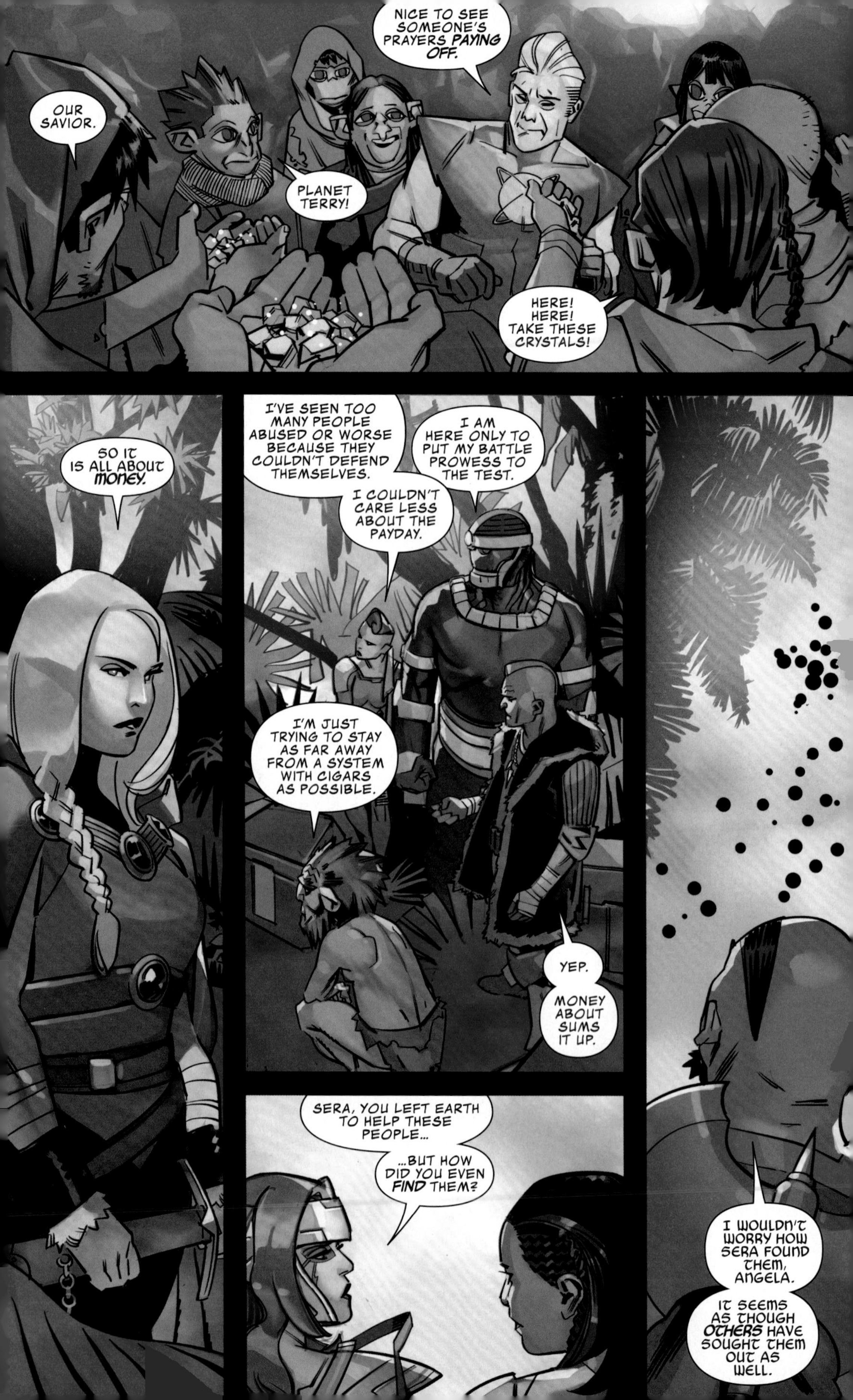
OUR SAVIOR.
NICE TO SEE SOMEONE'S PRAYERS PAYING OFF.
PLANET TERRY!
HERE! HERE! TAKE THESE CRYSTALS!
SO IT IS ALL ABOUT MONEY.
I'VE SEEN TOO MANY PEOPLE ABUSED OR WORSE BECAUSE THEY COULDN'T DEFEND THEMSELVES.
I COULDN'T CARE LESS ABOUT THE PAYDAY.
I AM HERE ONLY TO PUT MY BATTLE PROWESS TO THE TEST.
I'M JUST TRYING TO STAY AS FAR AWAY FROM A SYSTEM WITH CIGARS AS POSSIBLE.
YEP.
MONEY ABOUT SUMS IT UP.
SERA, YOU LEFT EARTH TO HELP THESE PEOPLE...
...BUT HOW DID YOU EVEN FIND THEM?
I WOULDN'T WORRY HOW SERA FOUND THEM, ANGELA.
IT SEEMS AS THOUGH OTHERS HAVE SOUGHT THEM OUT AS WELL.

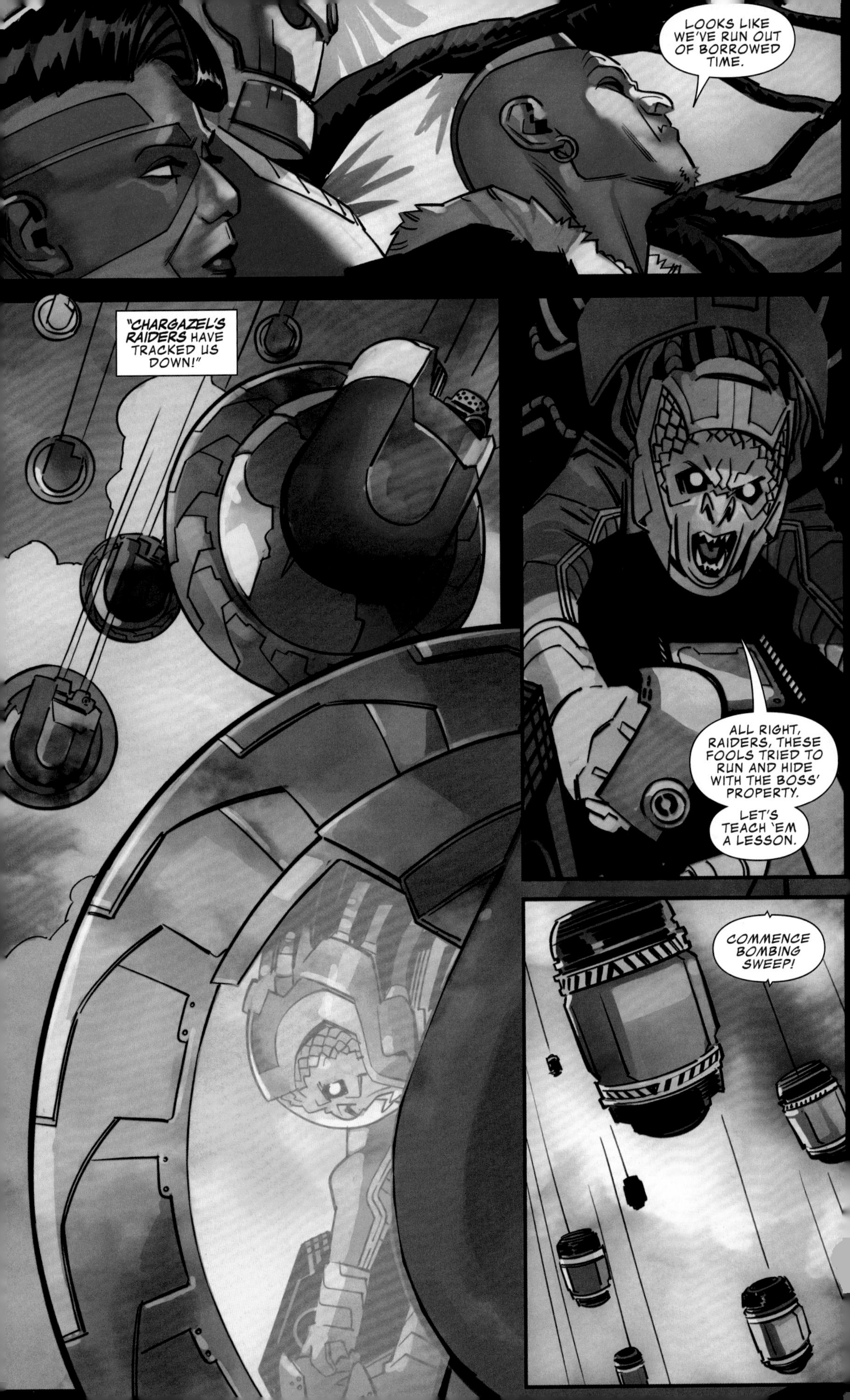
LOOKS LIKE WE'VE RUN OUT OF BORROWED TIME.
"CHARGAZEL'S RAIDERS HAVE TRACKED US DOWN!"
ALL RIGHT, RAIDERS, THESE FOOLS TRIED TO RUN AND HIDE WITH THE BOSS' PROPERTY.
LET'S TEACH 'EM A LESSON.
COMMENCE BOMBING SWEEP!

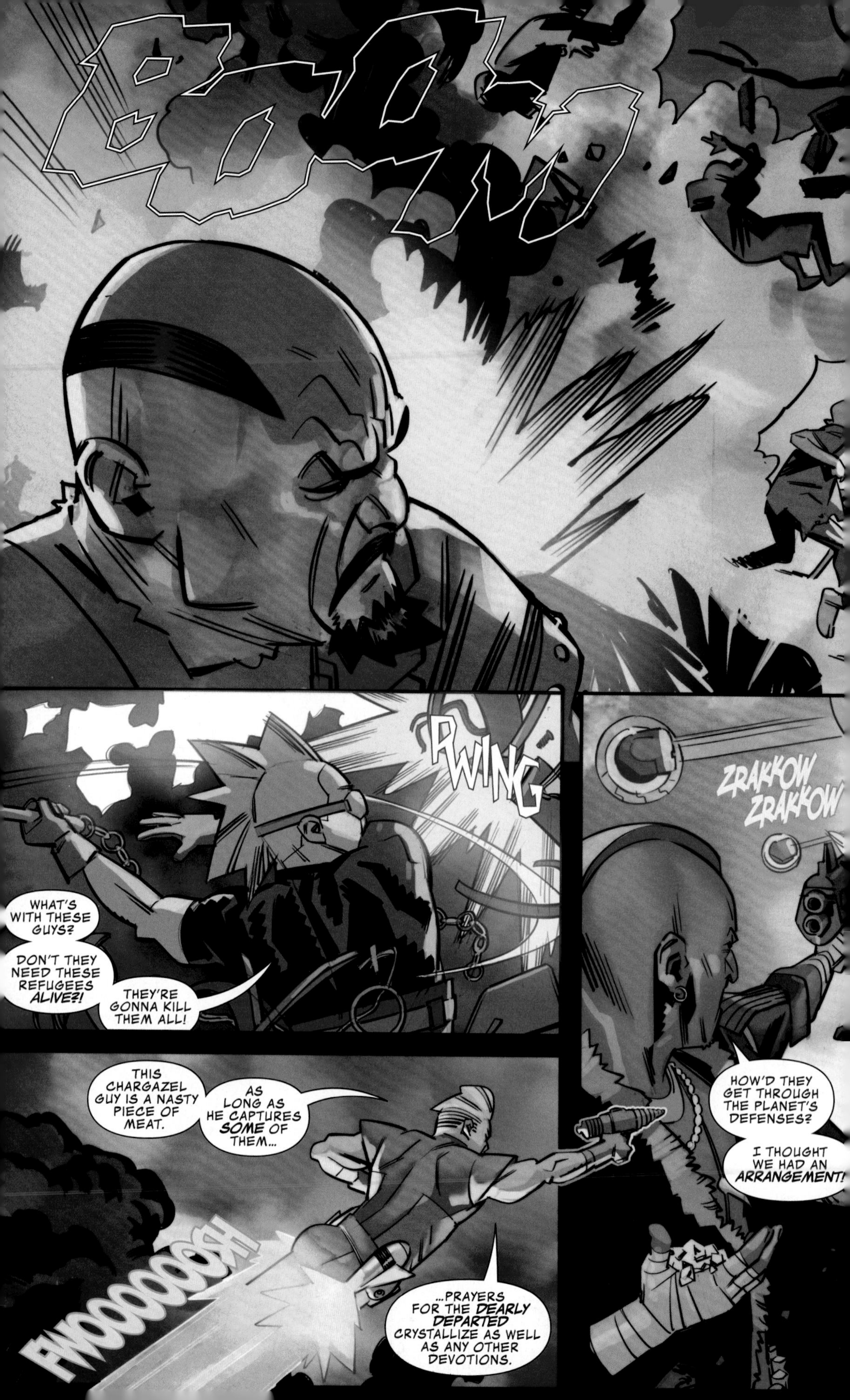
BOOM
RWING
WHAT'S WITH THESE GUYS?
DON'T THEY NEED THESE REFUGEES ALIVE?!
THEY'RE GONNA KILL THEM ALL!
ZRAKKOW ZRAKKOW
HOW'D THEY GET THROUGH THE PLANET'S DEFENSES?
I THOUGHT WE HAD AN ARRANGEMENT!
THIS CHARGAZEL GUY IS A NASTY PIECE OF MEAT.
AS LONG AS HE CAPTURES SOME OF THEM...
FWOOOOOOSH
...PRAYERS FOR THE DEARLY DEPARTED CRYSTALLIZE AS WELL AS ANY OTHER DEVOTIONS.

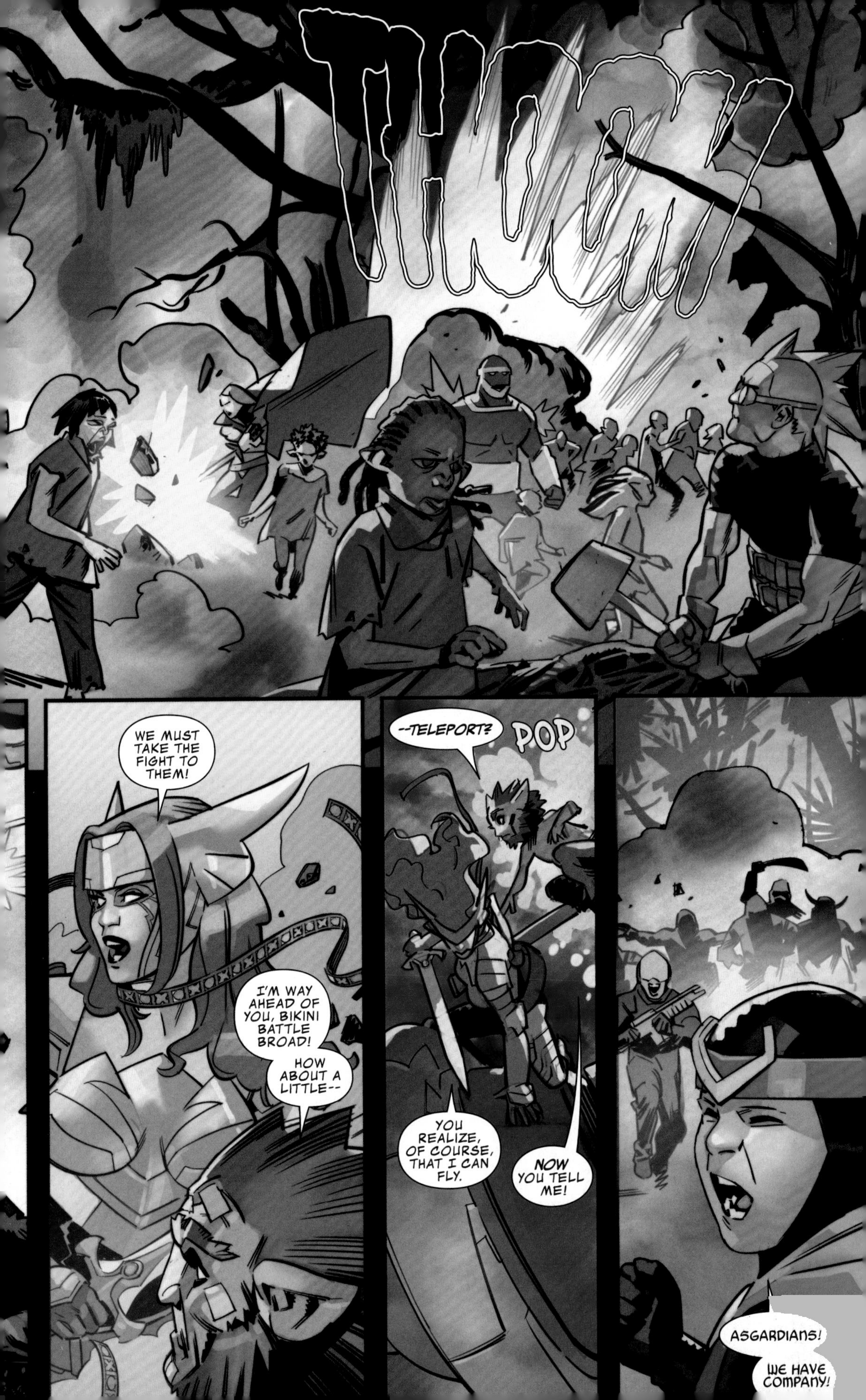

THOOM
WE MUST TAKE THE FIGHT TO THEM!
I'M WAY AHEAD OF YOU, BIKINI BATTLE BROAD!
HOW ABOUT A LITTLE--
--TELEPORT?
POP
YOU REALIZE, OF COURSE, THAT I CAN FLY.
NOW YOU TELL ME!
ASGARDIANS!
WE HAVE COMPANY!

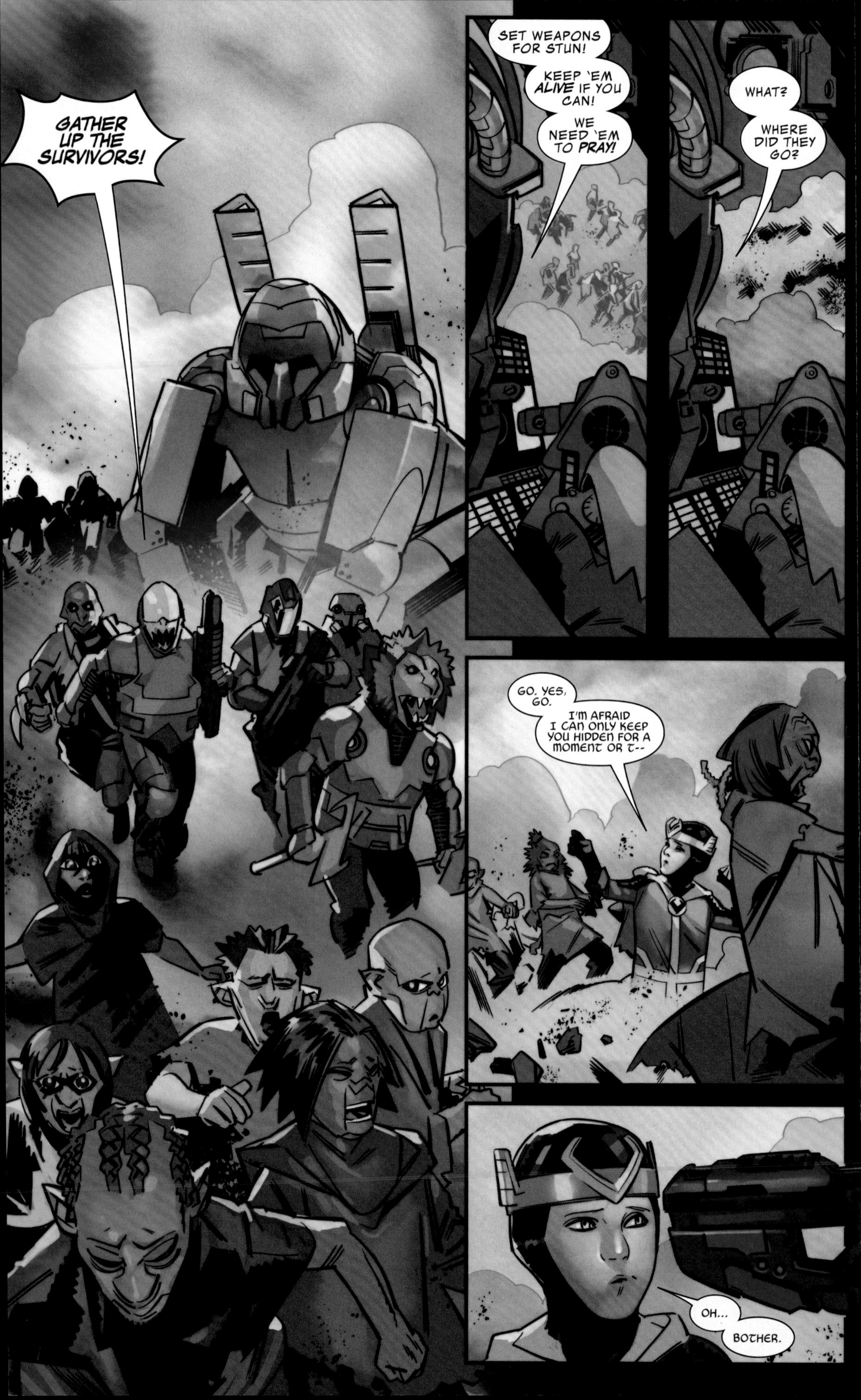
GATHER UP THE SURVIVORS!
SET WEAPONS FOR STUN!
KEEP 'EM ALIVE IF YOU CAN!
WE NEED 'EM TO PRAY!
WHAT?
WHERE DID THEY GO?
GO. YES, GO.
I'M AFRAID I CAN ONLY KEEP YOU HIDDEN FOR A MOMENT OR T--
OH...
BOTHER.

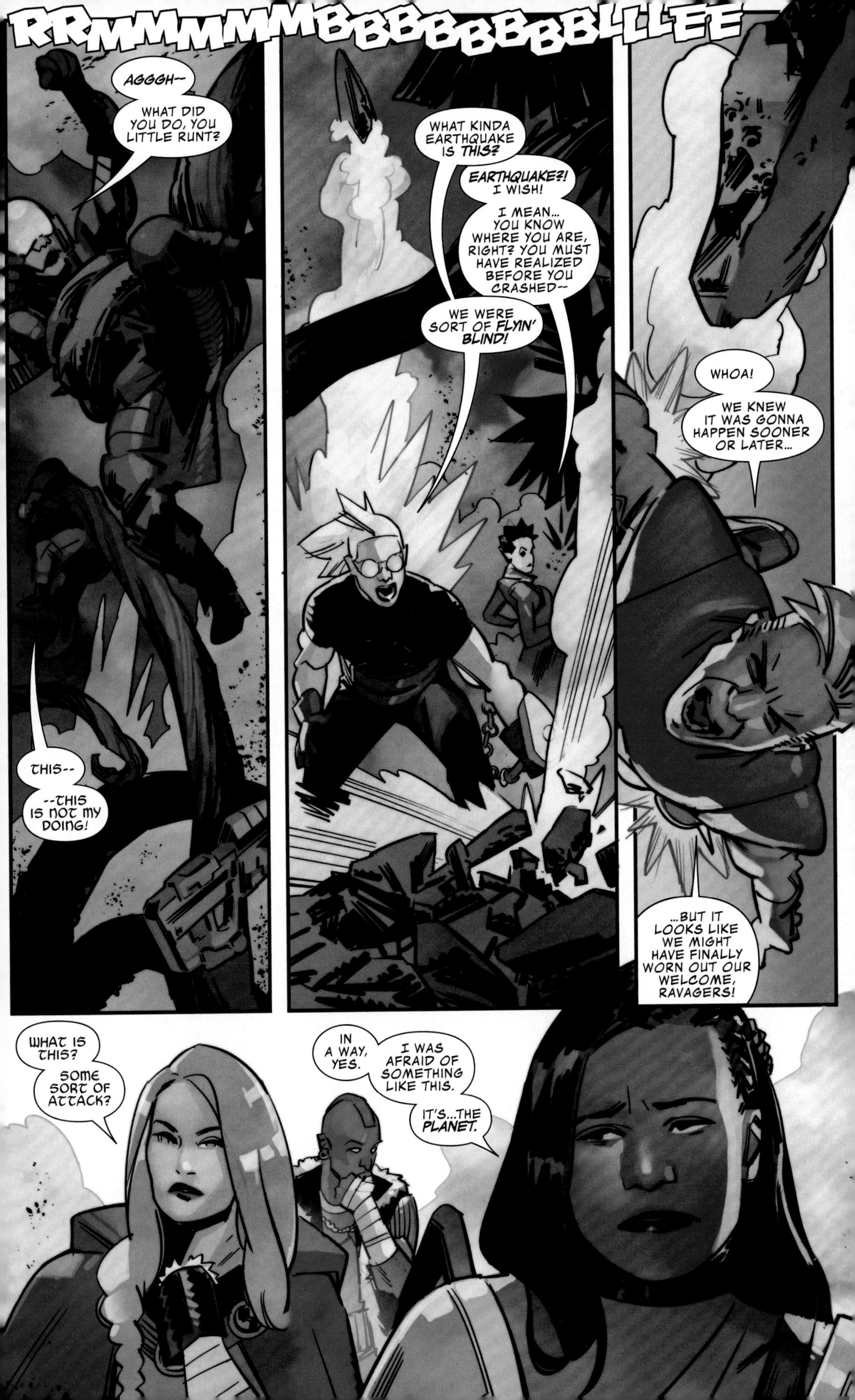
RRMMMMMMBBBBBBBBLLLEE
AGGGH--
WHAT DID YOU DO, YOU LITTLE RUNT?
THIS--
--THIS IS NOT MY DOING!
WHAT KINDA EARTHQUAKE IS THIS?
EARTHQUAKE?! I WISH!
I MEAN... YOU KNOW WHERE YOU ARE, RIGHT? YOU MUST HAVE REALIZED BEFORE YOU CRASHED--
WE WERE SORT OF FLYIN' BLIND!
WHOA!
WE KNEW IT WAS GONNA HAPPEN SOONER OR LATER...
...BUT IT LOOKS LIKE WE MIGHT HAVE FINALLY WORN OUT OUR WELCOME, RAVAGERS!
WHAT IS THIS?
SOME SORT OF ATTACK?
IN A WAY, YES.
I WAS AFRAID OF SOMETHING LIKE THIS.
IT'S...THE PLANET.

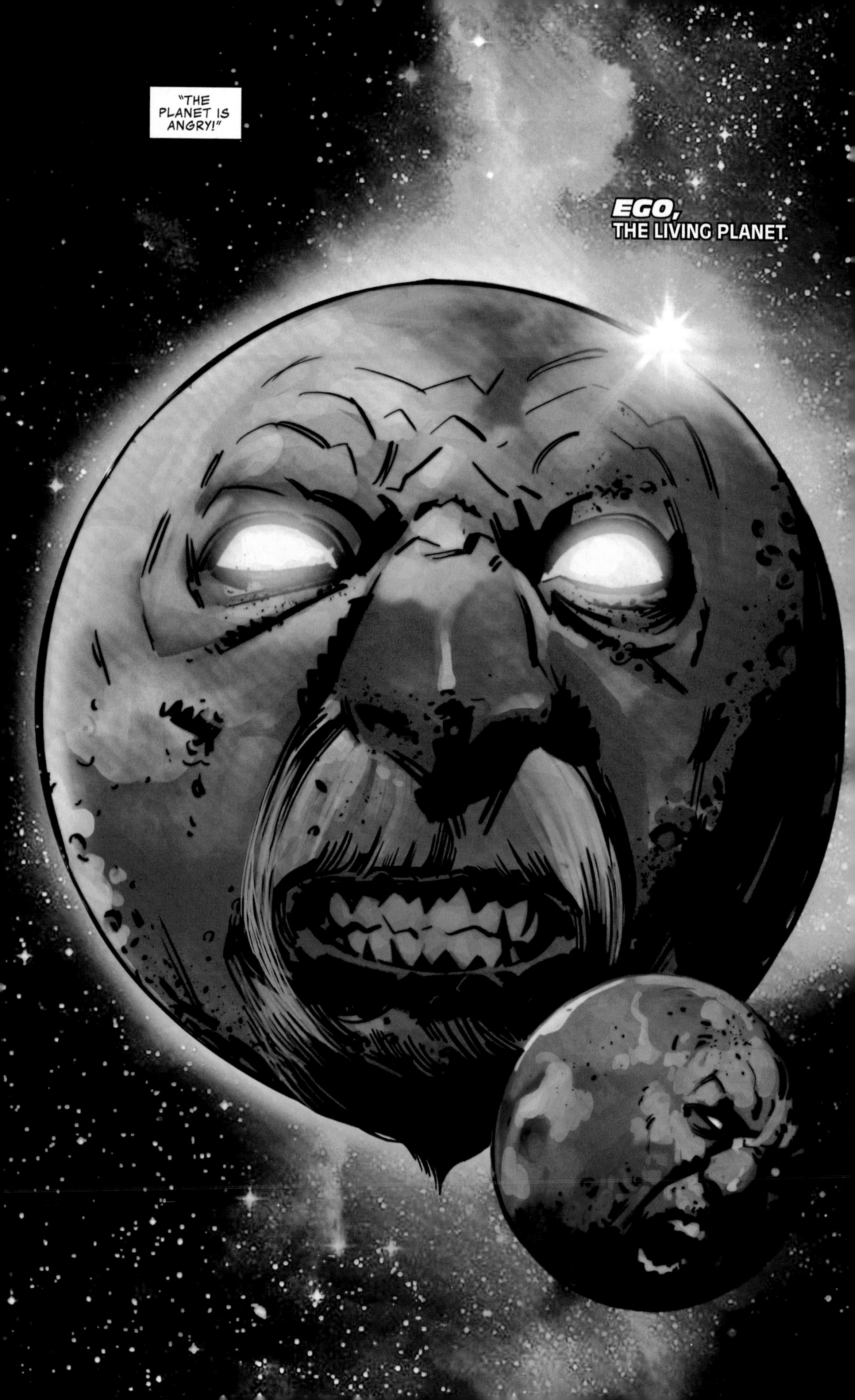
"THE PLANET IS ANGRY!"
EGO, THE LIVING PLANET.

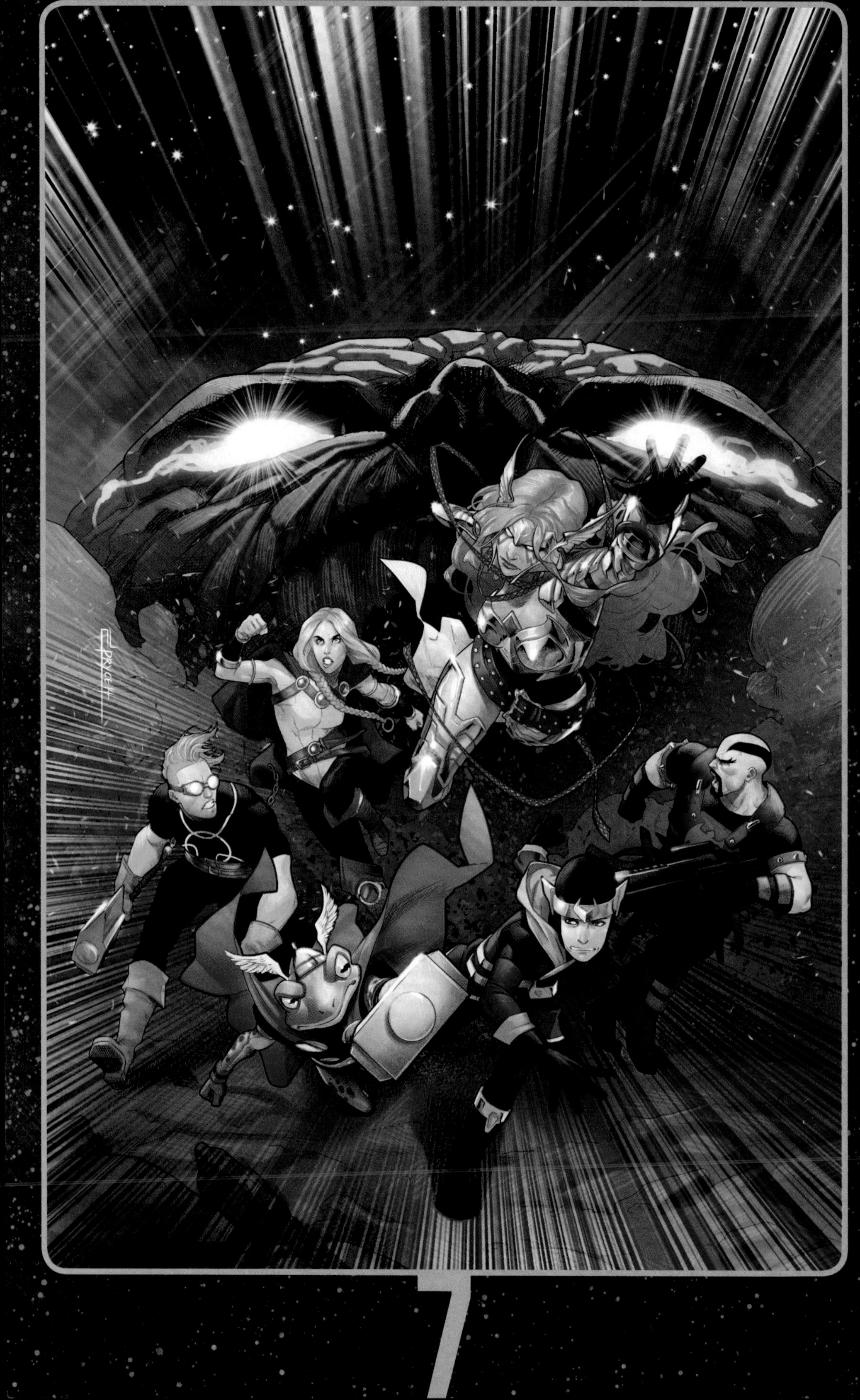
7

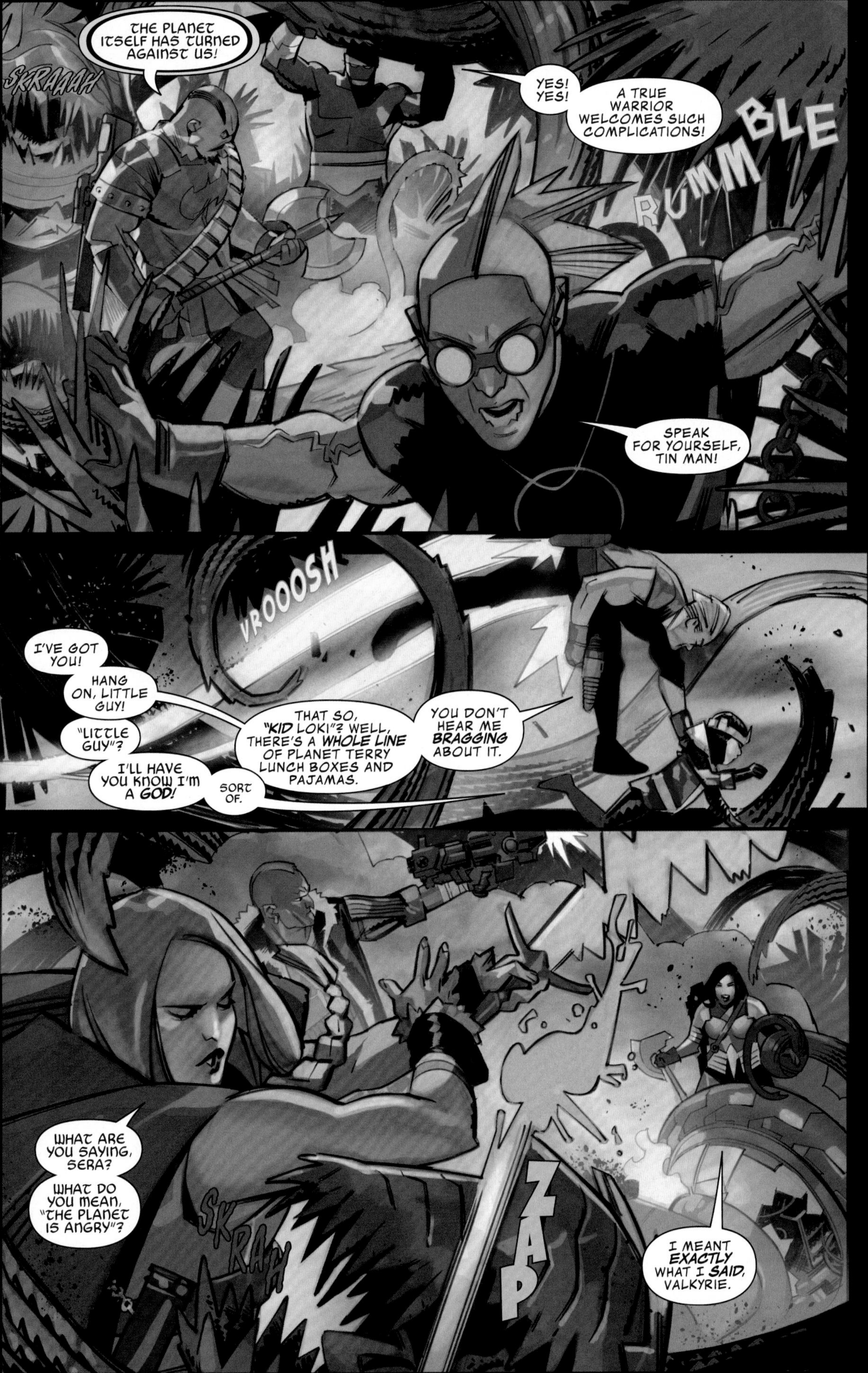
SKRAAAH
THE PLANET ITSELF HAS TURNED AGAINST US!
YES! YES!
A TRUE WARRIOR WELCOMES SUCH COMPLICATIONS!
RUMMBLE
SPEAK FOR YOURSELF, TIN MAN!
VROOOSH
I'VE GOT YOU!
HANG ON, LITTLE GUY!
"LITTLE GUY"?
I'LL HAVE YOU KNOW I'M A GOD!
SORT OF.
THAT SO, "KID LOKI"? WELL, THERE'S A WHOLE LINE OF PLANET TERRY LUNCH BOXES AND PAJAMAS.
YOU DON'T HEAR ME BRAGGING ABOUT IT.
WHAT ARE YOU SAYING, SERA?
WHAT DO YOU MEAN, "THE PLANET IS ANGRY"?
SKRAAH
ZAP
I MEANT EXACTLY WHAT I SAID, VALKYRIE.

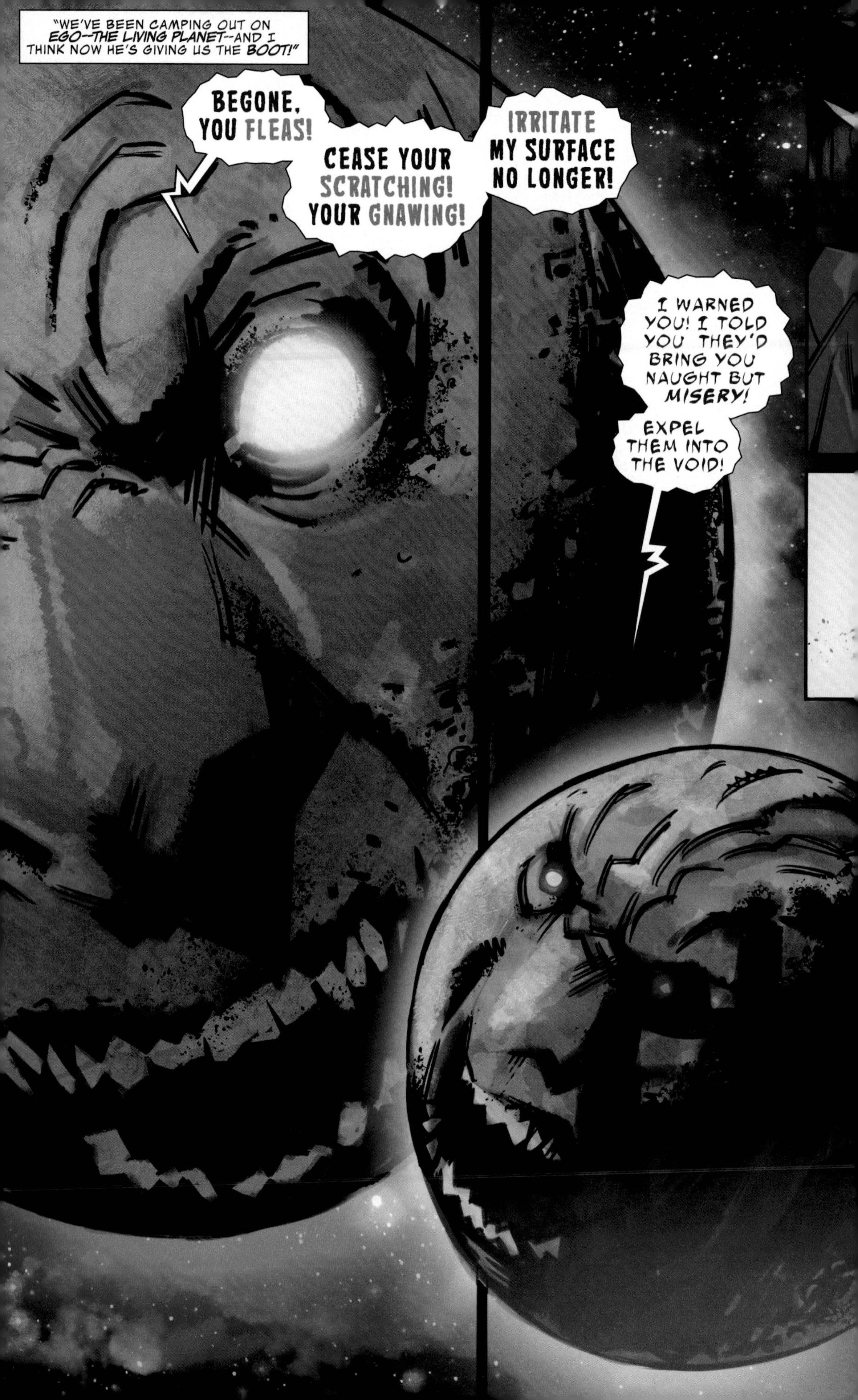
"WE'VE BEEN CAMPING OUT ON EGO--THE LIVING PLANET--AND I THINK NOW HE'S GIVING US THE BOOT!"
BEGONE, YOU FLEAS!
CEASE YOUR SCRATCHING! YOUR GNAWING!
IRRITATE MY SURFACE NO LONGER!
I WARNED YOU! I TOLD YOU THEY'D BRING YOU NAUGHT BUT MISERY!
EXPEL THEM INTO THE VOID!

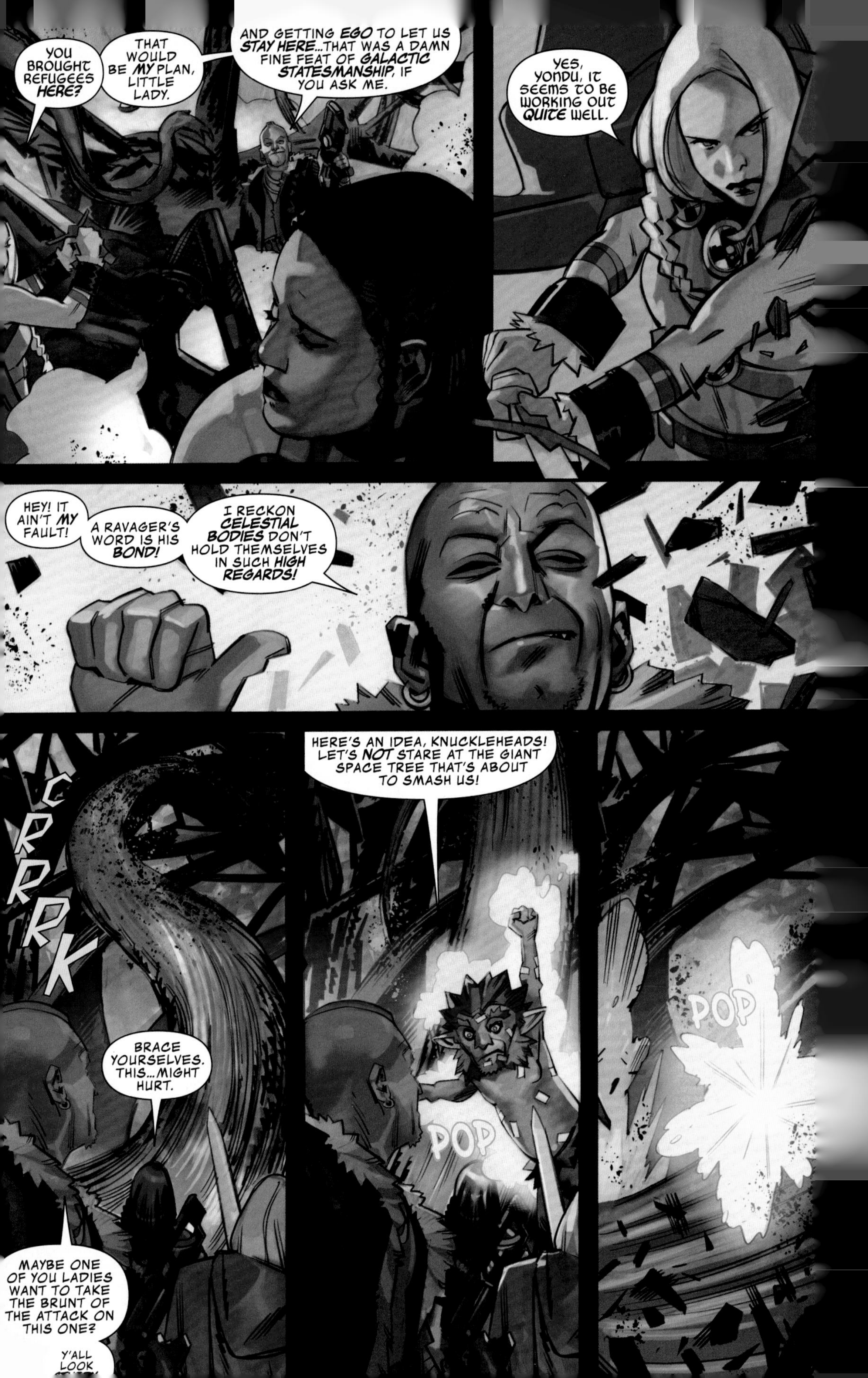
YOU BROUGHT REFUGEES HERE?
THAT WOULD BE MY PLAN, LITTLE LADY.
AND GETTING EGO TO LET US STAY HERE...THAT WAS A DAMN FINE FEAT OF GALACTIC STATESMANSHIP, IF YOU ASK ME.
YES, YONDU, IT SEEMS TO BE WORKING OUT QUITE WELL.
HEY! IT AIN'T MY FAULT!
A RAVAGER'S WORD IS HIS BOND!
I RECKON CELESTIAL BODIES DON'T HOLD THEMSELVES IN SUCH HIGH REGARDS!
CRRRK
BRACE YOURSELVES. THIS...MIGHT HURT.
MAYBE ONE OF YOU LADIES WANT TO TAKE THE BRUNT OF THE ATTACK ON THIS ONE?
Y'ALL LOOK
HERE'S AN IDEA, KNUCKLEHEADS! LET'S NOT STARE AT THE GIANT SPACE TREE THAT'S ABOUT TO SMASH US!
POP
POP

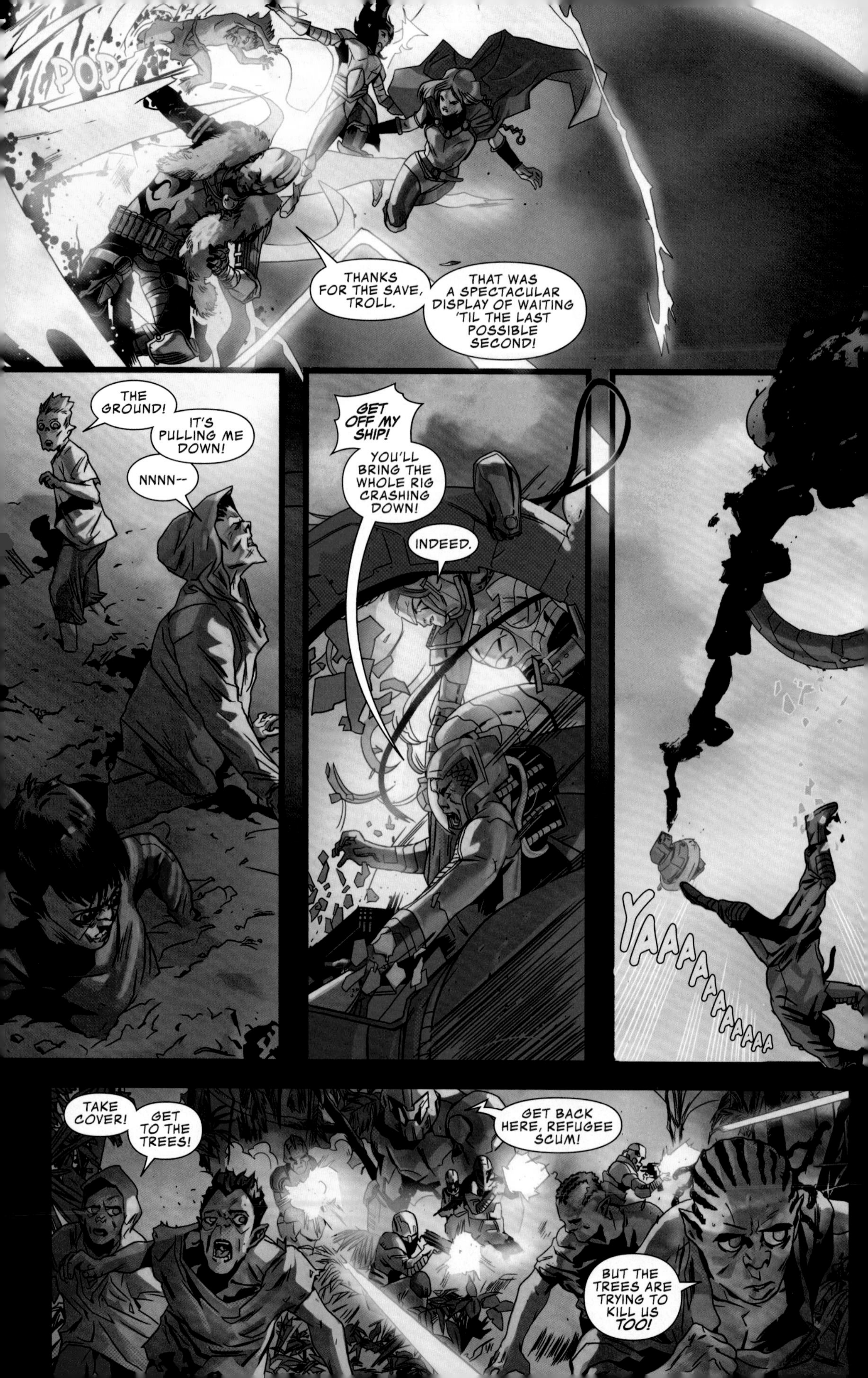
POP
THANKS FOR THE SAVE, TROLL.
THAT WAS A SPECTACULAR DISPLAY OF WAITING 'TIL THE LAST POSSIBLE SECOND!
THE GROUND!
IT'S PULLING ME DOWN!
NNNN--
GET OFF MY SHIP!
YOU'LL BRING THE WHOLE RIG CRASHING DOWN!
INDEED.
YAAAAAAAAAAA
TAKE COVER!
GET TO THE TREES!
GET BACK HERE, REFUGEE SCUM!
BUT THE TREES ARE TRYING TO KILL US TOO!

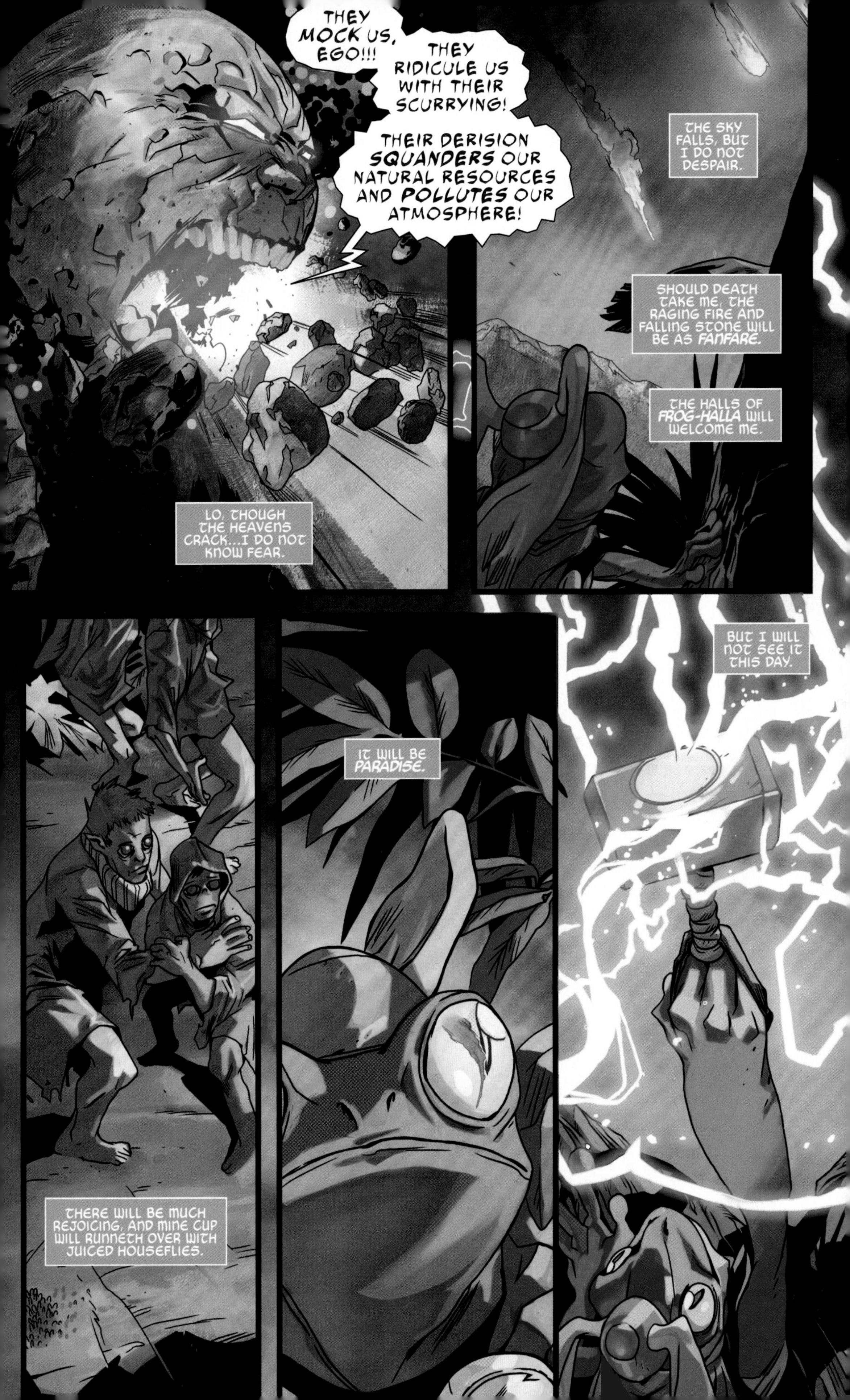
THEY MOCK US, EGO!!!
THEY RIDICULE US WITH THEIR SCURRYING!
THEIR DERISION SQUANDERS OUR NATURAL RESOURCES AND POLLUTES OUR ATMOSPHERE!
LO, THOUGH THE HEAVENS CRACK...I DO NOT KNOW FEAR.
THE SKY FALLS, BUT I DO NOT DESPAIR.
SHOULD DEATH TAKE ME, THE RAGING FIRE AND FALLING STONE WILL BE AS FANFARE.
THE HALLS OF FROG-HALLA WILL WELCOME ME.
BUT I WILL NOT SEE IT THIS DAY.
IT WILL BE PARADISE.
THERE WILL BE MUCH REJOICING, AND MINE CUP WILL RUNNETH OVER WITH JUICED HOUSEFLIES.

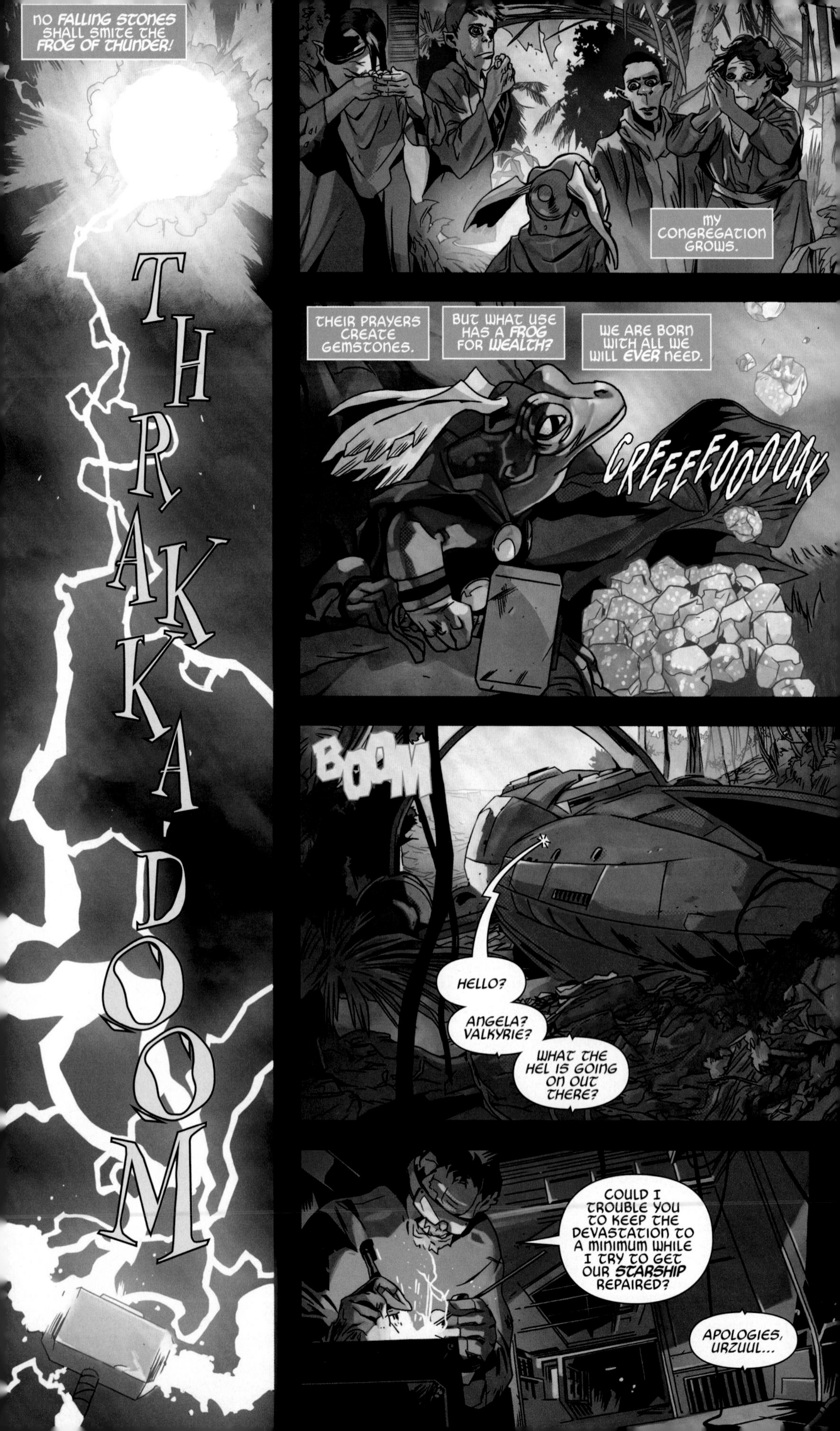
NO FALLING STONES SHALL SMITE THE FROG OF THUNDER!
THRAKKA-DOOM
MY CONGREGATION GROWS.
THEIR PRAYERS CREATE GEMSTONES.
BUT WHAT USE HAS A FROG FOR WEALTH?
WE ARE BORN WITH ALL WE WILL EVER NEED.
GREEEFOOOOAK
BOOM
HELLO?
ANGELA? VALKYRIE?
WHAT THE HEL IS GOING ON OUT THERE?
COULD I TROUBLE YOU TO KEEP THE DEVASTATION TO A MINIMUM WHILE I TRY TO GET OUR STARSHIP REPAIRED?
APOLOGIES, URZUUL...

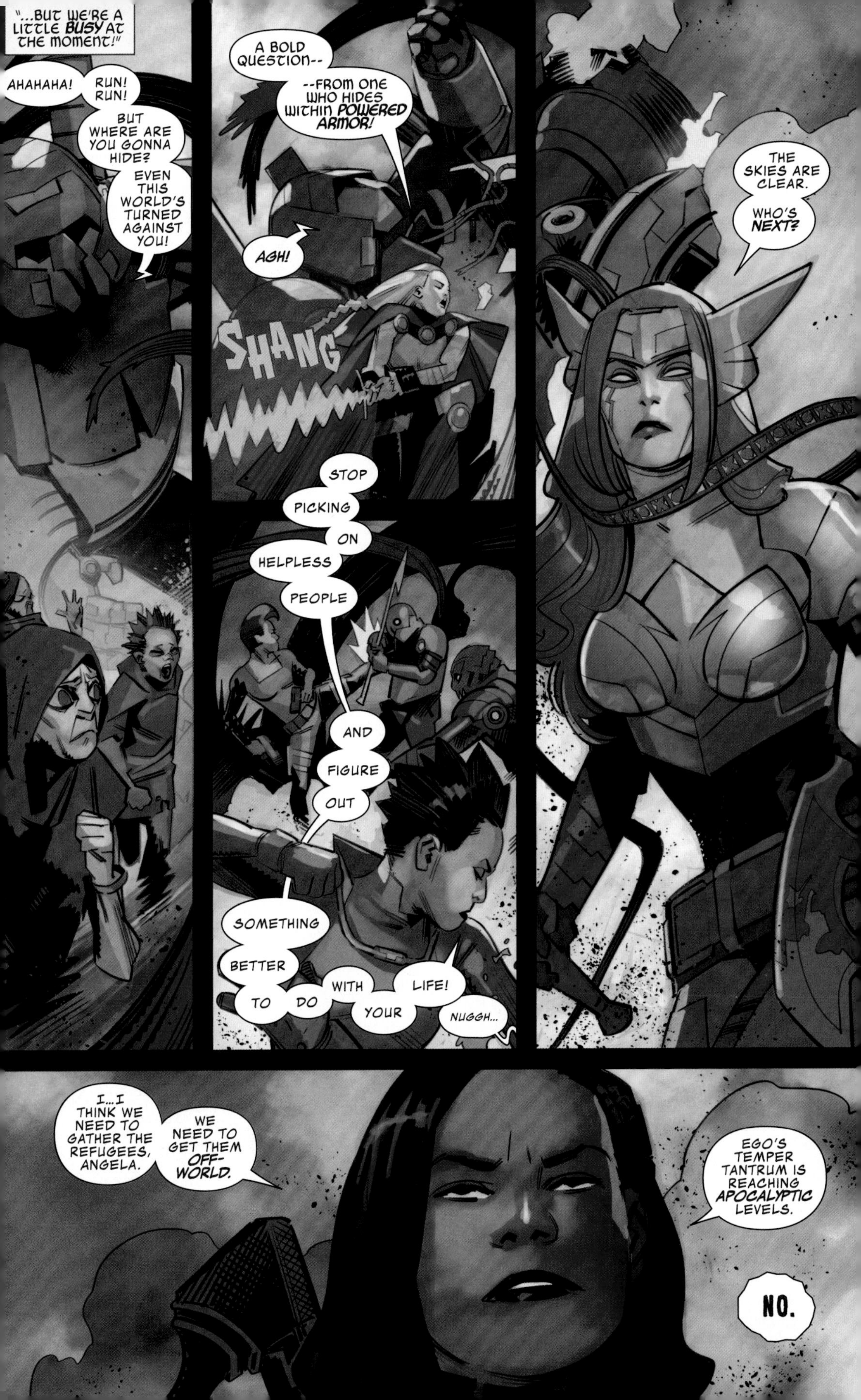
"...BUT WE'RE A LITTLE BUSY AT THE MOMENT!"
AHAHAHA!
RUN! RUN!
BUT WHERE ARE YOU GONNA HIDE?
EVEN THIS WORLD'S TURNED AGAINST YOU!
A BOLD QUESTION--
--FROM ONE WHO HIDES WITHIN POWERED ARMOR!
AGH!
SHANG
THE SKIES ARE CLEAR.
WHO'S NEXT?
STOP PICKING ON HELPLESS PEOPLE AND FIGURE OUT SOMETHING BETTER TO DO WITH YOUR LIFE!
NUGGH...
I...I THINK WE NEED TO GATHER THE REFUGEES, ANGELA.
WE NEED TO GET THEM OFF-WORLD.
EGO'S TEMPER TANTRUM IS REACHING APOCALYPTIC LEVELS.
NO.

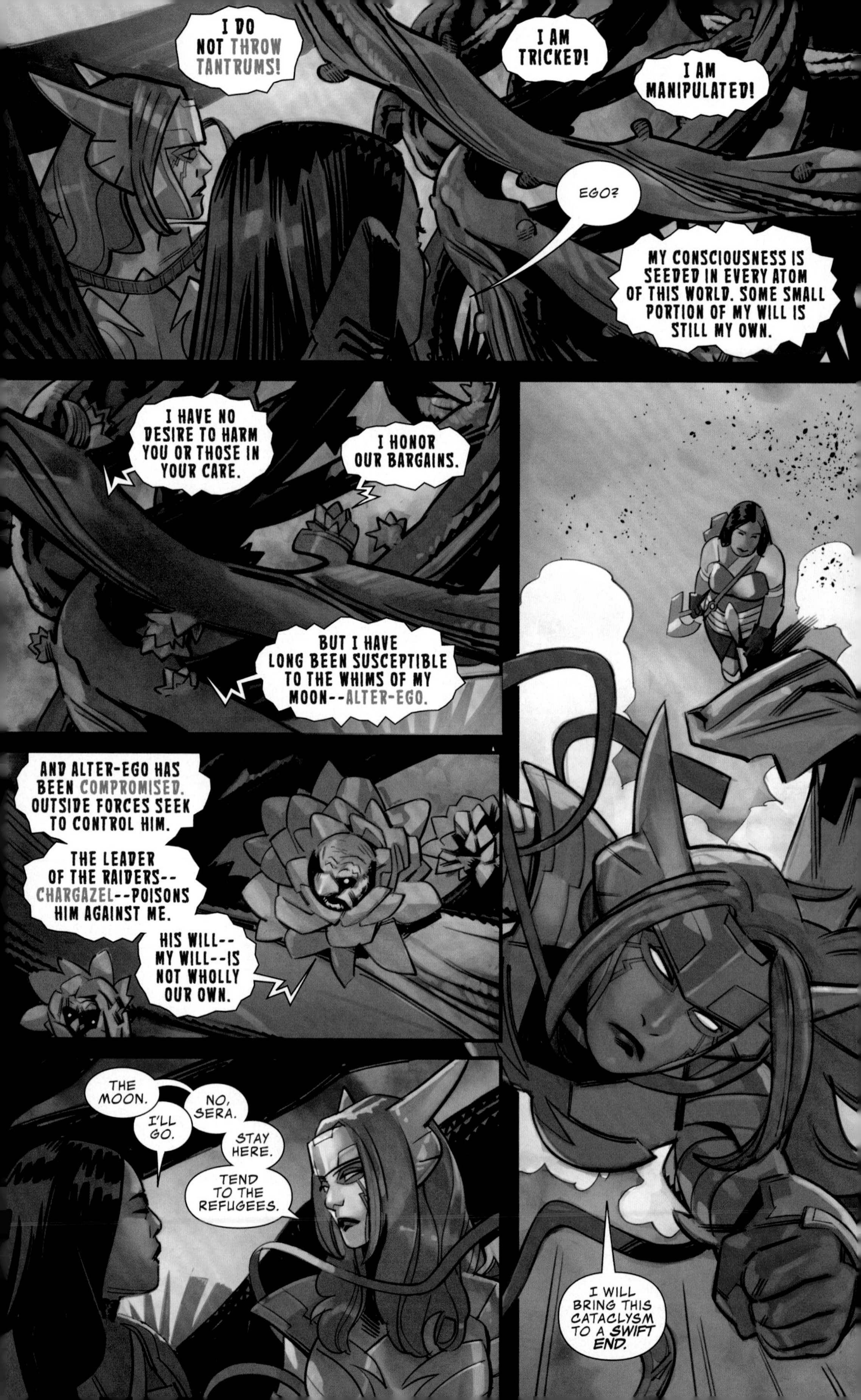
I DO NOT THROW TANTRUMS!
I AM TRICKED!
I AM MANIPULATED!
EGO?
MY CONSCIOUSNESS IS SEEDED IN EVERY ATOM OF THIS WORLD. SOME SMALL PORTION OF MY WILL IS STILL MY OWN.
I HAVE NO DESIRE TO HARM YOU OR THOSE IN YOUR CARE.
I HONOR OUR BARGAINS.
BUT I HAVE LONG BEEN SUSCEPTIBLE TO THE WHIMS OF MY MOON--ALTER-EGO.
AND ALTER-EGO HAS BEEN COMPROMISED. OUTSIDE FORCES SEEK TO CONTROL HIM.
THE LEADER OF THE RAIDERS--CHARGAZEL--POISONS HIM AGAINST ME.
HIS WILL--MY WILL--IS NOT WHOLLY OUR OWN.
THE MOON.
I'LL GO.
NO, SERA.
STAY HERE.
TEND TO THE REFUGEES.
I WILL BRING THIS CATACLYSM TO A SWIFT END.

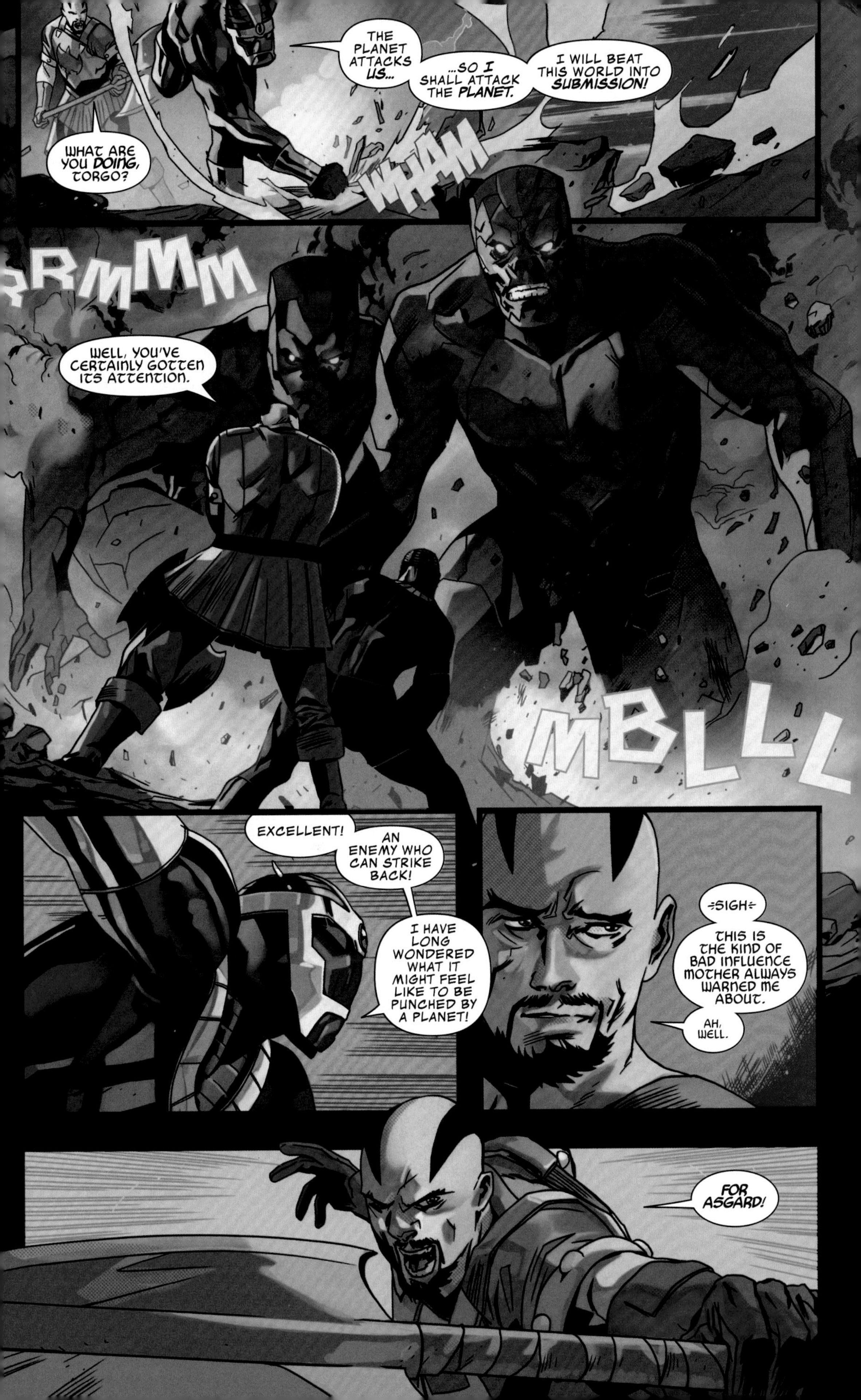

WHAT ARE YOU DOING, TORGO?
THE PLANET ATTACKS US...
...SO I SHALL ATTACK THE PLANET.
I WILL BEAT THIS WORLD INTO SUBMISSION!
WHAM
RRMMM
WELL, YOU'VE CERTAINLY GOTTEN ITS ATTENTION.
MBLLL
EXCELLENT!
AN ENEMY WHO CAN STRIKE BACK!
I HAVE LONG WONDERED WHAT IT MIGHT FEEL LIKE TO BE PUNCHED BY A PLANET!
SIGH
THIS IS THE KIND OF BAD INFLUENCE MOTHER ALWAYS WARNED ME ABOUT.
AH, WELL.
FOR ASGARD!

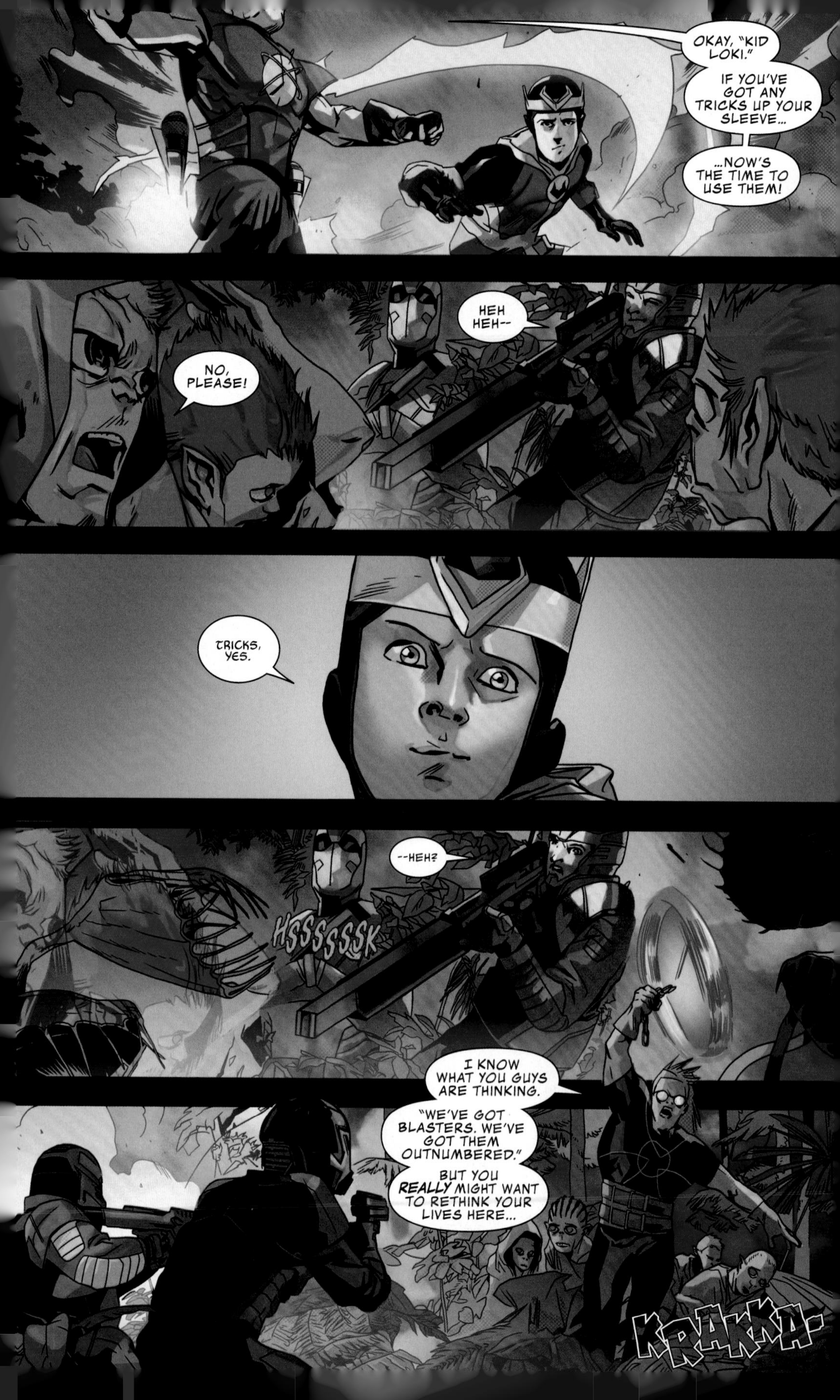
OKAY, "KID LOKI."
IF YOU'VE GOT ANY TRICKS UP YOUR SLEEVE...
...NOW'S THE TIME TO USE THEM!
HEH HEH--
NO, PLEASE!
TRICKS, YES.
--HEH?
HSSSSSSK
I KNOW WHAT YOU GUYS ARE THINKING.
"WE'VE GOT BLASTERS. WE'VE GOT THEM OUTNUMBERED."
BUT YOU REALLY MIGHT WANT TO RETHINK YOUR LIVES HERE...
KRAKKA-

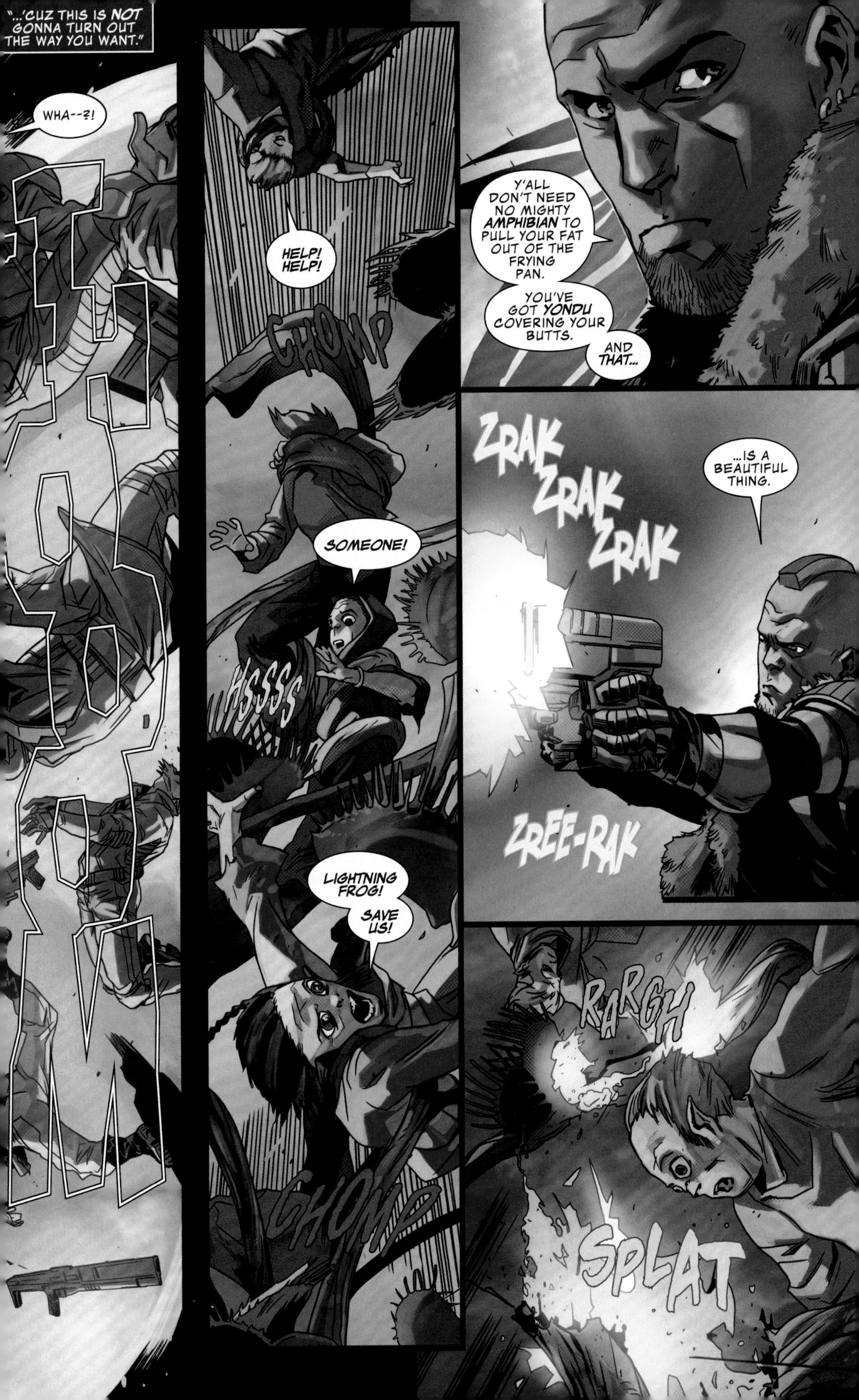
"...'CUZ THIS IS NOT GONNA TURN OUT THE WAY YOU WANT."
WHA--?!
HELP! HELP!
CHOMP
SOMEONE!
HSSSS
LIGHTNING FROG!
SAVE US!
CHOMP
Y'ALL DON'T NEED NO MIGHTY AMPHIBIAN TO PULL YOUR FAT OUT OF THE FRYING PAN.
YOU'VE GOT YONDU COVERING YOUR BUTTS.
AND THAT...
ZRAK ZRAK ZRAK
...IS A BEAUTIFUL THING.
ZREE-RAK
RARGH
SPLAT

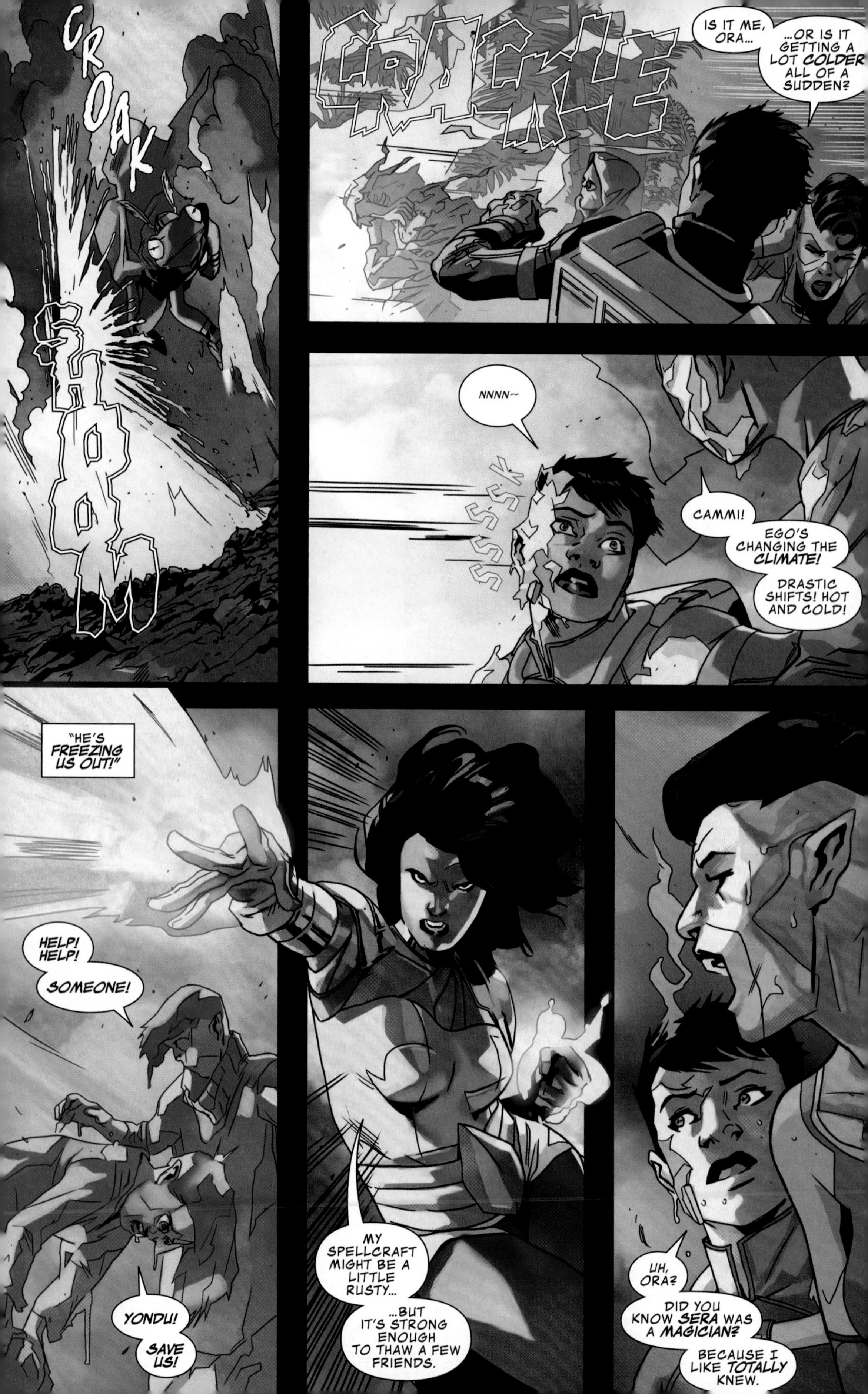
CROAK
BOOM
CRACKLE
IS IT ME, ORA...
...OR IS IT GETTING A LOT COLDER ALL OF A SUDDEN?
NNNN--
SSSSK
CAMMI!
EGO'S CHANGING THE CLIMATE!
DRASTIC SHIFTS! HOT AND COLD!
"HE'S FREEZING US OUT!"
HELP! HELP!
SOMEONE!
YONDU!
SAVE US!
MY SPELLCRAFT MIGHT BE A LITTLE RUSTY...
...BUT IT'S STRONG ENOUGH TO THAW A FEW FRIENDS.
UH, ORA?
DID YOU KNOW SERA WAS A MAGICIAN?
BECAUSE I LIKE TOTALLY KNEW.

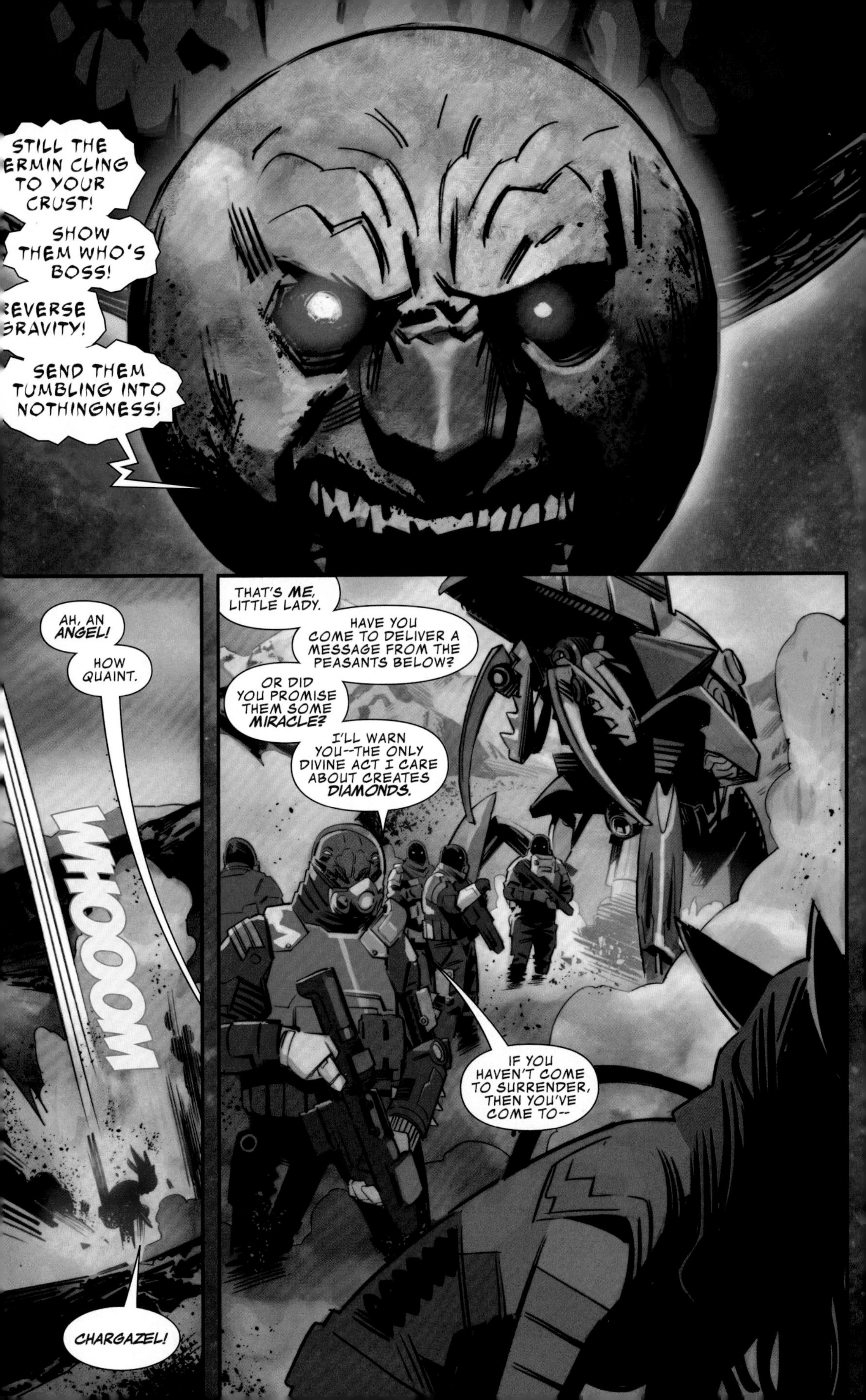

STILL THE ERMIN CLING TO YOUR CRUST!
SHOW THEM WHO'S BOSS!
EVERSE RAVITY!
SEND THEM TUMBLING INTO NOTHINGNESS!
AH, AN ANGEL!
HOW QUAINT.
WHOOOOM
CHARGAZEL!
THAT'S ME, LITTLE LADY.
HAVE YOU COME TO DELIVER A MESSAGE FROM THE PEASANTS BELOW?
OR DID YOU PROMISE THEM SOME MIRACLE?
I'LL WARN YOU--THE ONLY DIVINE ACT I CARE ABOUT CREATES DIAMONDS.
IF YOU HAVEN'T COME TO SURRENDER, THEN YOU'VE COME TO--

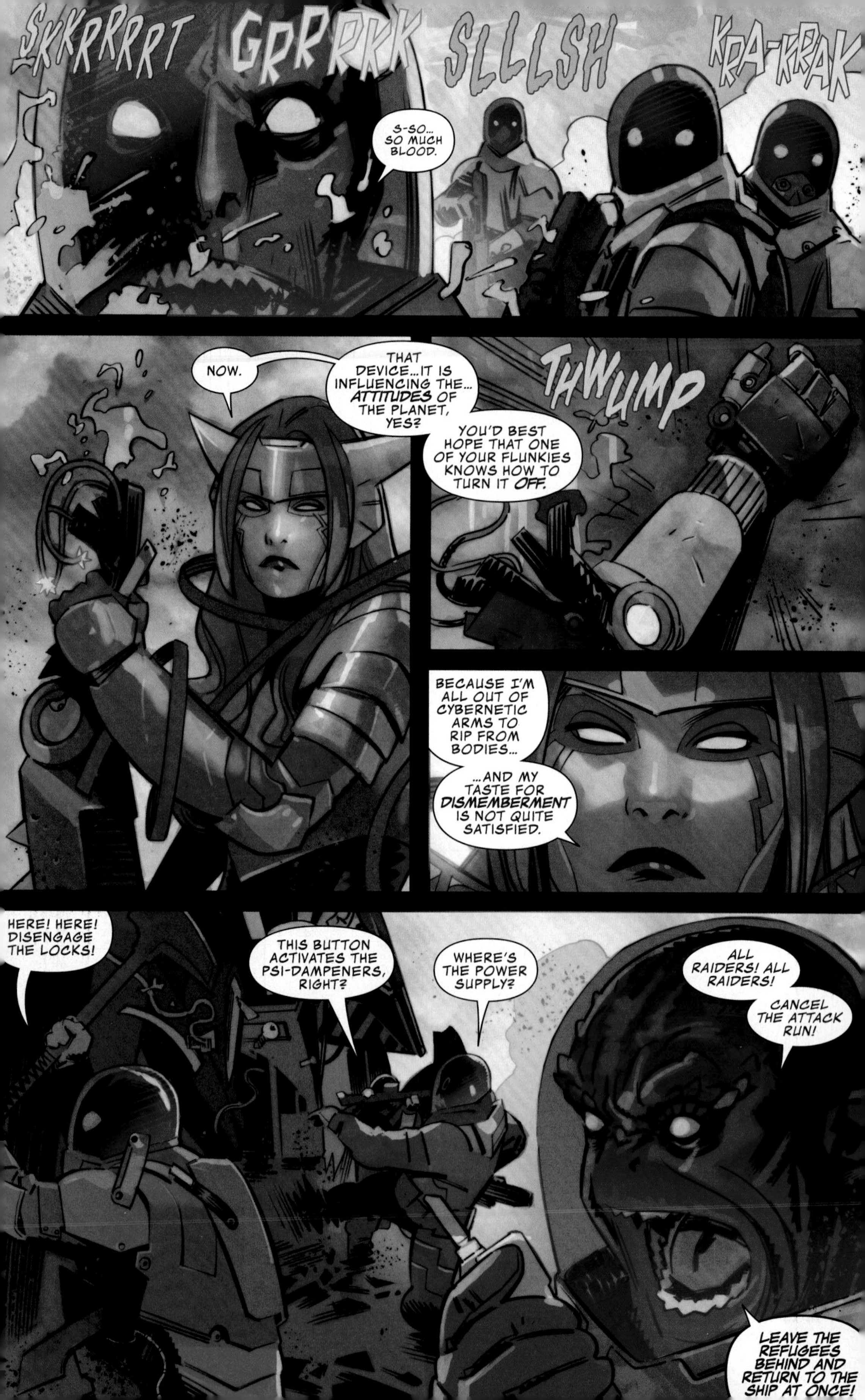
SKKRRRRT
GRRRRK
SLLLSH
KRA-KRAK
S-SO... SO MUCH BLOOD.
NOW.
THAT DEVICE...IT IS INFLUENCING THE... ATTITUDES OF THE PLANET, YES?
YOU'D BEST HOPE THAT ONE OF YOUR FLUNKIES KNOWS HOW TO TURN IT OFF.
THWUMP
BECAUSE I'M ALL OUT OF CYBERNETIC ARMS TO RIP FROM BODIES...
...AND MY TASTE FOR DISMEMBERMENT IS NOT QUITE SATISFIED.
HERE! HERE! DISENGAGE THE LOCKS!
THIS BUTTON ACTIVATES THE PSI-DAMPENERS, RIGHT?
WHERE'S THE POWER SUPPLY?
ALL RAIDERS! ALL RAIDERS!
CANCEL THE ATTACK RUN!
LEAVE THE REFUGEES BEHIND AND RETURN TO THE SHIP AT ONCE!

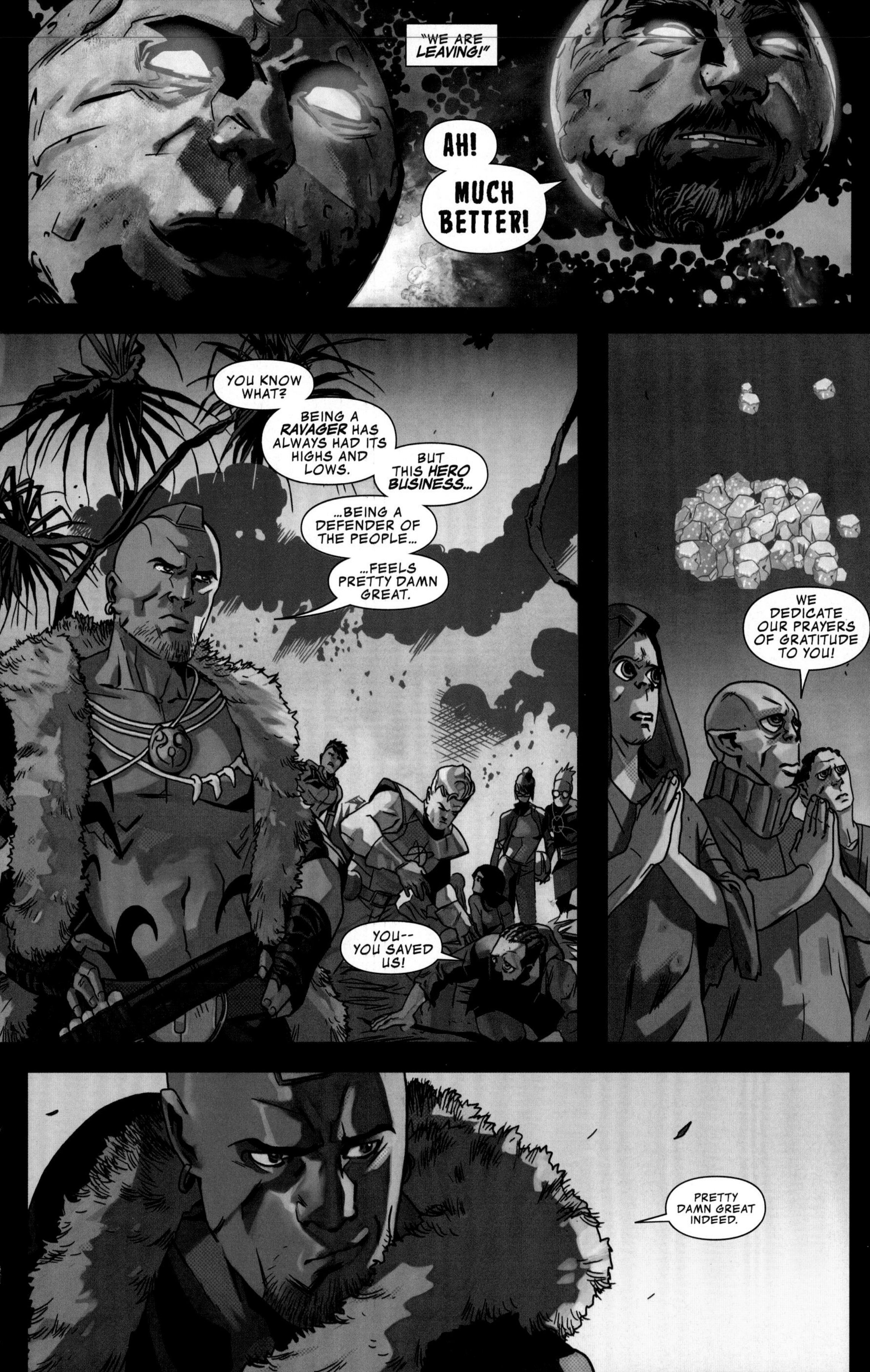
"WE ARE LEAVING!"
AH!
MUCH BETTER!
YOU KNOW WHAT?
BEING A RAVAGER HAS ALWAYS HAD ITS HIGHS AND LOWS.
BUT THIS HERO BUSINESS...
...BEING A DEFENDER OF THE PEOPLE...
...FEELS PRETTY DAMN GREAT.
YOU-- YOU SAVED US!
WE DEDICATE OUR PRAYERS OF GRATITUDE TO YOU!
PRETTY DAMN GREAT INDEED.

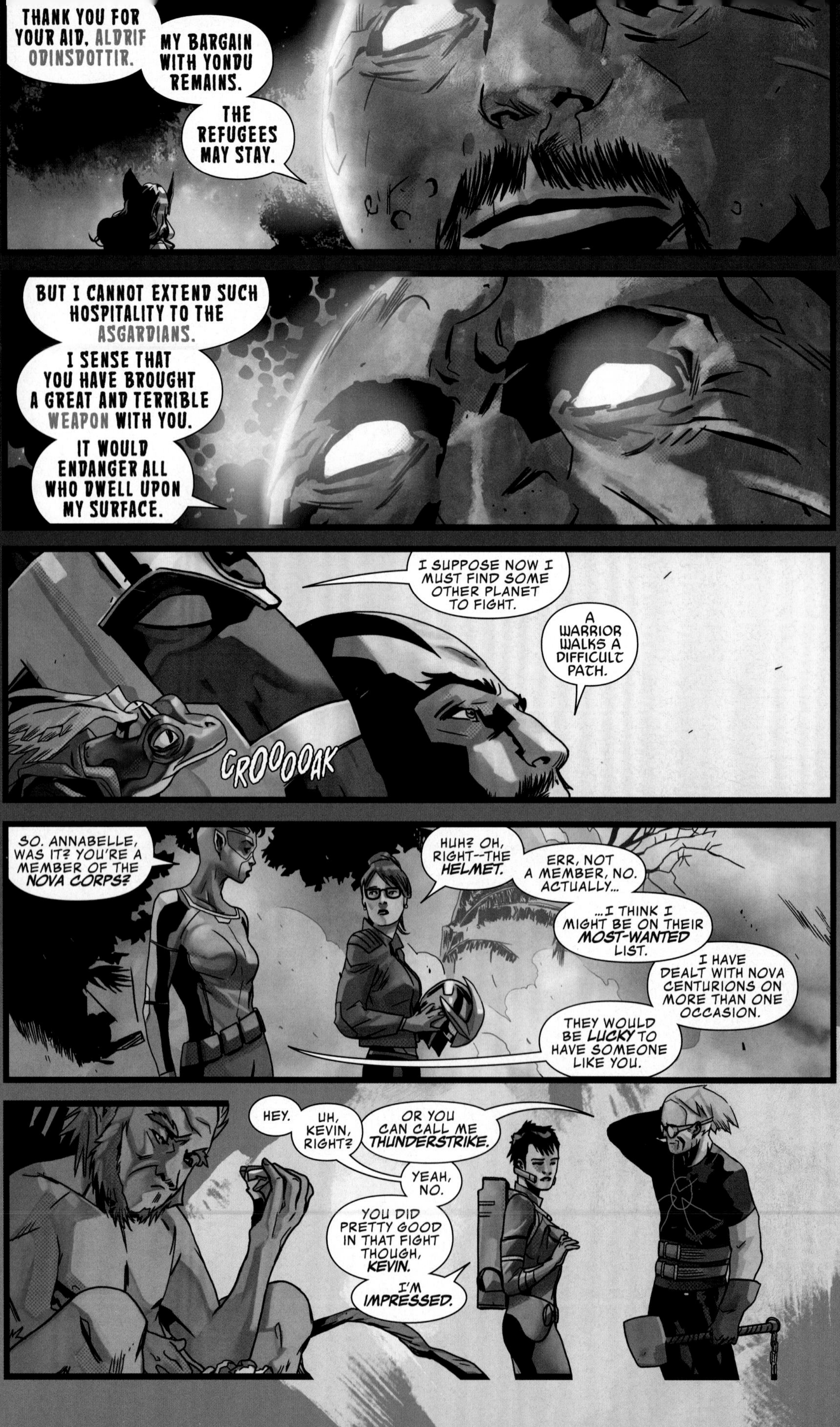
THANK YOU FOR YOUR AID, ALDRIF ODINSDOTTIR.
MY BARGAIN WITH YONDU REMAINS.
THE REFUGEES MAY STAY.
BUT I CANNOT EXTEND SUCH HOSPITALITY TO THE ASGARDIANS.
I SENSE THAT YOU HAVE BROUGHT A GREAT AND TERRIBLE WEAPON WITH YOU.
IT WOULD ENDANGER ALL WHO DWELL UPON MY SURFACE.
I SUPPOSE NOW I MUST FIND SOME OTHER PLANET TO FIGHT.
A WARRIOR WALKS A DIFFICULT PATH.
CROOOOAK
SO. ANNABELLE, WAS IT? YOU'RE A MEMBER OF THE NOVA CORPS?
HUH? OH, RIGHT--THE HELMET.
ERR, NOT A MEMBER, NO. ACTUALLY...
...I THINK I MIGHT BE ON THEIR MOST-WANTED LIST.
I HAVE DEALT WITH NOVA CENTURIONS ON MORE THAN ONE OCCASION.
THEY WOULD BE LUCKY TO HAVE SOMEONE LIKE YOU.
HEY.
UH, KEVIN, RIGHT?
OR YOU CAN CALL ME THUNDERSTRIKE.
YEAH, NO.
YOU DID PRETTY GOOD IN THAT FIGHT THOUGH, KEVIN.
I'M IMPRESSED.

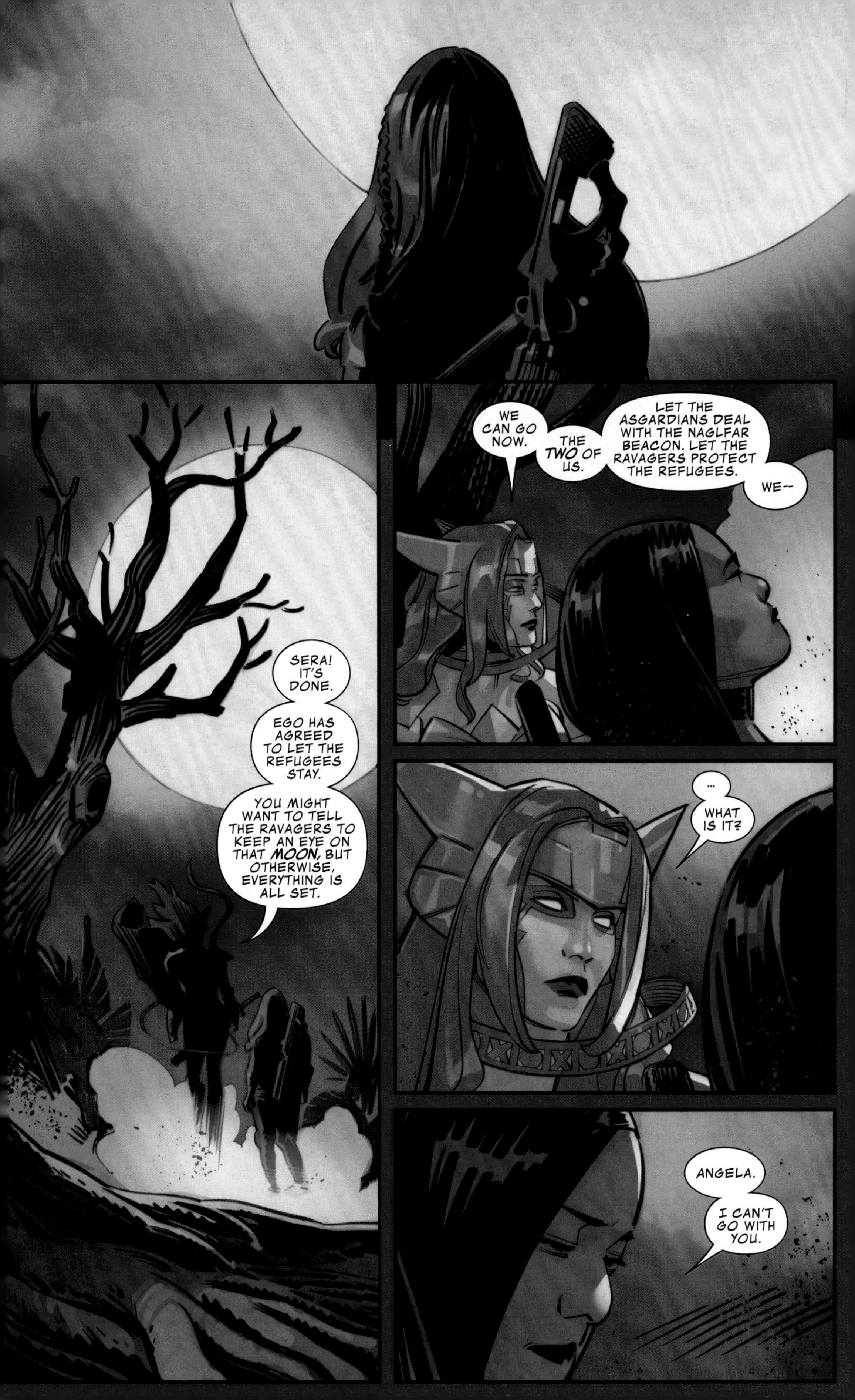
SERA! IT'S DONE.
EGO HAS AGREED TO LET THE REFUGEES STAY.
YOU MIGHT WANT TO TELL THE RAVAGERS TO KEEP AN EYE ON THAT MOON, BUT OTHERWISE, EVERYTHING IS ALL SET.
WE CAN GO NOW.
THE TWO OF US.
LET THE ASGARDIANS DEAL WITH THE NAGLFAR BEACON. LET THE RAVAGERS PROTECT THE REFUGEES.
WE--
...
WHAT IS IT?
ANGELA.
I CAN'T GO WITH YOU.

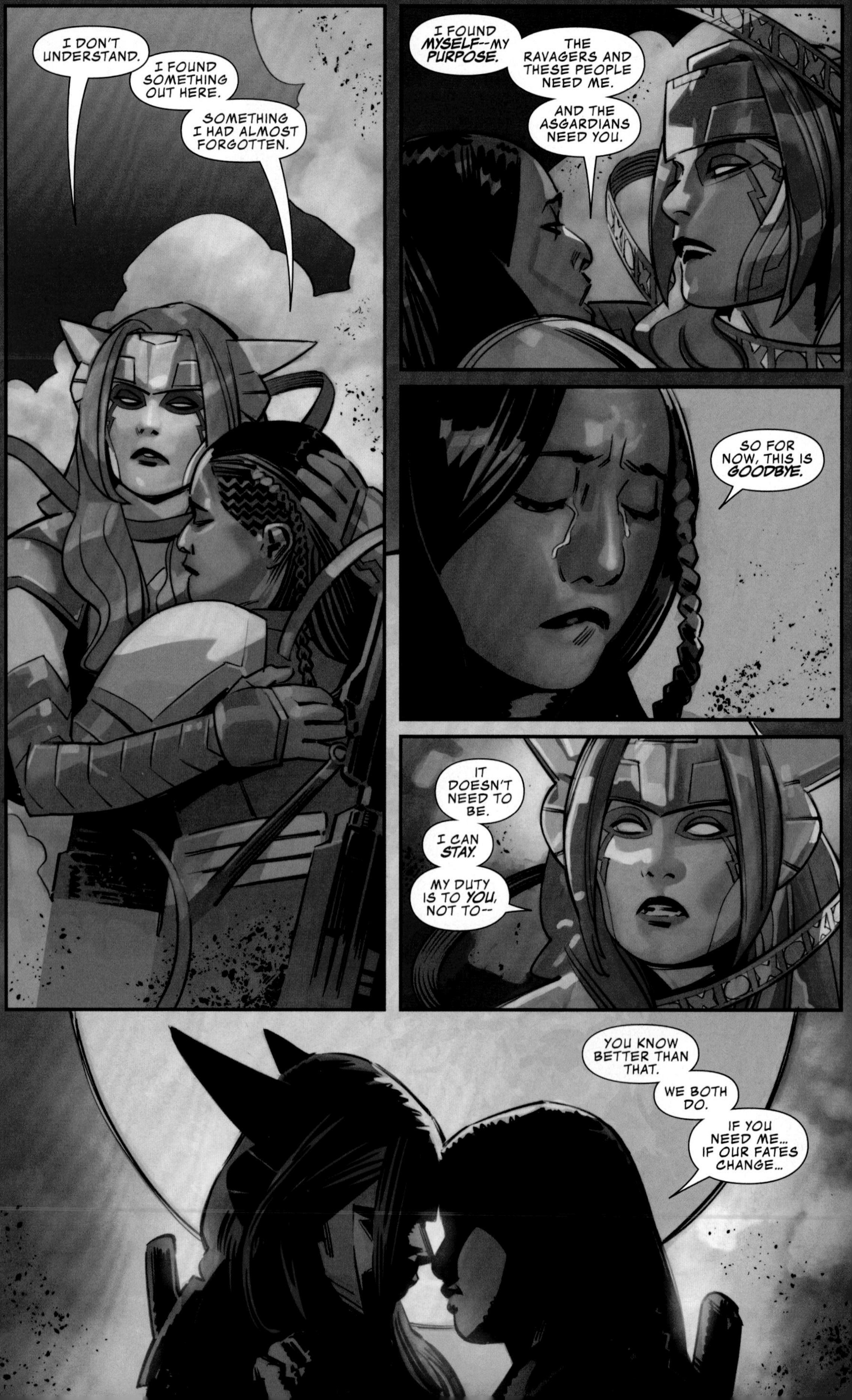
I DON'T UNDERSTAND.
I FOUND SOMETHING OUT HERE.
SOMETHING I HAD ALMOST FORGOTTEN.
I FOUND MYSELF--MY PURPOSE.
THE RAVAGERS AND THESE PEOPLE NEED ME.
AND THE ASGARDIANS NEED YOU.
SO FOR NOW, THIS IS GOODBYE.
IT DOESN'T NEED TO BE.
I CAN STAY.
MY DUTY IS TO YOU, NOT TO--
YOU KNOW BETTER THAN THAT.
WE BOTH DO.
IF YOU NEED ME... IF OUR FATES CHANGE...

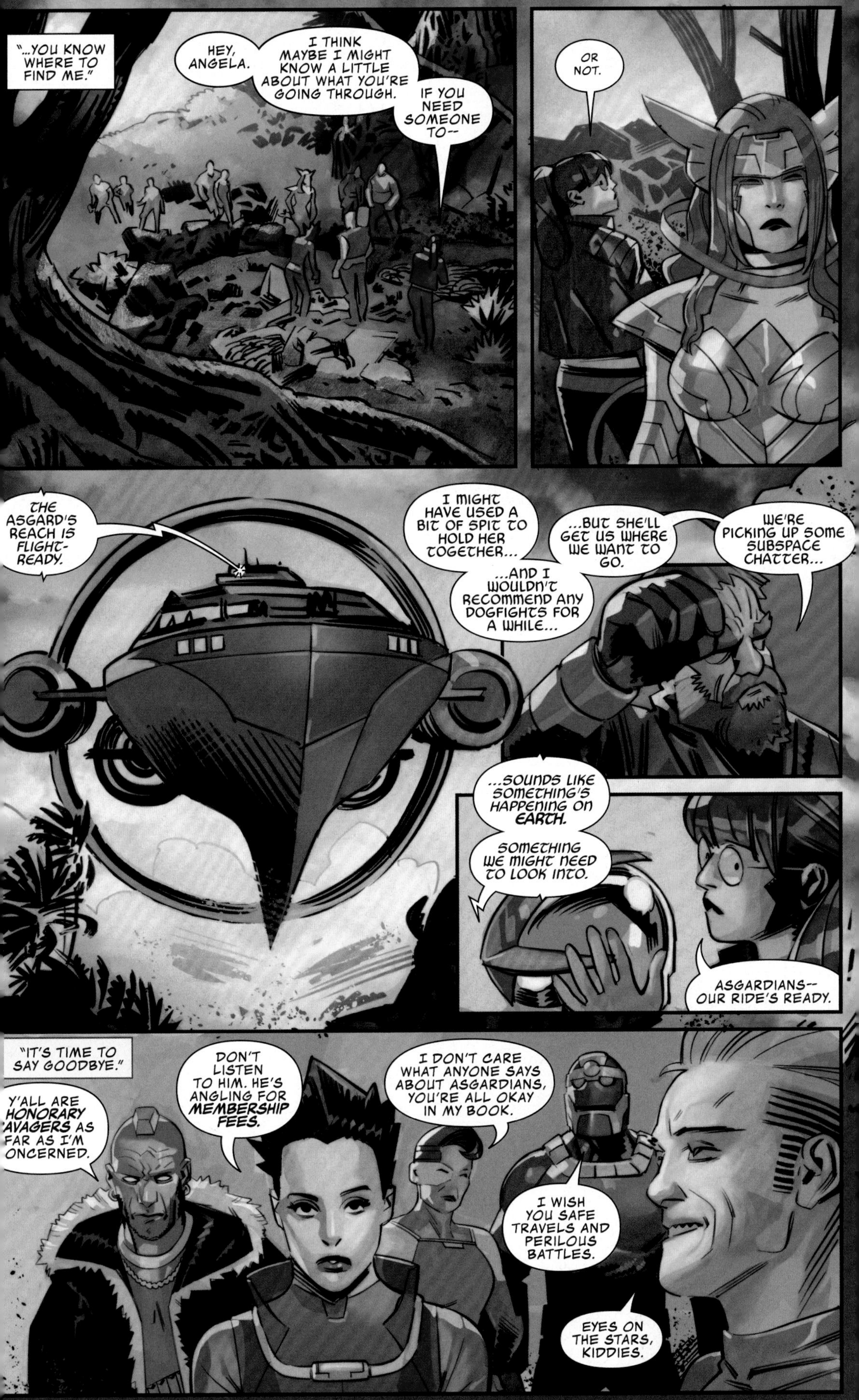
"...YOU KNOW WHERE TO FIND ME."
HEY, ANGELA.
I THINK MAYBE I MIGHT KNOW A LITTLE ABOUT WHAT YOU'RE GOING THROUGH.
IF YOU NEED SOMEONE TO--
OR NOT.
THE ASGARD'S REACH IS FLIGHT-READY.
I MIGHT HAVE USED A BIT OF SPIT TO HOLD HER TOGETHER...
...AND I WOULDN'T RECOMMEND ANY DOGFIGHTS FOR A WHILE...
...BUT SHE'LL GET US WHERE WE WANT TO GO.
WE'RE PICKING UP SOME SUBSPACE CHATTER...
...SOUNDS LIKE SOMETHING'S HAPPENING ON EARTH.
SOMETHING WE MIGHT NEED TO LOOK INTO.
ASGARDIANS-- OUR RIDE'S READY.
"IT'S TIME TO SAY GOODBYE."
Y'ALL ARE HONORARY RAVAGERS AS FAR AS I'M CONCERNED.
DON'T LISTEN TO HIM. HE'S ANGLING FOR MEMBERSHIP FEES.
I DON'T CARE WHAT ANYONE SAYS ABOUT ASGARDIANS, YOU'RE ALL OKAY IN MY BOOK.
I WISH YOU SAFE TRAVELS AND PERILOUS BATTLES.
EYES ON THE STARS, KIDDIES.

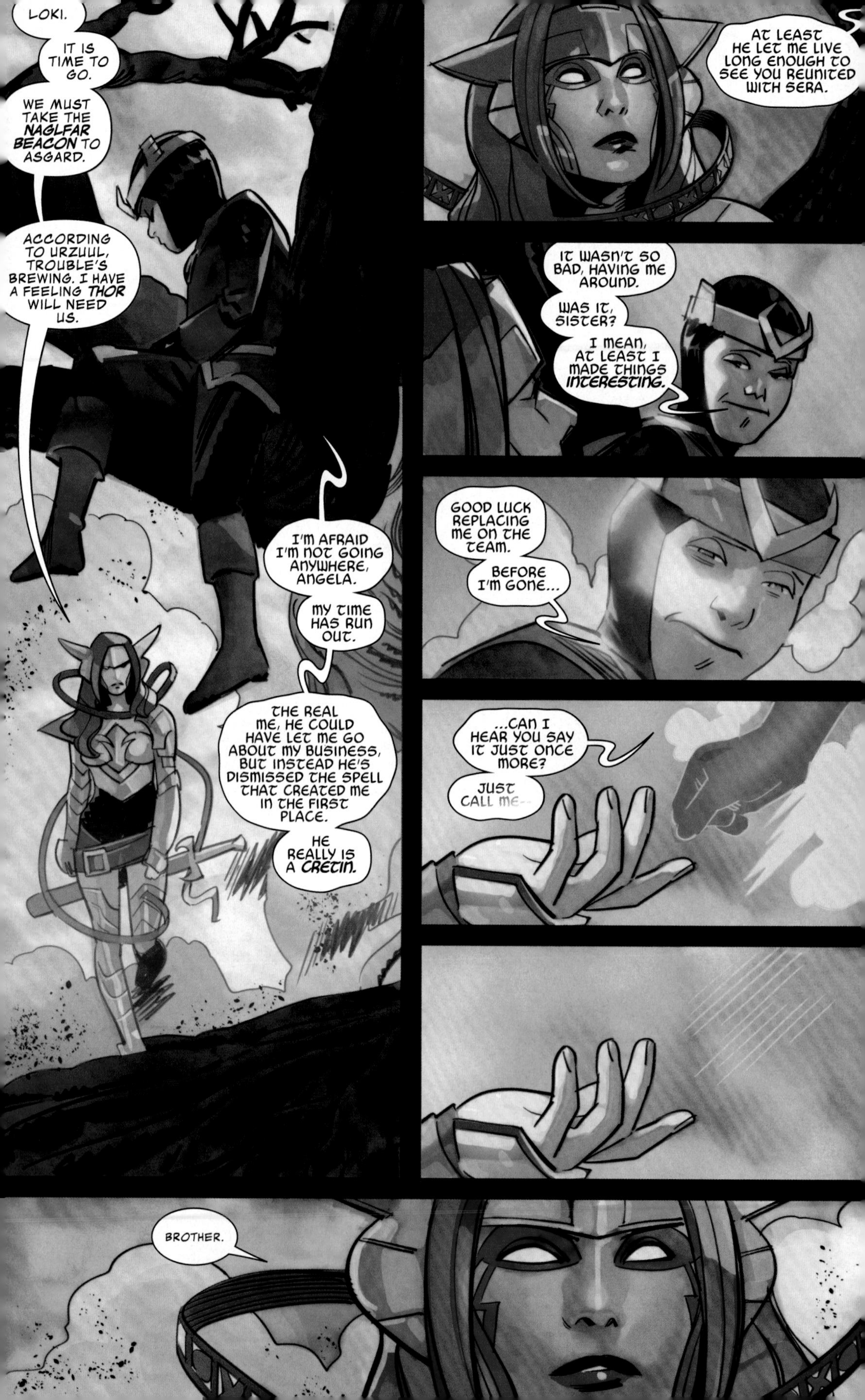
LOKI.
IT IS TIME TO GO.
WE MUST TAKE THE NAGLFAR BEACON TO ASGARD.
ACCORDING TO URZUUL, TROUBLE'S BREWING. I HAVE A FEELING THOR WILL NEED US.
I'M AFRAID I'M NOT GOING ANYWHERE, ANGELA.
MY TIME HAS RUN OUT.
THE REAL ME, HE COULD HAVE LET ME GO ABOUT MY BUSINESS, BUT INSTEAD HE'S DISMISSED THE SPELL THAT CREATED ME IN THE FIRST PLACE.
HE REALLY IS A CRETIN.
AT LEAST HE LET ME LIVE LONG ENOUGH TO SEE YOU REUNITED WITH SERA.
IT WASN'T SO BAD, HAVING ME AROUND.
WAS IT, SISTER?
I MEAN, AT LEAST I MADE THINGS INTERESTING.
GOOD LUCK REPLACING ME ON THE TEAM.
BEFORE I'M GONE...
...CAN I HEAR YOU SAY IT JUST ONCE MORE?
JUST CALL ME--
BROTHER.

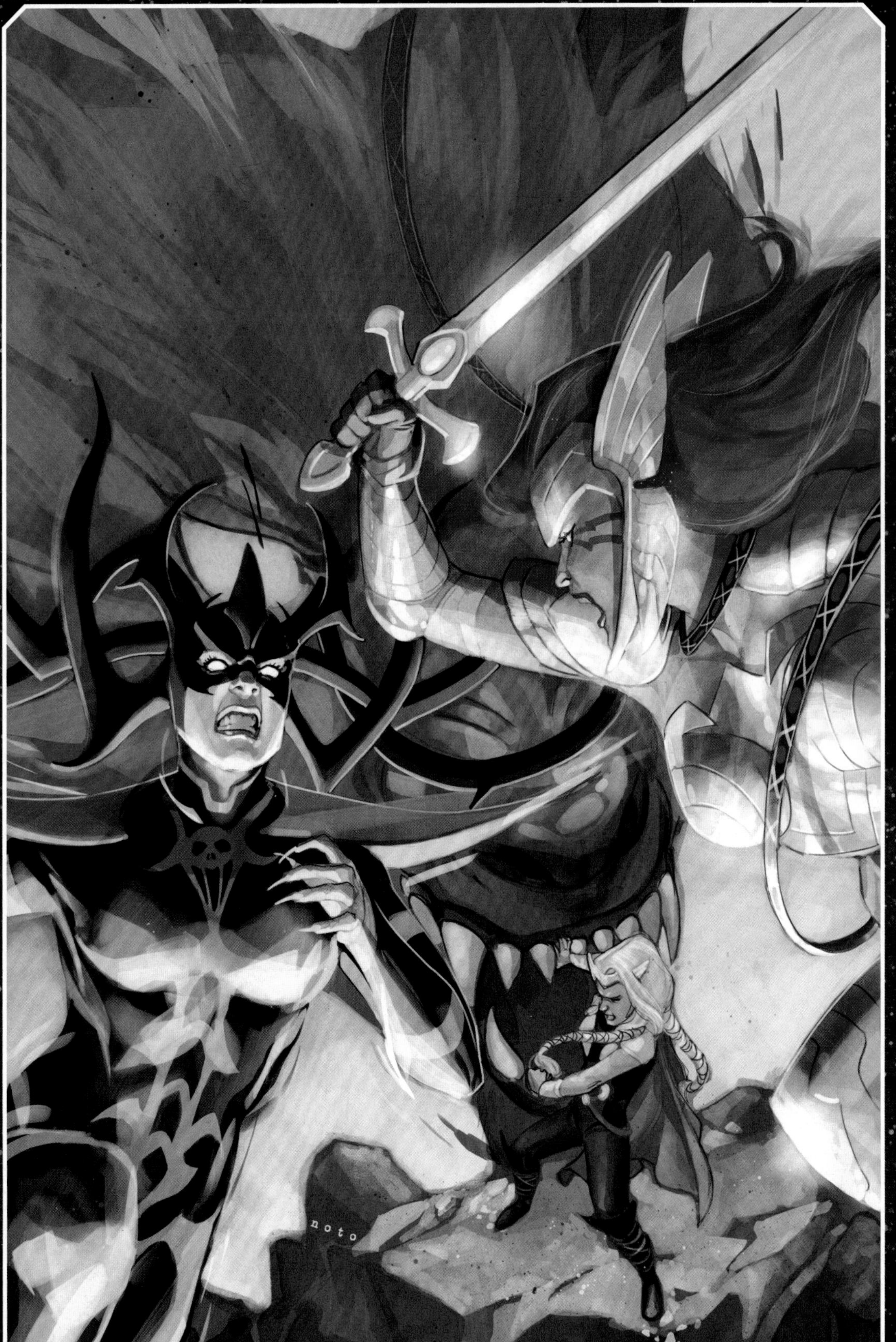
noto

PHIL NOTO

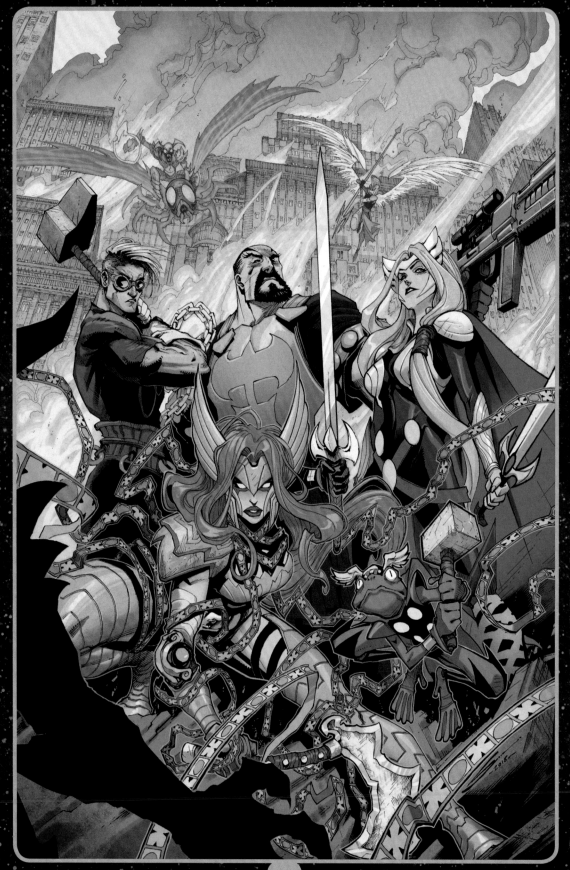

8

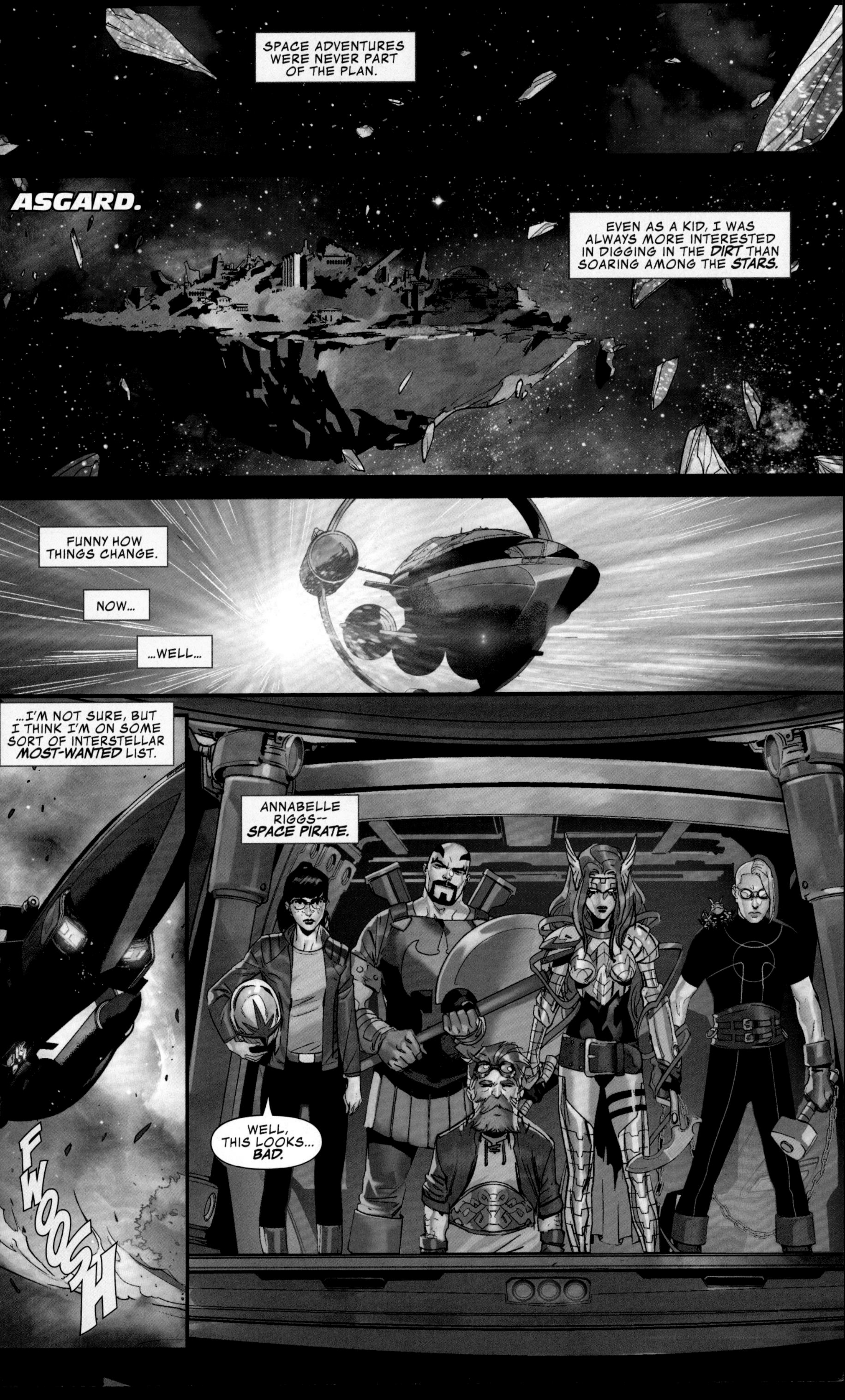

SPACE ADVENTURES WERE NEVER PART OF THE PLAN.
ASGARD.
EVEN AS A KID, I WAS ALWAYS MORE INTERESTED IN DIGGING IN THE DIRT THAN SOARING AMONG THE STARS.
FUNNY HOW THINGS CHANGE.
NOW...
...WELL...
...I'M NOT SURE, BUT I THINK I'M ON SOME SORT OF INTERSTELLAR MOST-WANTED LIST.
ANNABELLE RIGGS-- SPACE PIRATE.
WELL, THIS LOOKS... BAD.
FWOOOSH

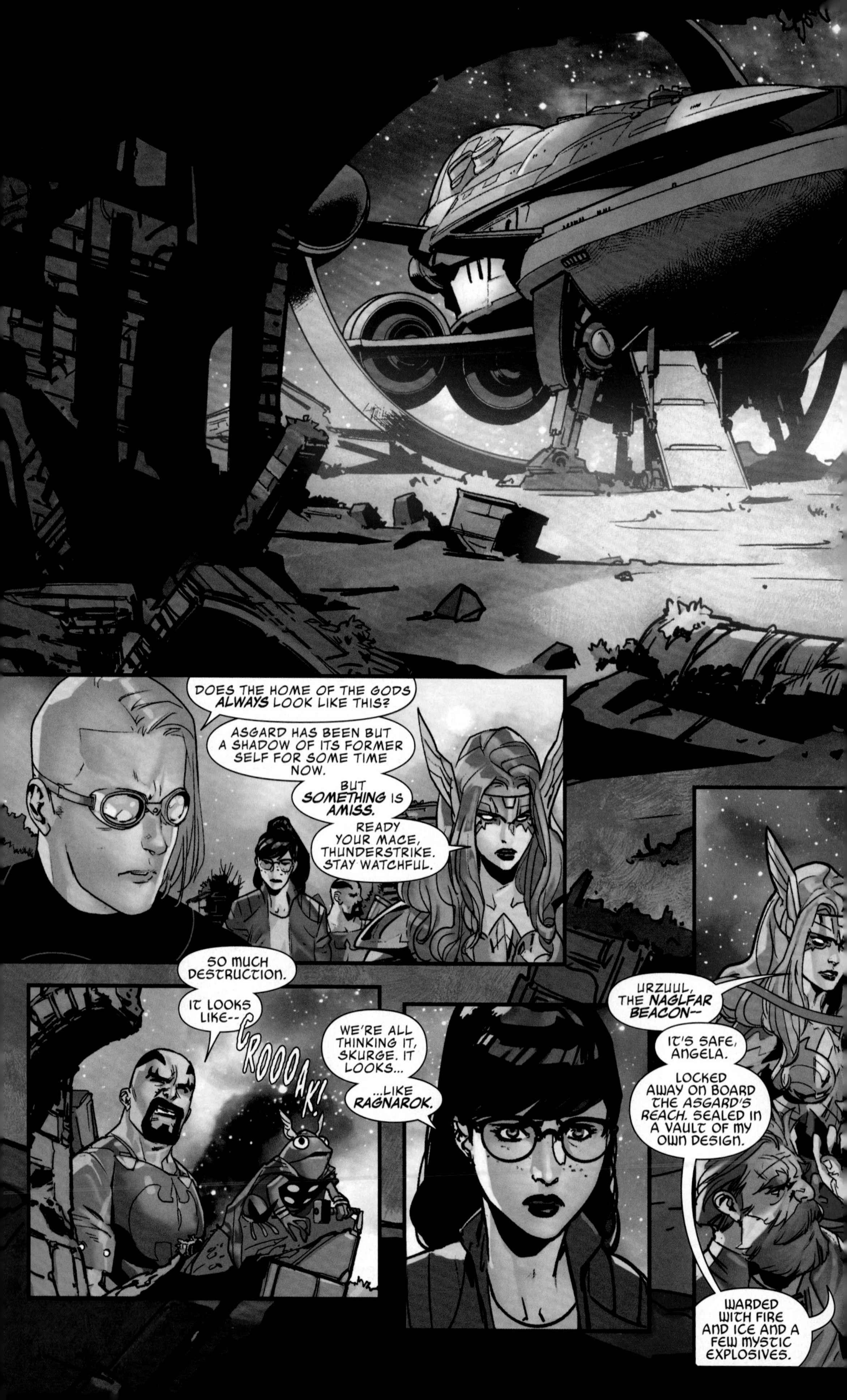
DOES THE HOME OF THE GODS ALWAYS LOOK LIKE THIS?
ASGARD HAS BEEN BUT A SHADOW OF ITS FORMER SELF FOR SOME TIME NOW.
BUT SOMETHING IS AMISS.
READY YOUR MACE, THUNDERSTRIKE. STAY WATCHFUL.
SO MUCH DESTRUCTION.
IT LOOKS LIKE--
CROOOAK!
WE'RE ALL THINKING IT, SKURGE. IT LOOKS...
...LIKE RAGNAROK.
URZUUL, THE NAGLFAR BEACON--
IT'S SAFE, ANGELA.
LOCKED AWAY ON BOARD THE ASGARD'S REACH. SEALED IN A VAULT OF MY OWN DESIGN.
WARDED WITH FIRE AND ICE AND A FEW MYSTIC EXPLOSIVES.

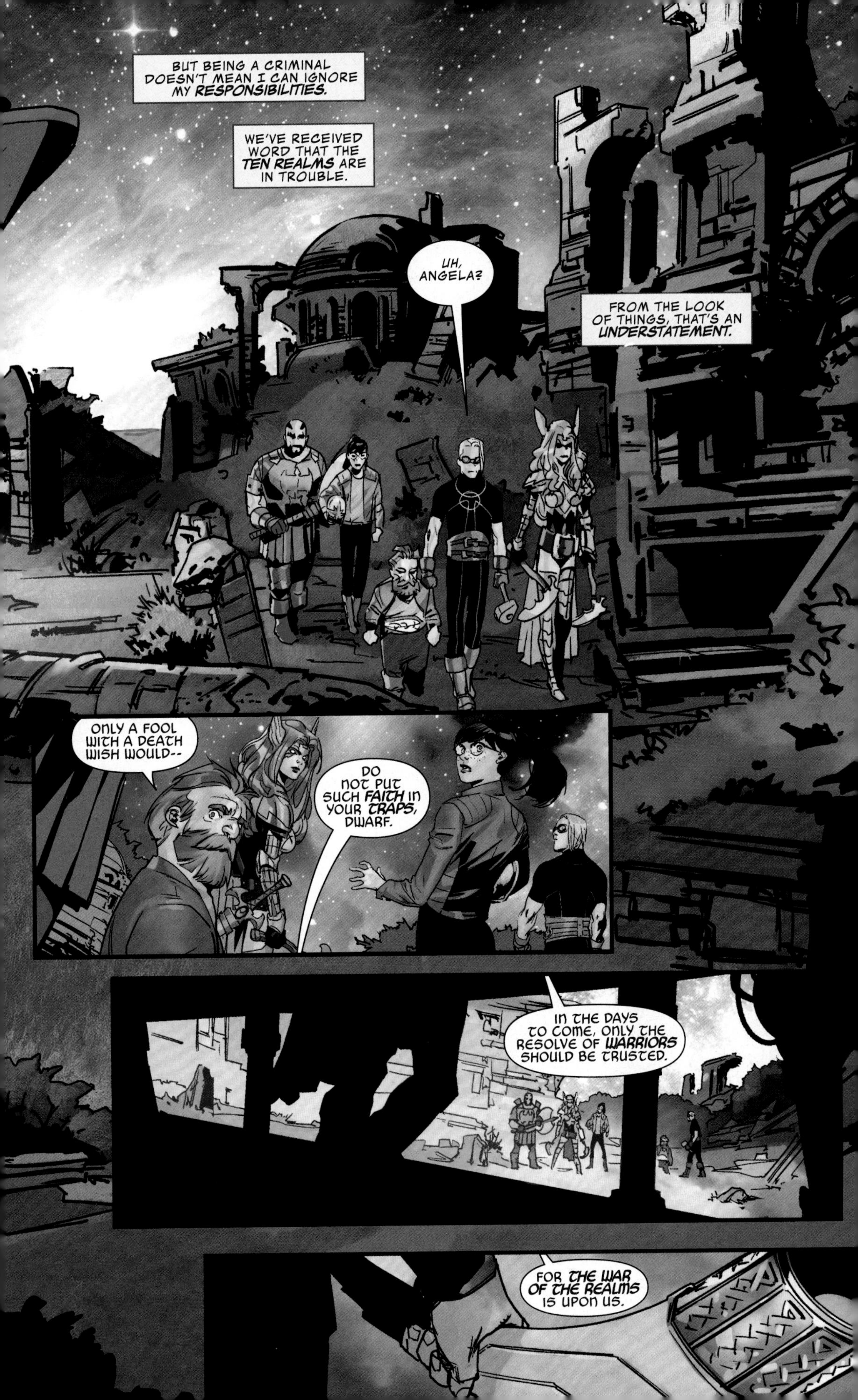

BUT BEING A CRIMINAL DOESN'T MEAN I CAN IGNORE MY RESPONSIBILITIES.
WE'VE RECEIVED WORD THAT THE TEN REALMS ARE IN TROUBLE.
UH, ANGELA?
FROM THE LOOK OF THINGS, THAT'S AN UNDERSTATEMENT.
ONLY A FOOL WITH A DEATH WISH WOULD--
DO NOT PUT SUCH FAITH IN YOUR TRAPS, DWARF.
IN THE DAYS TO COME, ONLY THE RESOLVE OF WARRIORS SHOULD BE TRUSTED.
FOR THE WAR OF THE REALMS IS UPON US.

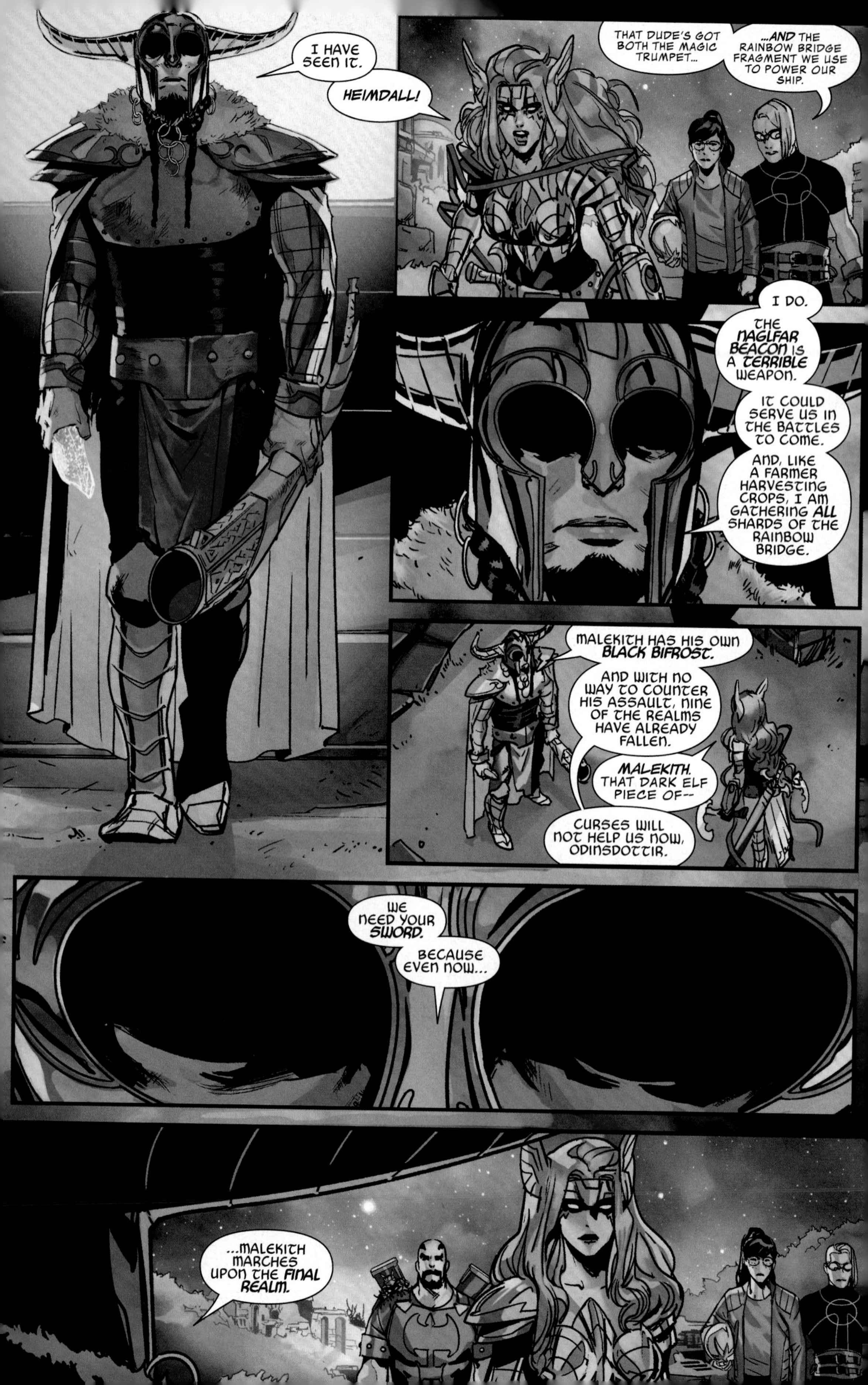

I HAVE SEEN IT.
HEIMDALL!
THAT DUDE'S GOT BOTH THE MAGIC TRUMPET...
...AND THE RAINBOW BRIDGE FRAGMENT WE USE TO POWER OUR SHIP.
I DO.
THE NAGLFAR BEACON IS A TERRIBLE WEAPON.
IT COULD SERVE US IN THE BATTLES TO COME.
AND, LIKE A FARMER HARVESTING CROPS, I AM GATHERING ALL SHARDS OF THE RAINBOW BRIDGE.
MALEKITH HAS HIS OWN BLACK BIFROST.
AND WITH NO WAY TO COUNTER HIS ASSAULT, NINE OF THE REALMS HAVE ALREADY FALLEN.
MALEKITH. THAT DARK ELF PIECE OF--
CURSES WILL NOT HELP US NOW, ODINSDOTTIR.
WE NEED YOUR SWORD.
BECAUSE EVEN NOW...
...MALEKITH MARCHES UPON THE FINAL REALM.

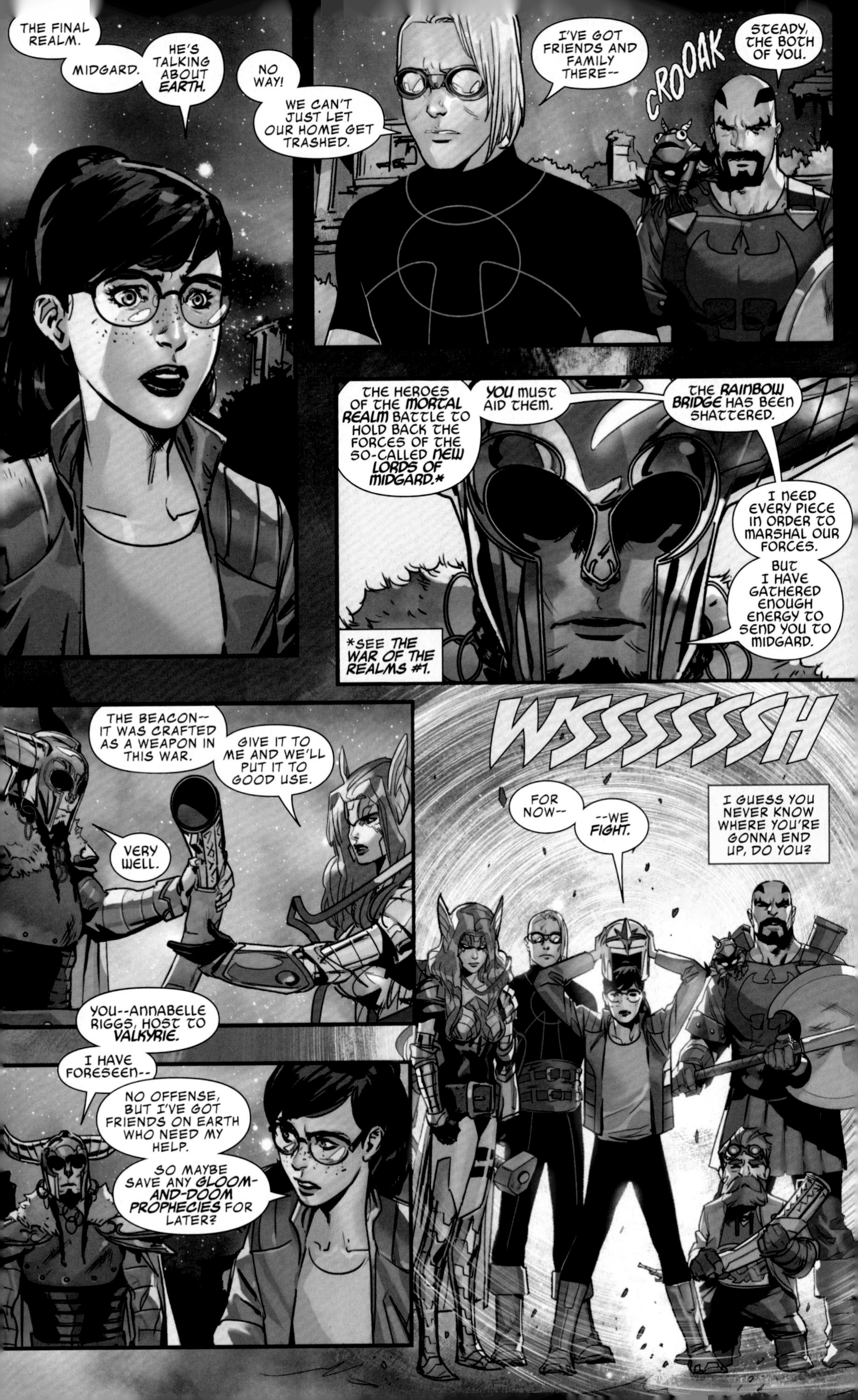
THE FINAL REALM.
MIDGARD.
HE'S TALKING ABOUT EARTH.
NO WAY!
WE CAN'T JUST LET OUR HOME GET TRASHED.
I'VE GOT FRIENDS AND FAMILY THERE--
CROOAK
STEADY, THE BOTH OF YOU.
THE HEROES OF THE MORTAL REALM BATTLE TO HOLD BACK THE FORCES OF THE SO-CALLED NEW LORDS OF MIDGARD.*
YOU MUST AID THEM.
THE RAINBOW BRIDGE HAS BEEN SHATTERED.
I NEED EVERY PIECE IN ORDER TO MARSHAL OUR FORCES.
BUT I HAVE GATHERED ENOUGH ENERGY TO SEND YOU TO MIDGARD.
*SEE THE WAR OF THE REALMS #1.
THE BEACON-- IT WAS CRAFTED AS A WEAPON IN THIS WAR.
GIVE IT TO ME AND WE'LL PUT IT TO GOOD USE.
VERY WELL.
YOU--ANNABELLE RIGGS, HOST TO VALKYRIE.
I HAVE FORESEEN--
NO OFFENSE, BUT I'VE GOT FRIENDS ON EARTH WHO NEED MY HELP.
SO MAYBE SAVE ANY GLOOM-AND-DOOM PROPHECIES FOR LATER?
WSSSSSH
FOR NOW--
--WE FIGHT.
I GUESS YOU NEVER KNOW WHERE YOU'RE GONNA END UP, DO YOU?

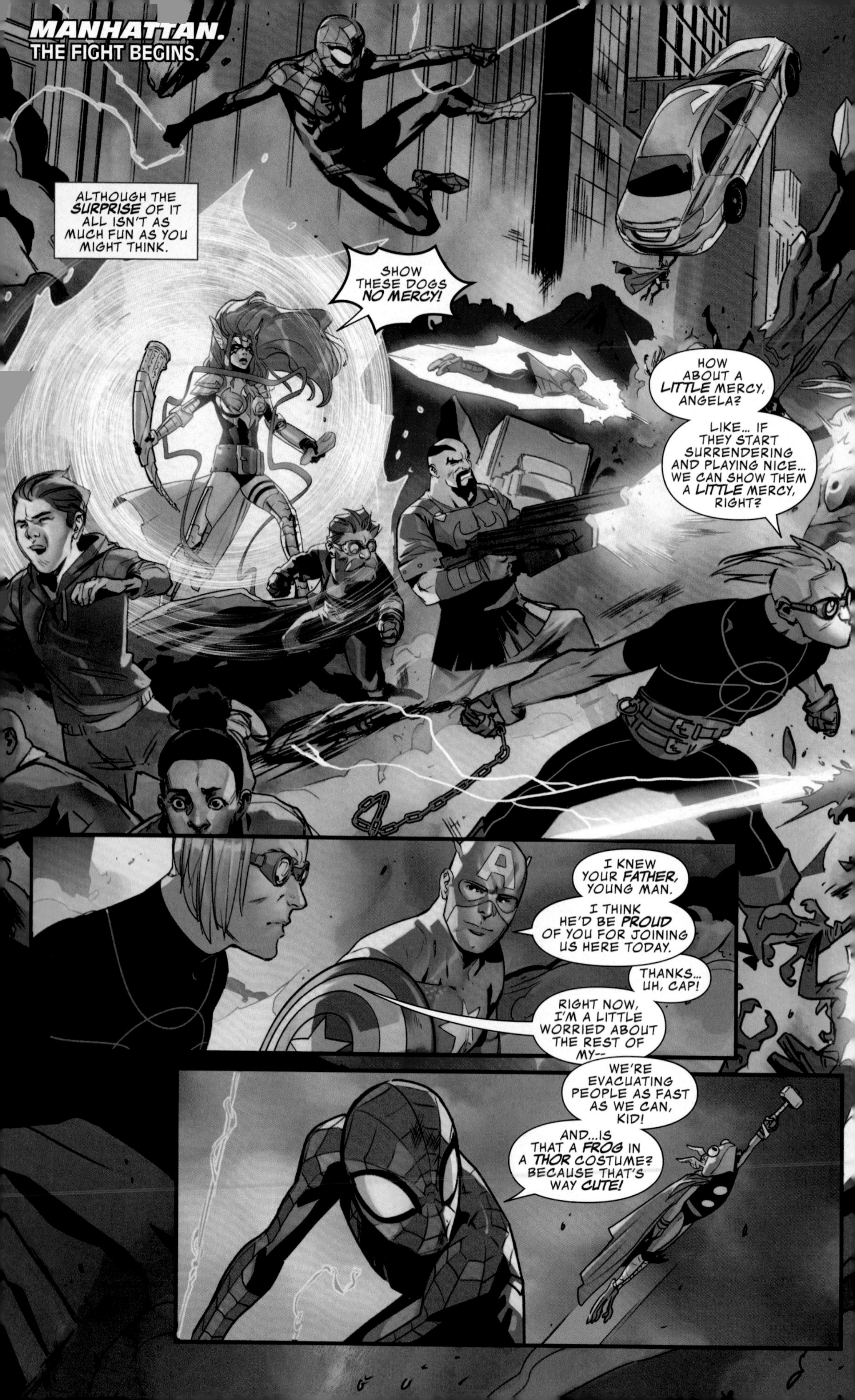
MANHATTAN.
THE FIGHT BEGINS.
ALTHOUGH THE SURPRISE OF IT ALL ISN'T AS MUCH FUN AS YOU MIGHT THINK.
SHOW THESE DOGS NO MERCY!
HOW ABOUT A LITTLE MERCY, ANGELA?
LIKE... IF THEY START SURRENDERING AND PLAYING NICE... WE CAN SHOW THEM A LITTLE MERCY, RIGHT?
I KNEW YOUR FATHER, YOUNG MAN.
I THINK HE'D BE PROUD OF YOU FOR JOINING US HERE TODAY.
THANKS... UH, CAP!
RIGHT NOW, I'M A LITTLE WORRIED ABOUT THE REST OF MY--
WE'RE EVACUATING PEOPLE AS FAST AS WE CAN, KID!
AND...IS THAT A FROG IN A THOR COSTUME? BECAUSE THAT'S WAY CUTE!

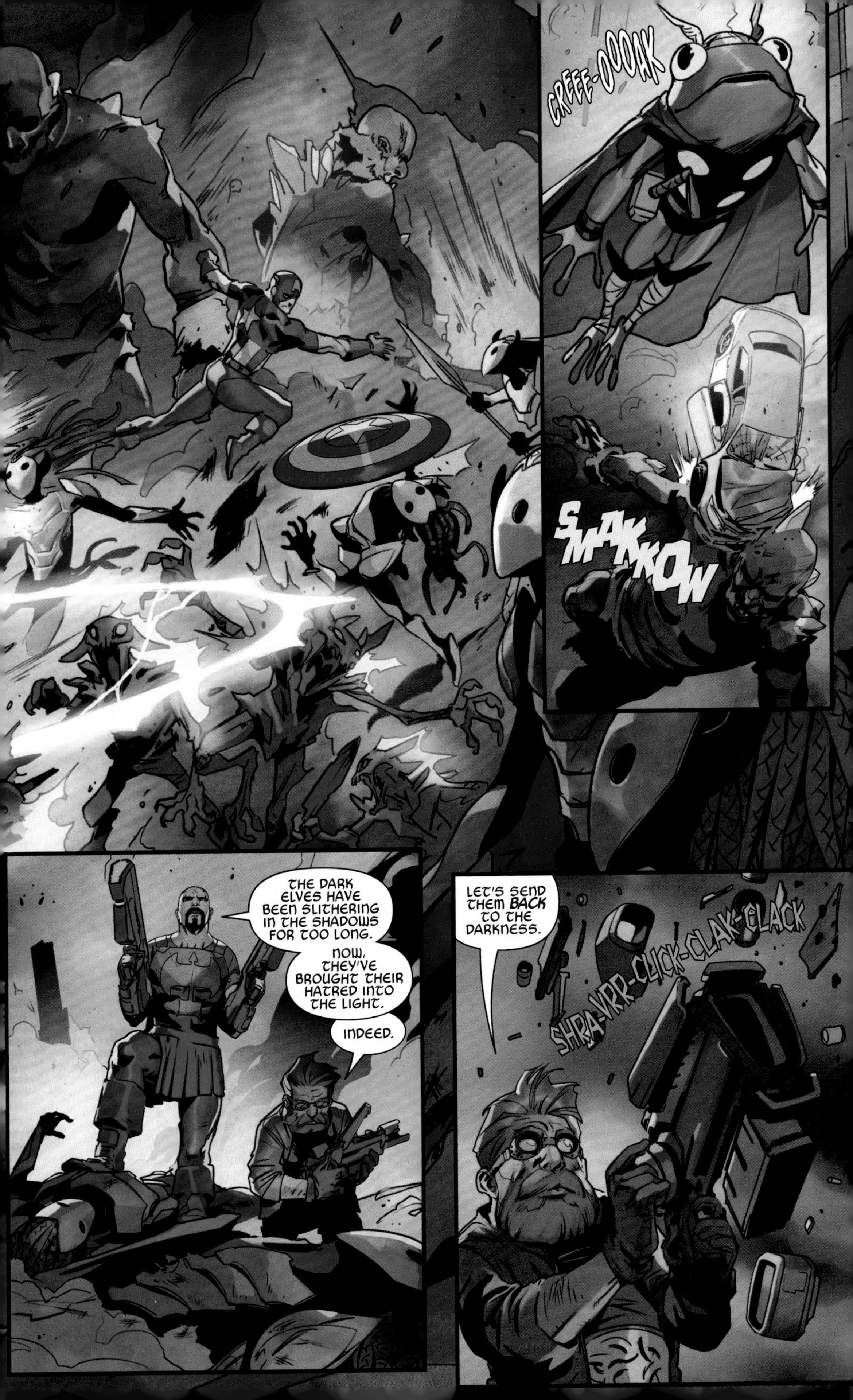
CREEE-OOOAK
SMAKKOW
THE DARK ELVES HAVE BEEN SLITHERING IN THE SHADOWS FOR TOO LONG.
NOW, THEY'VE BROUGHT THEIR HATRED INTO THE LIGHT.
INDEED.
LET'S SEND THEM **BACK** TO THE DARKNESS.
SHRA-VRR-CLICK-CLAK-CLACK

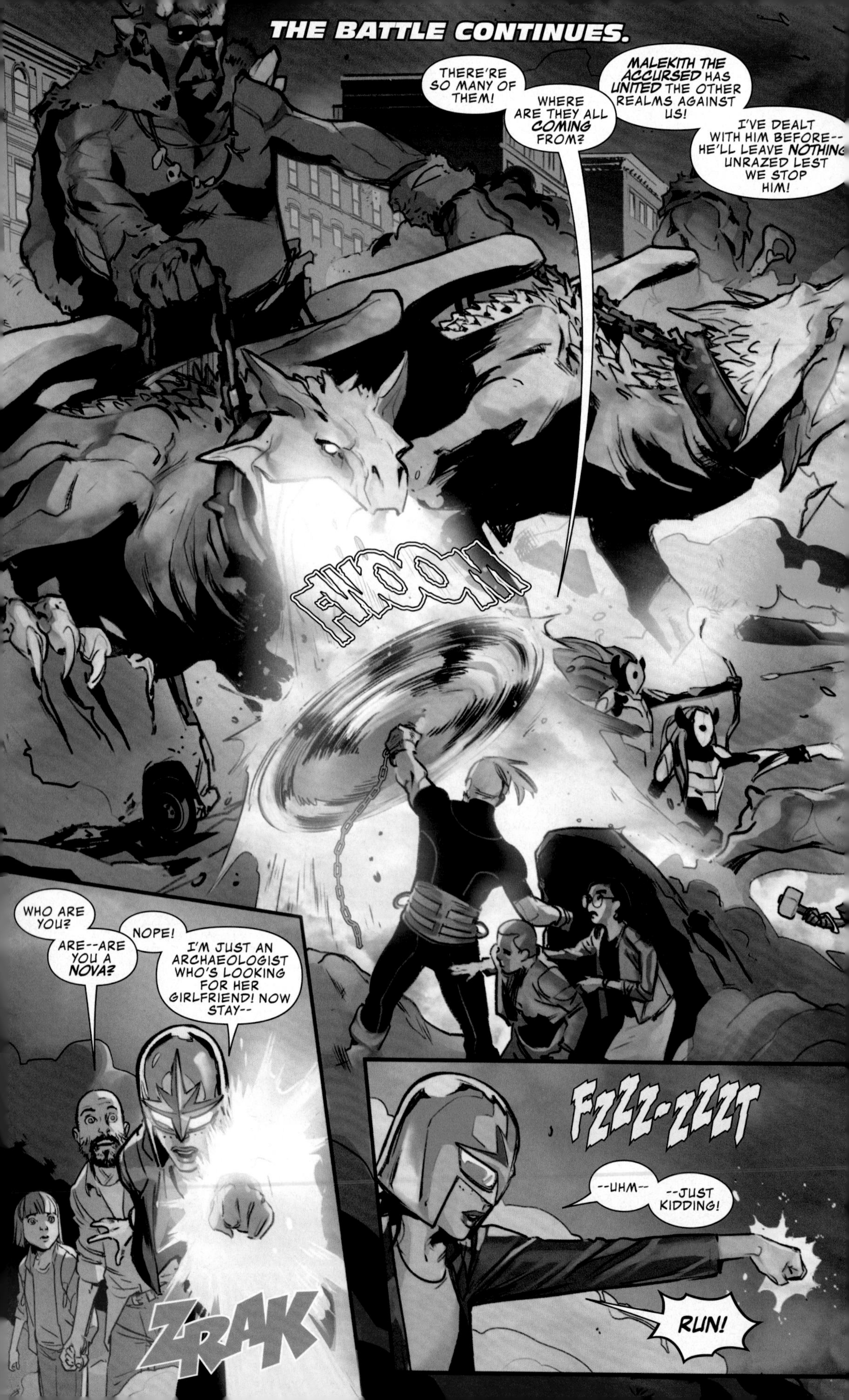
THE BATTLE CONTINUES.
THERE'RE SO MANY OF THEM!
WHERE ARE THEY ALL COMING FROM?
MALEKITH THE ACCURSED HAS UNITED THE OTHER REALMS AGAINST US!
I'VE DEALT WITH HIM BEFORE-- HE'LL LEAVE NOTHING UNRAZED LEST WE STOP HIM!
FWOOM
WHO ARE YOU?
ARE--ARE YOU A NOVA?
NOPE!
I'M JUST AN ARCHAEOLOGIST WHO'S LOOKING FOR HER GIRLFRIEND! NOW STAY--
ZRAK
FZZZ-ZZZT
--UHM--
--JUST KIDDING!
RUN!

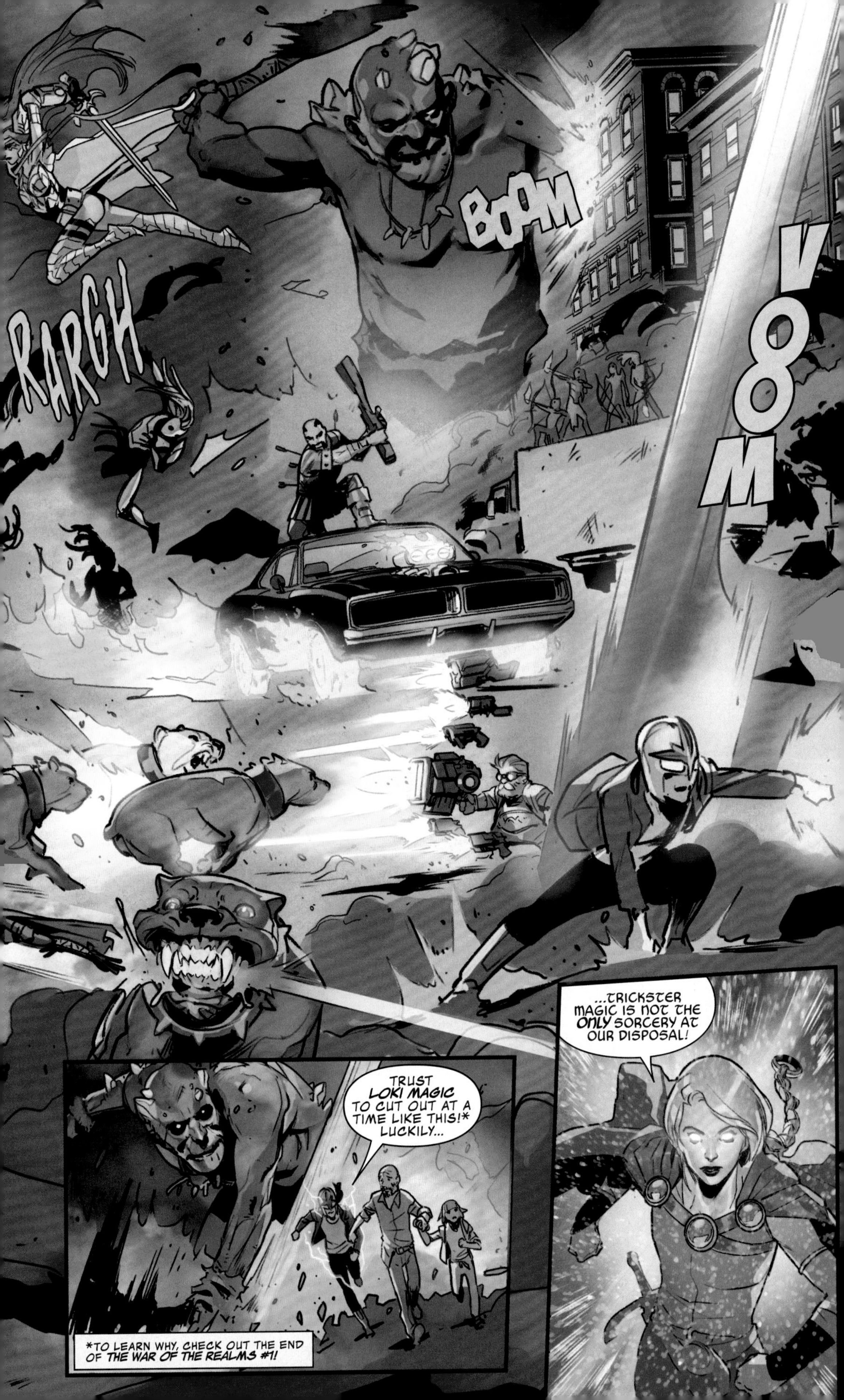
BOOM
RARGH
VOOM
TRUST LOKI MAGIC TO CUT OUT AT A TIME LIKE THIS!* LUCKILY...
...TRICKSTER MAGIC IS NOT THE ONLY SORCERY AT OUR DISPOSAL!
*TO LEARN WHY, CHECK OUT THE END OF THE WAR OF THE REALMS #1!

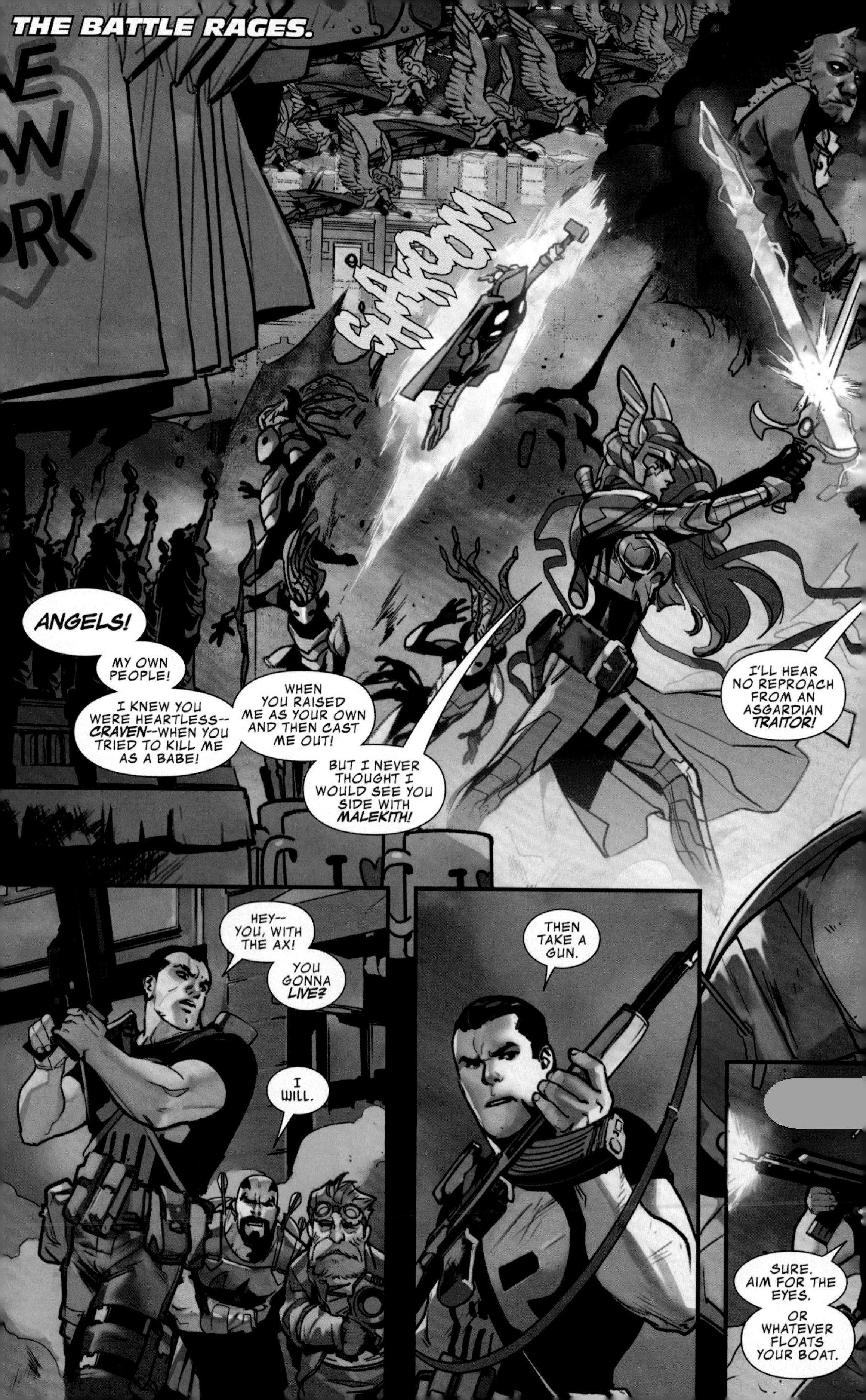
THE BATTLE RAGES.
SHRAKOOM
ANGELS!
MY OWN PEOPLE!
I KNEW YOU WERE HEARTLESS-- CRAVEN--WHEN YOU TRIED TO KILL ME AS A BABE!
WHEN YOU RAISED ME AS YOUR OWN AND THEN CAST ME OUT!
BUT I NEVER THOUGHT I WOULD SEE YOU SIDE WITH MALEKITH!
I'LL HEAR NO REPROACH FROM AN ASGARDIAN TRAITOR!
HEY-- YOU, WITH THE AX!
YOU GONNA LIVE?
I WILL.
THEN TAKE A GUN.
SURE. AIM FOR THE EYES.
OR WHATEVER FLOATS YOUR BOAT.

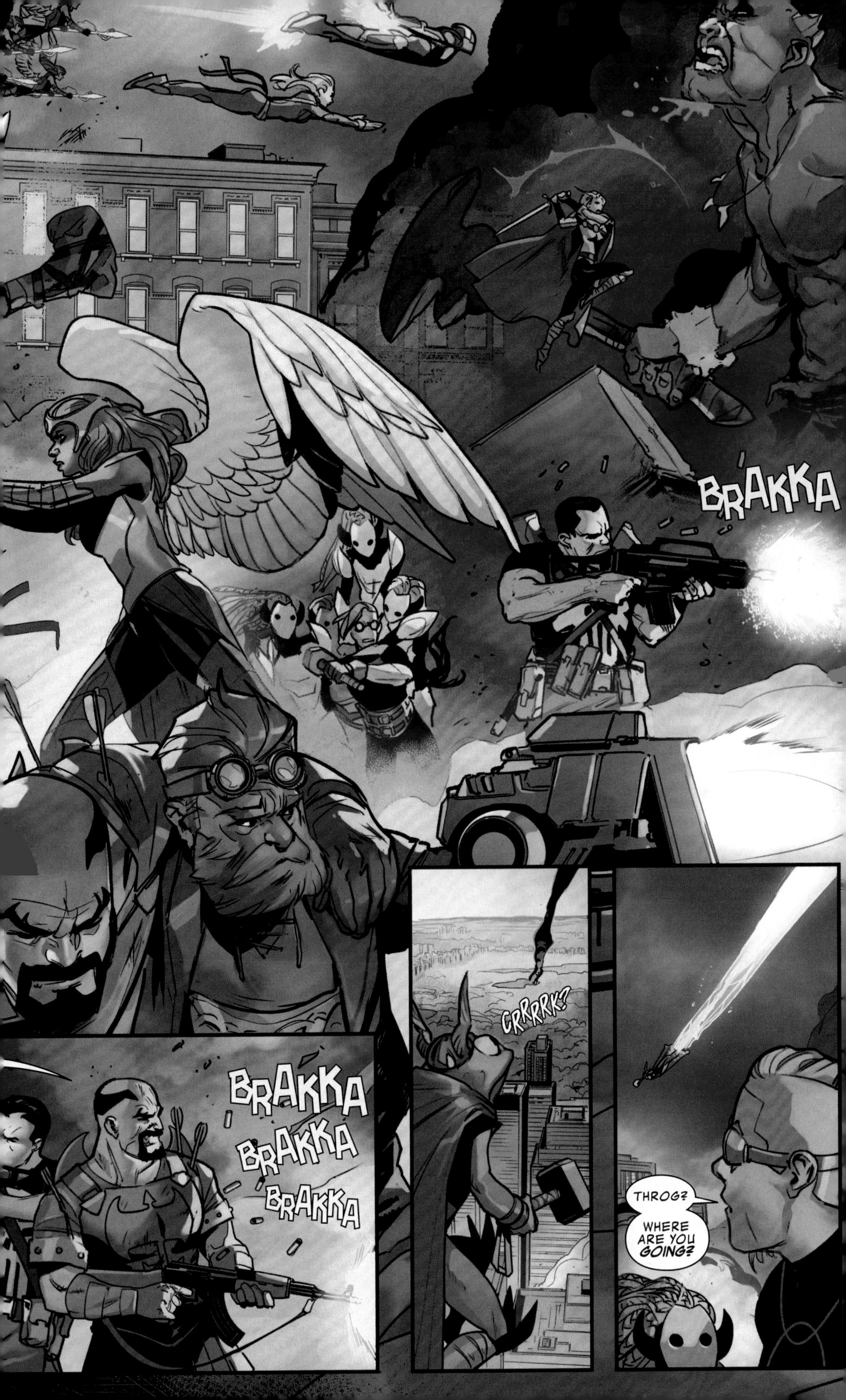
BRAKKA
BRAKKA
BRAKKA
BRAKKA
CRRRRK?
THROG?
WHERE ARE YOU GOING?

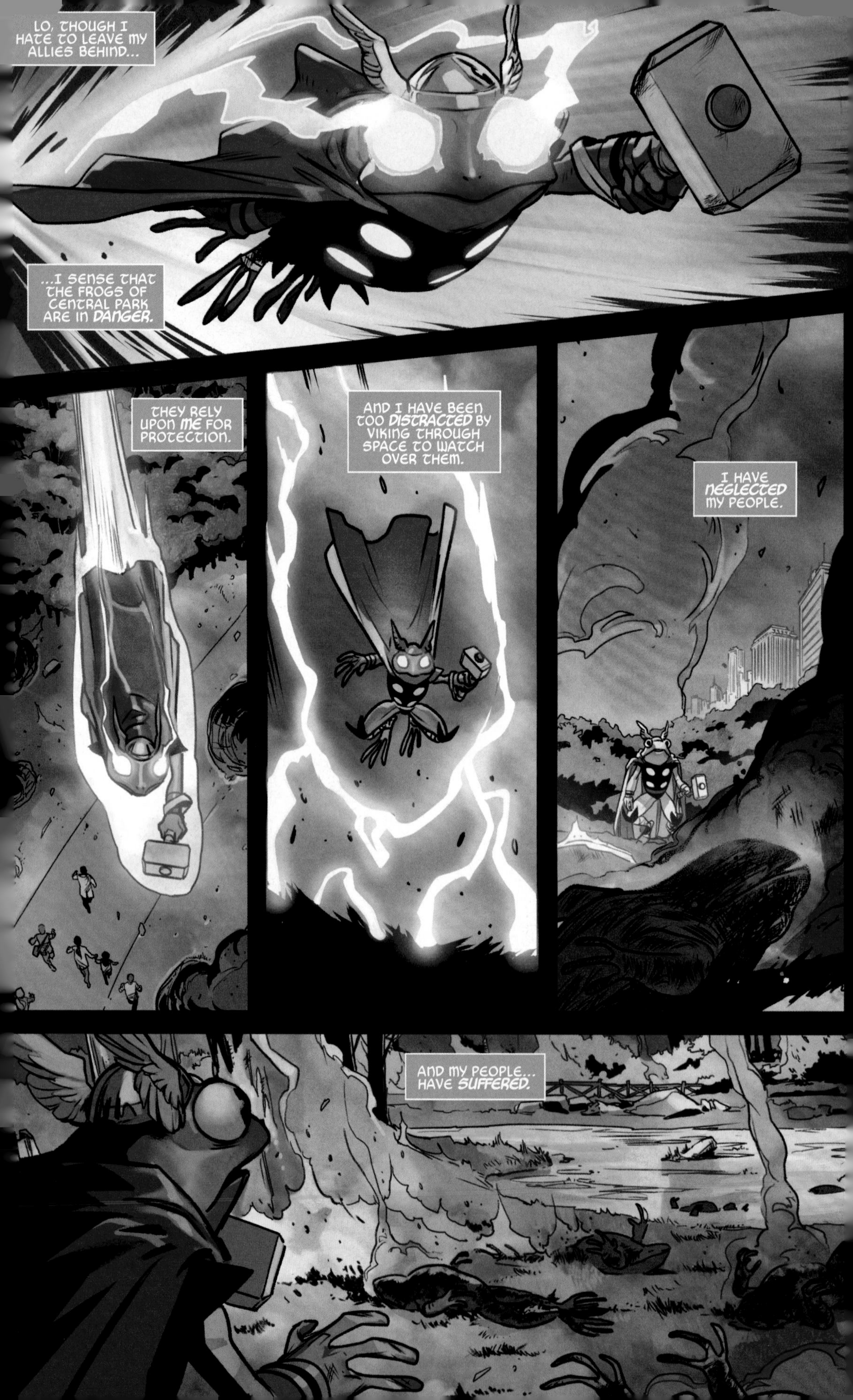
LO, THOUGH I HATE TO LEAVE MY ALLIES BEHIND...
...I SENSE THAT THE FROGS OF CENTRAL PARK ARE IN DANGER.
THEY RELY UPON ME FOR PROTECTION.
AND I HAVE BEEN TOO DISTRACTED BY VIKING THROUGH SPACE TO WATCH OVER THEM.
I HAVE NEGLECTED MY PEOPLE.
AND MY PEOPLE... HAVE SUFFERED.

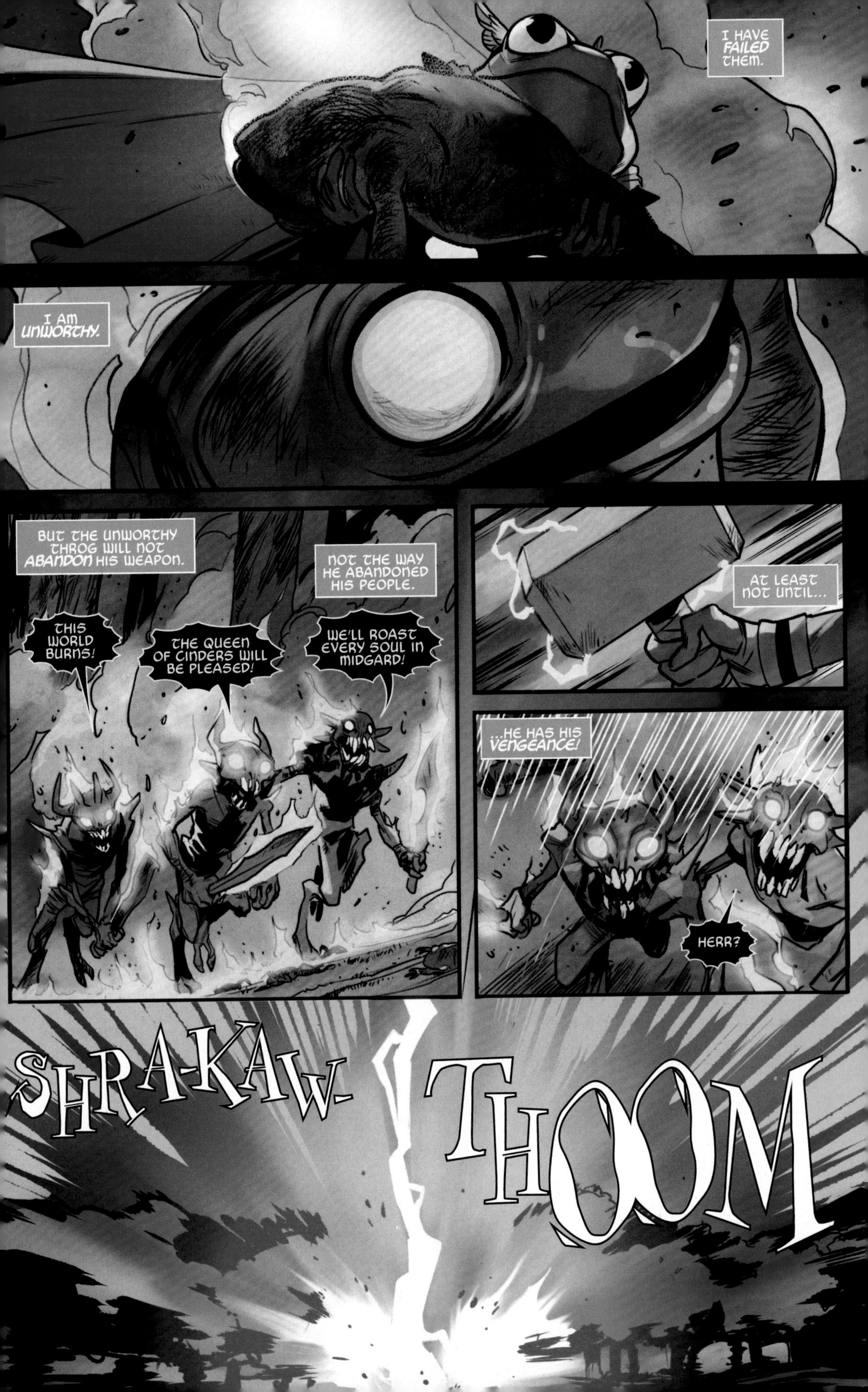
I HAVE FAILED THEM.
I AM UNWORTHY.
BUT THE UNWORTHY THROG WILL NOT ABANDON HIS WEAPON.
NOT THE WAY HE ABANDONED HIS PEOPLE.
THIS WORLD BURNS!
THE QUEEN OF CINDERS WILL BE PLEASED!
WE'LL ROAST EVERY SOUL IN MIDGARD!
AT LEAST NOT UNTIL...
...HE HAS HIS VENGEANCE!
HERR?
SHRA-KAW-
THOOM

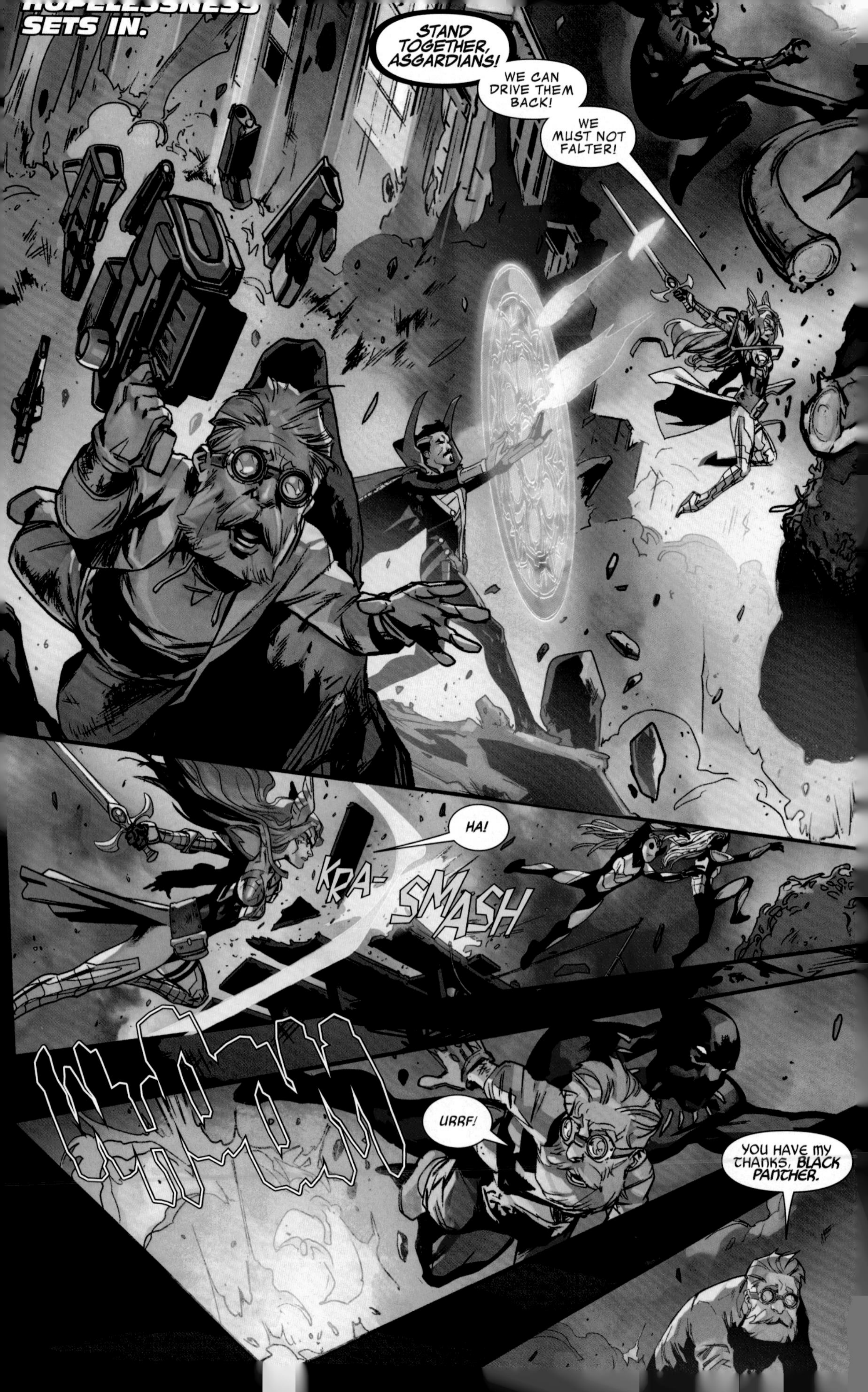
HOPELESSNESS
SETS IN.
STAND TOGETHER, ASGARDIANS!
WE CAN DRIVE THEM BACK!
WE MUST NOT FALTER!
HA!
KRA-
SMASH
URRF!
YOU HAVE MY THANKS, BLACK PANTHER.

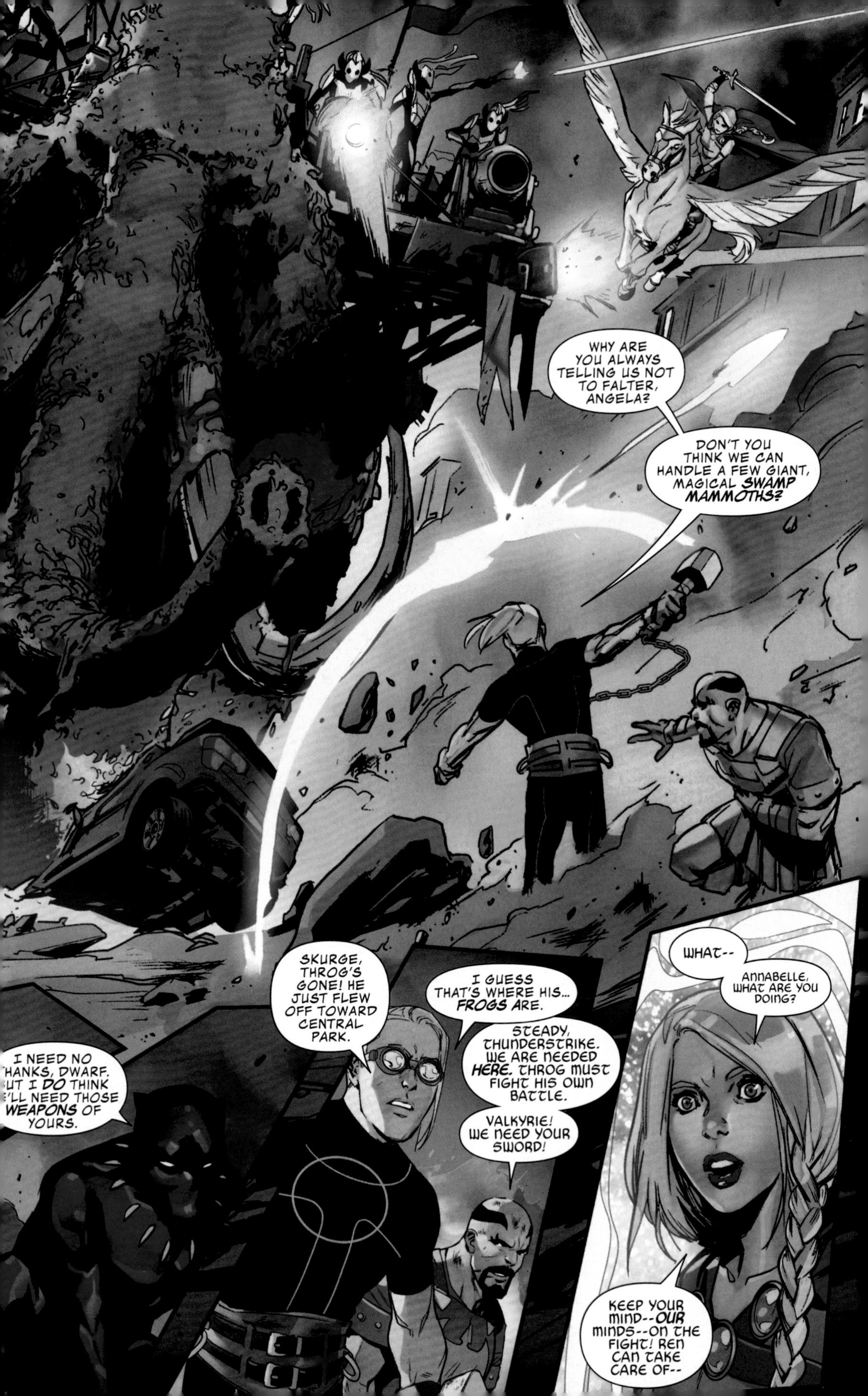
WHY ARE YOU ALWAYS TELLING US NOT TO FALTER, ANGELA?
DON'T YOU THINK WE CAN HANDLE A FEW GIANT, MAGICAL SWAMP MAMMOTHS?
SKURGE, THROG'S GONE! HE JUST FLEW OFF TOWARD CENTRAL PARK.
I GUESS THAT'S WHERE HIS... FROGS ARE.
STEADY, THUNDERSTRIKE. WE ARE NEEDED HERE. THROG MUST FIGHT HIS OWN BATTLE.
VALKYRIE! WE NEED YOUR SWORD!
I NEED NO THANKS, DWARF. UT I DO THINK 'LL NEED THOSE WEAPONS OF YOURS.
WHAT--
ANNABELLE, WHAT ARE YOU DOING?
KEEP YOUR MIND--OUR MINDS--ON THE FIGHT! REN CAN TAKE CARE OF--

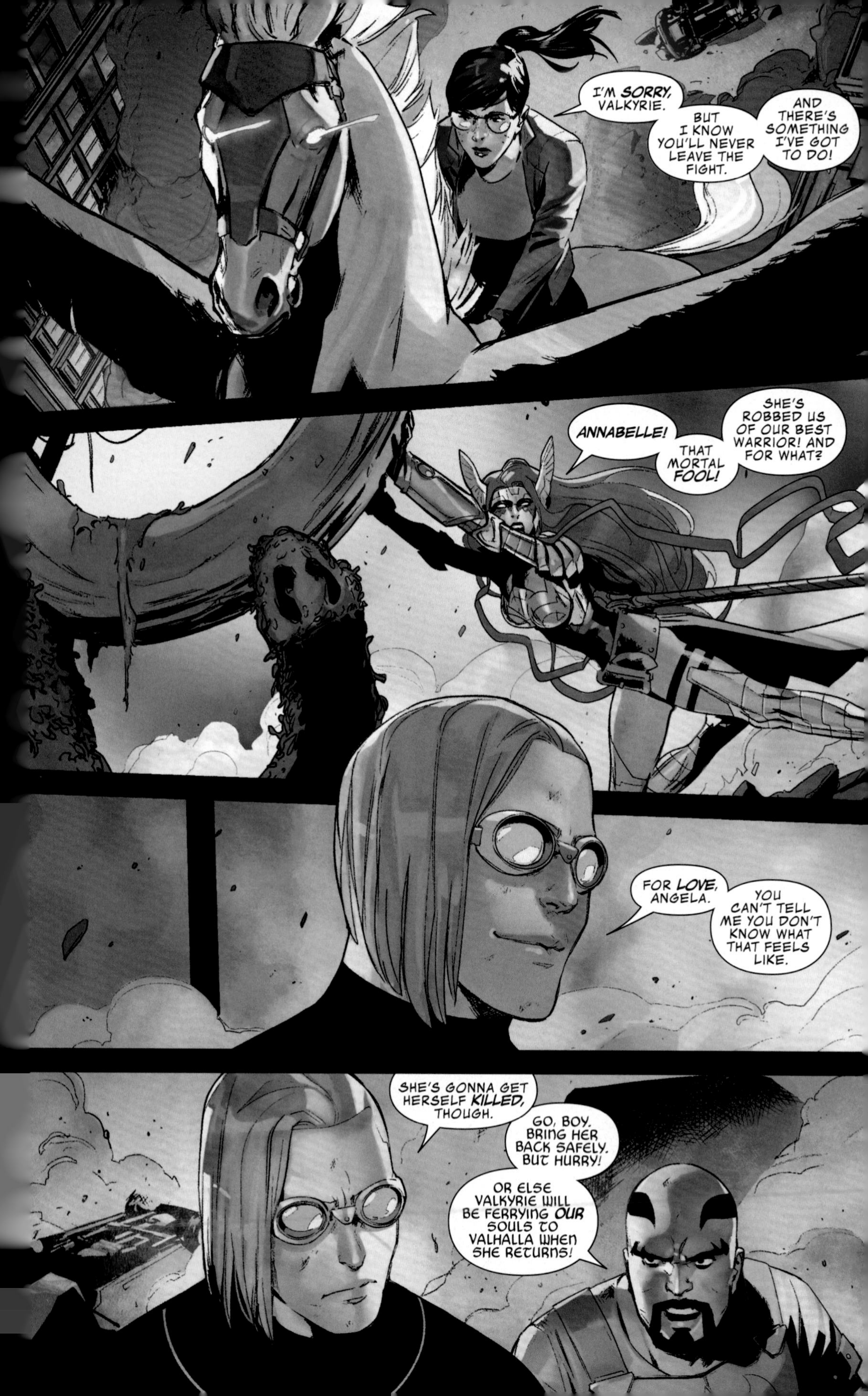
I'M SORRY, VALKYRIE.
BUT I KNOW YOU'LL NEVER LEAVE THE FIGHT.
AND THERE'S SOMETHING I'VE GOT TO DO!
ANNABELLE!
THAT MORTAL FOOL!
SHE'S ROBBED US OF OUR BEST WARRIOR! AND FOR WHAT?
FOR LOVE, ANGELA.
YOU CAN'T TELL ME YOU DON'T KNOW WHAT THAT FEELS LIKE.
SHE'S GONNA GET HERSELF KILLED, THOUGH.
GO, BOY. BRING HER BACK SAFELY. BUT HURRY!
OR ELSE VALKYRIE WILL BE FERRYING OUR SOULS TO VALHALLA WHEN SHE RETURNS!

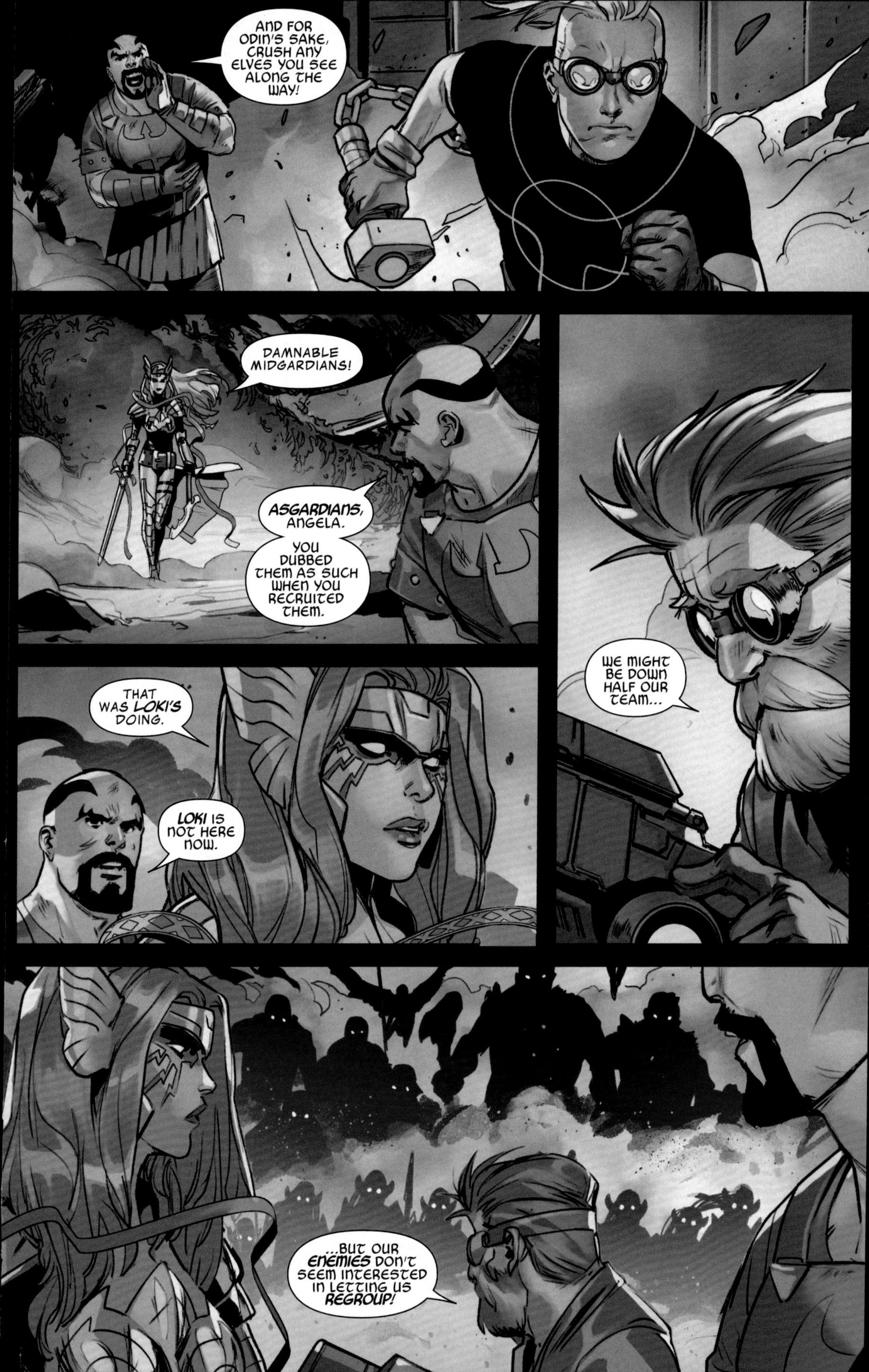
AND FOR ODIN'S SAKE, CRUSH ANY ELVES YOU SEE ALONG THE WAY!
DAMNABLE MIDGARDIANS!
ASGARDIANS, ANGELA.
YOU DUBBED THEM AS SUCH WHEN YOU RECRUITED THEM.
THAT WAS LOKI'S DOING.
LOKI IS NOT HERE NOW.
WE MIGHT BE DOWN HALF OUR TEAM...
...BUT OUR ENEMIES DON'T SEEM INTERESTED IN LETTING US REGROUP!

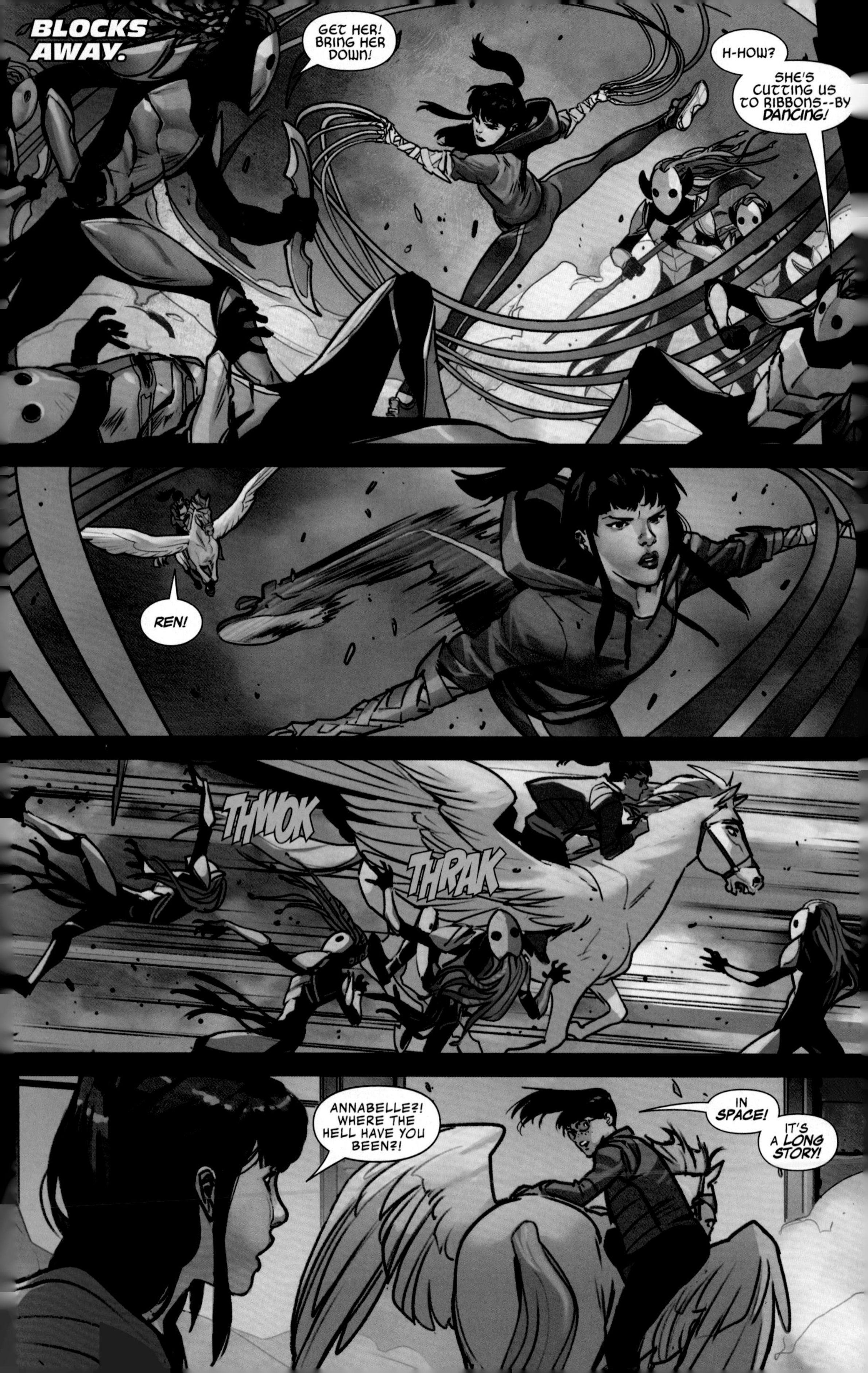
BLOCKS AWAY.
GET HER! BRING HER DOWN!
H-HOW?
SHE'S CUTTING US TO RIBBONS--BY DANCING!
REN!
THWOK
THRAK
ANNABELLE?! WHERE THE HELL HAVE YOU BEEN?!
IN SPACE!
IT'S A LONG STORY!

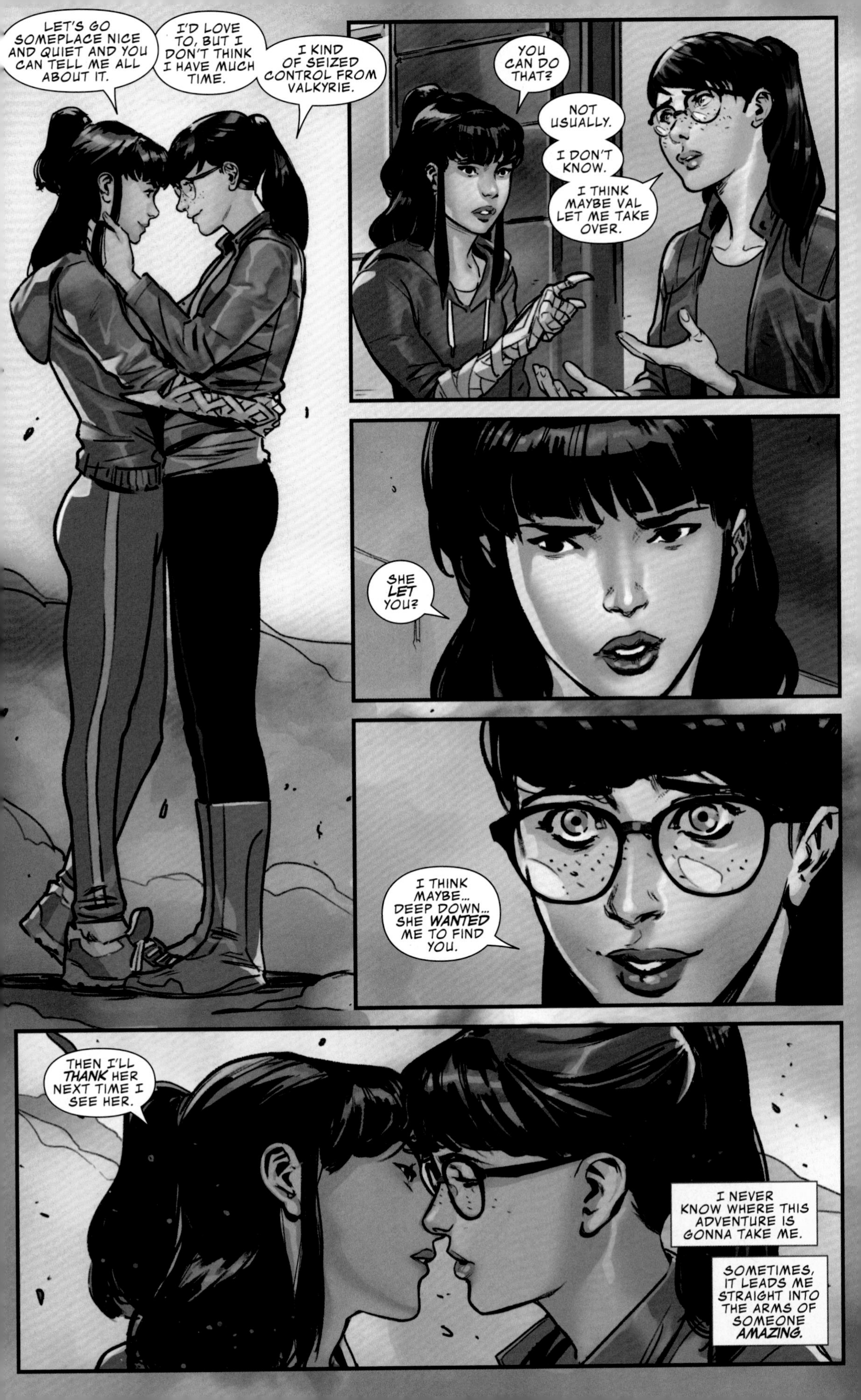
LET'S GO SOMEPLACE NICE AND QUIET AND YOU CAN TELL ME ALL ABOUT IT.
I'D LOVE TO, BUT I DON'T THINK I HAVE MUCH TIME.
I KIND OF SEIZED CONTROL FROM VALKYRIE.
YOU CAN DO THAT?
NOT USUALLY.
I DON'T KNOW.
I THINK MAYBE VAL LET ME TAKE OVER.
SHE *LET* YOU?
I THINK MAYBE... DEEP DOWN... SHE *WANTED* ME TO FIND YOU.
THEN I'LL *THANK* HER NEXT TIME I SEE HER.
I NEVER KNOW WHERE THIS ADVENTURE IS GONNA TAKE ME.
SOMETIMES, IT LEADS ME STRAIGHT INTO THE ARMS OF SOMEONE *AMAZING*.

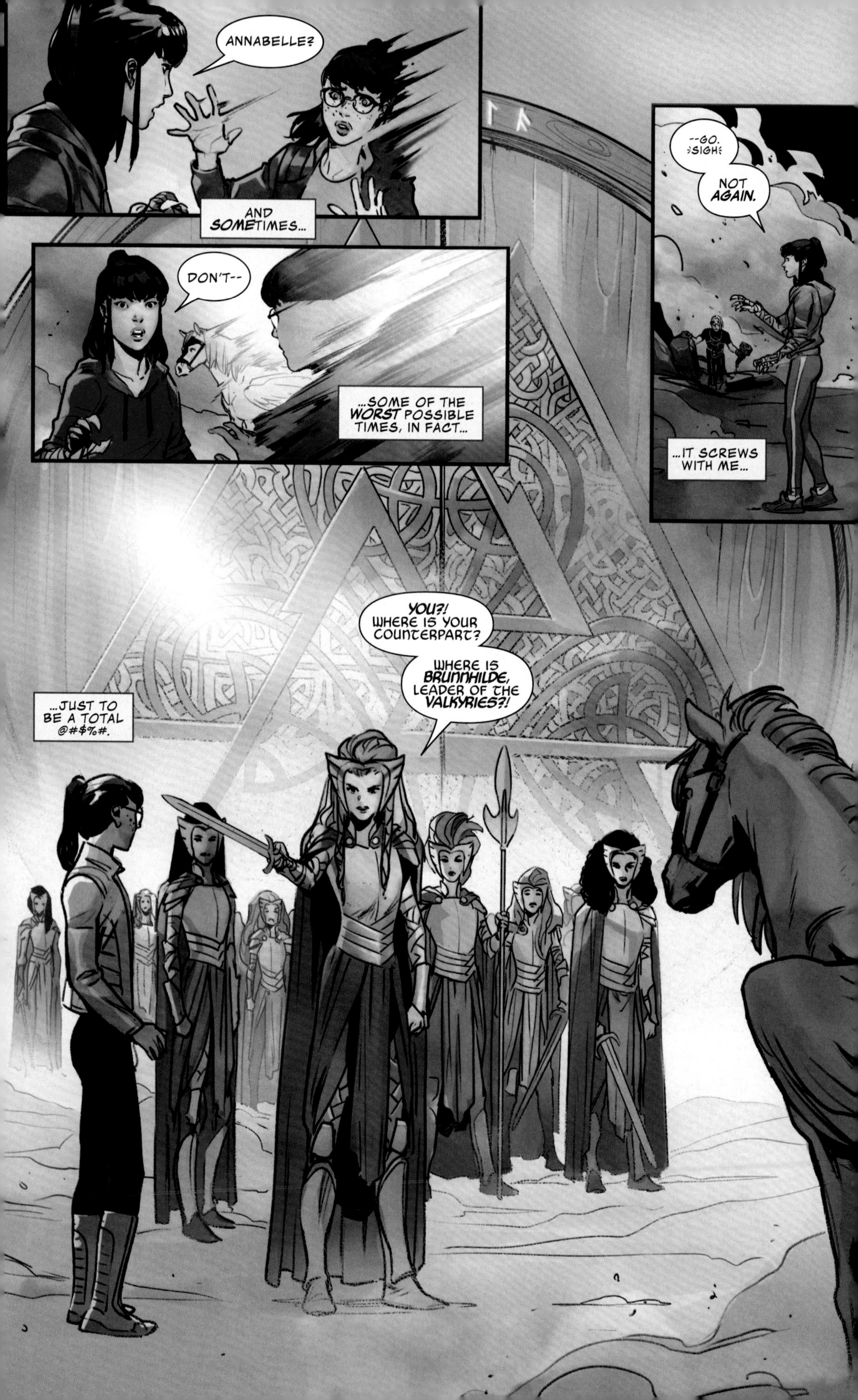
ANNABELLE?
AND SOMETIMES...
DON'T--
...SOME OF THE WORST POSSIBLE TIMES, IN FACT...
--GO.
SIGH
NOT AGAIN.
...IT SCREWS WITH ME...
...JUST TO BE A TOTAL @#$%#.
YOU?! WHERE IS YOUR COUNTERPART?
WHERE IS BRUNNHILDE, LEADER OF THE VALKYRIES?!

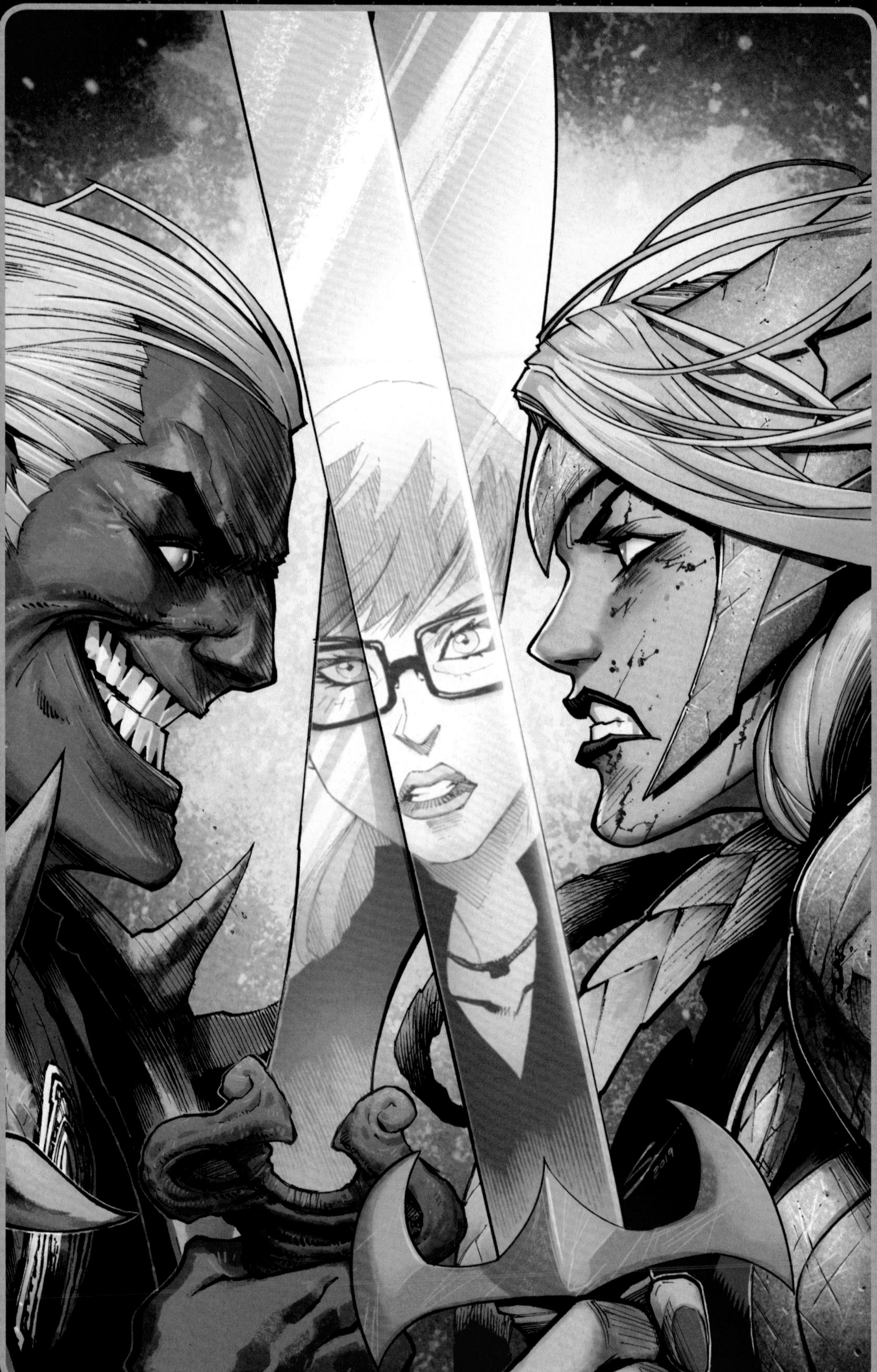

9

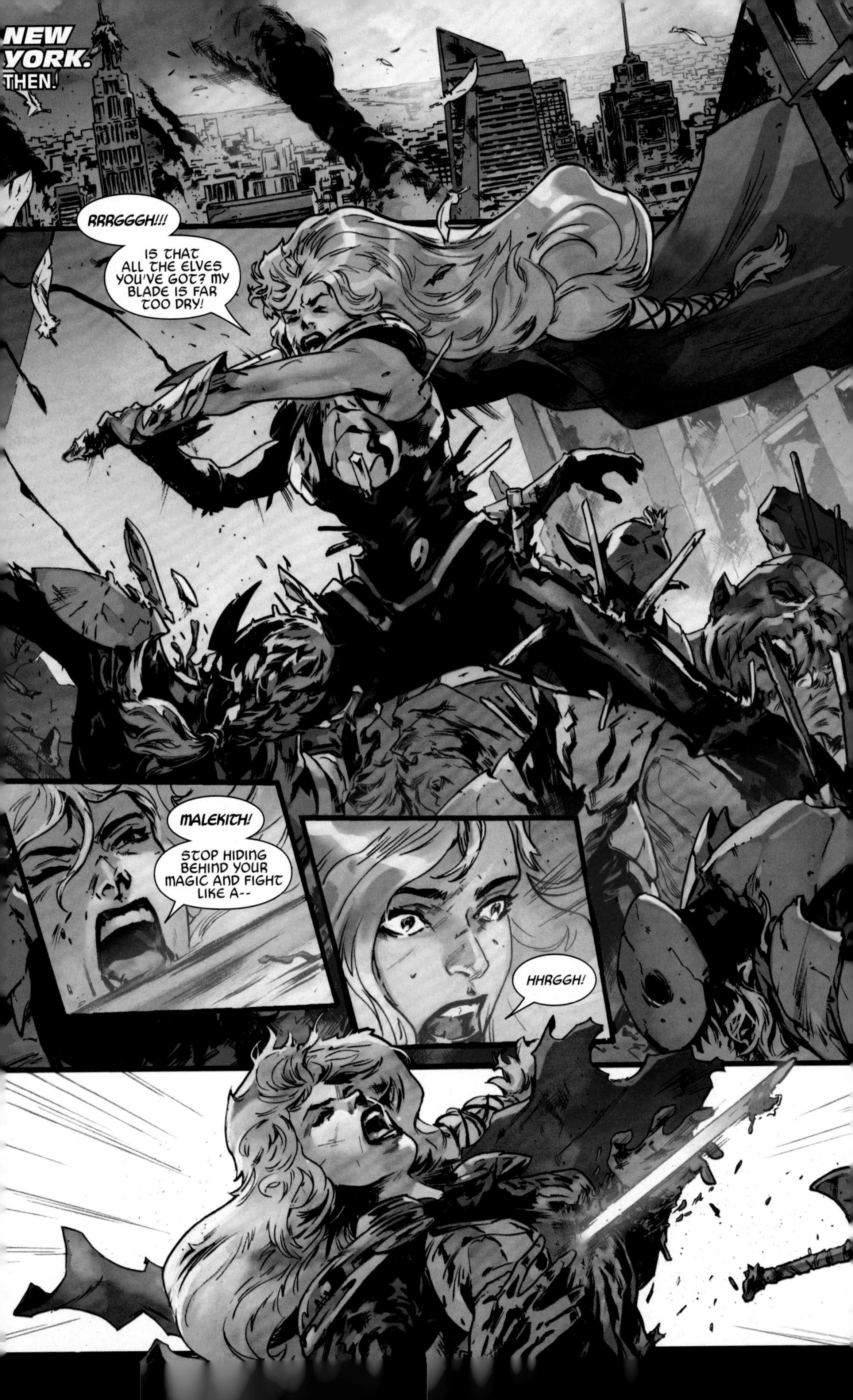
NEW YORK. THEN.
RRRGGGH!!!
IS THAT ALL THE ELVES YOU'VE GOT? MY BLADE IS FAR TOO DRY!
MALEKITH!
STOP HIDING BEHIND YOUR MAGIC AND FIGHT LIKE A--
HHRGGH!

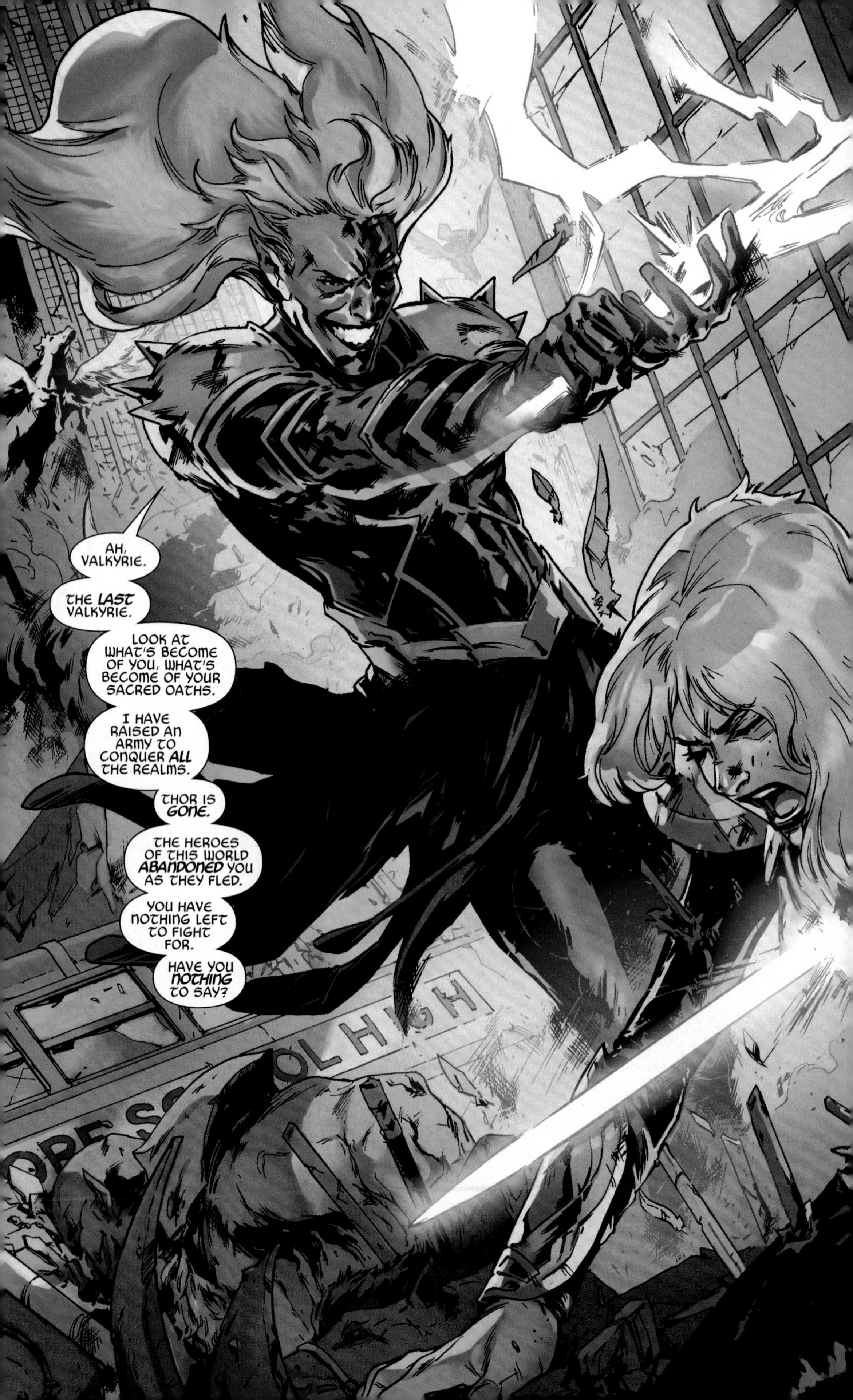
AH, VALKYRIE.
THE ***LAST*** VALKYRIE.
LOOK AT WHAT'S BECOME OF YOU, WHAT'S BECOME OF YOUR SACRED OATHS.
I HAVE RAISED AN ARMY TO CONQUER ***ALL*** THE REALMS.
THOR IS ***GONE.***
THE HEROES OF THIS WORLD ***ABANDONED*** YOU AS THEY FLED.
YOU HAVE NOTHING LEFT TO FIGHT FOR.
HAVE YOU ***NOTHING*** TO SAY?

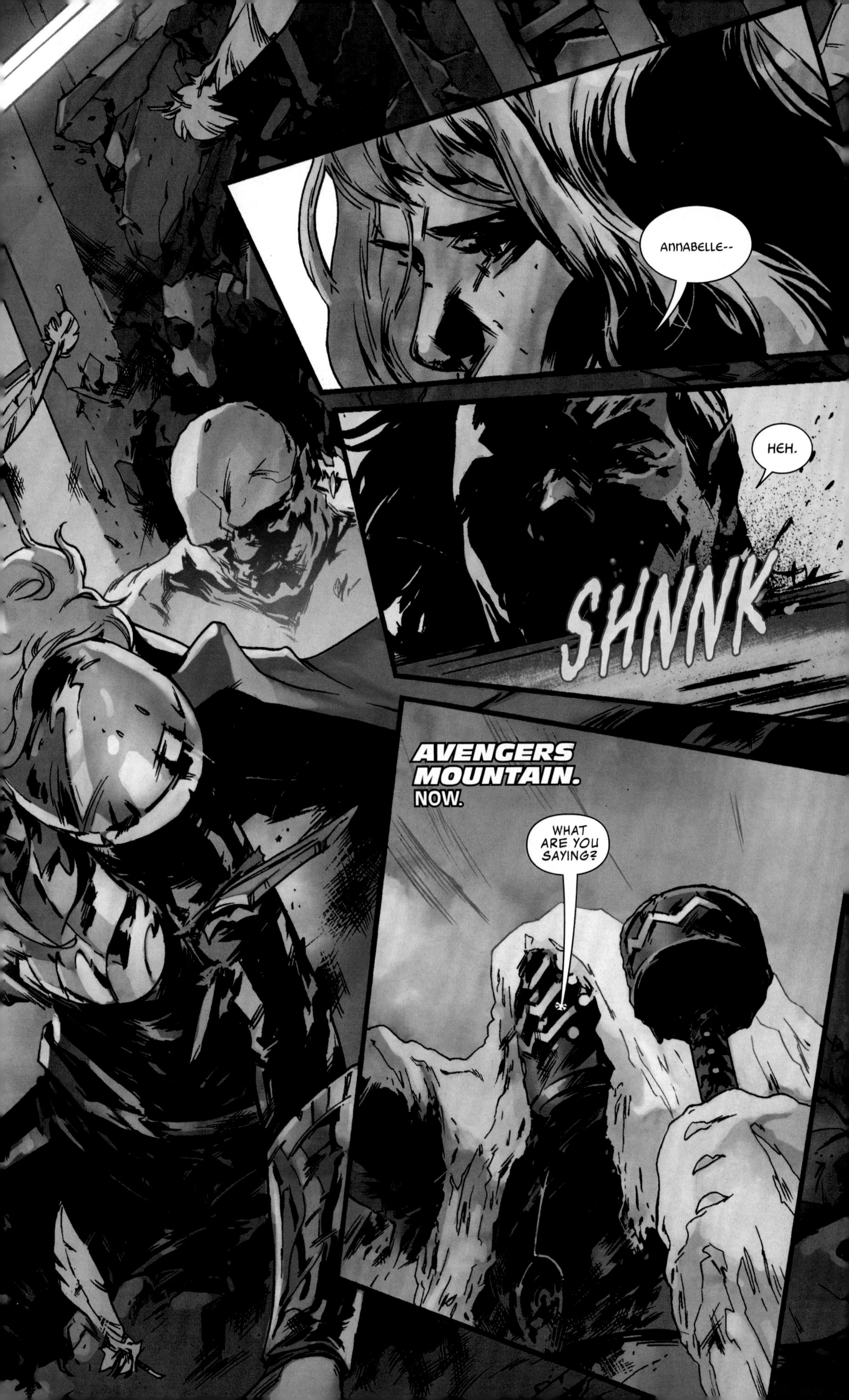
ANNABELLE--
HEH.
SHNNK
AVENGERS MOUNTAIN. NOW.
WHAT ARE YOU SAYING?

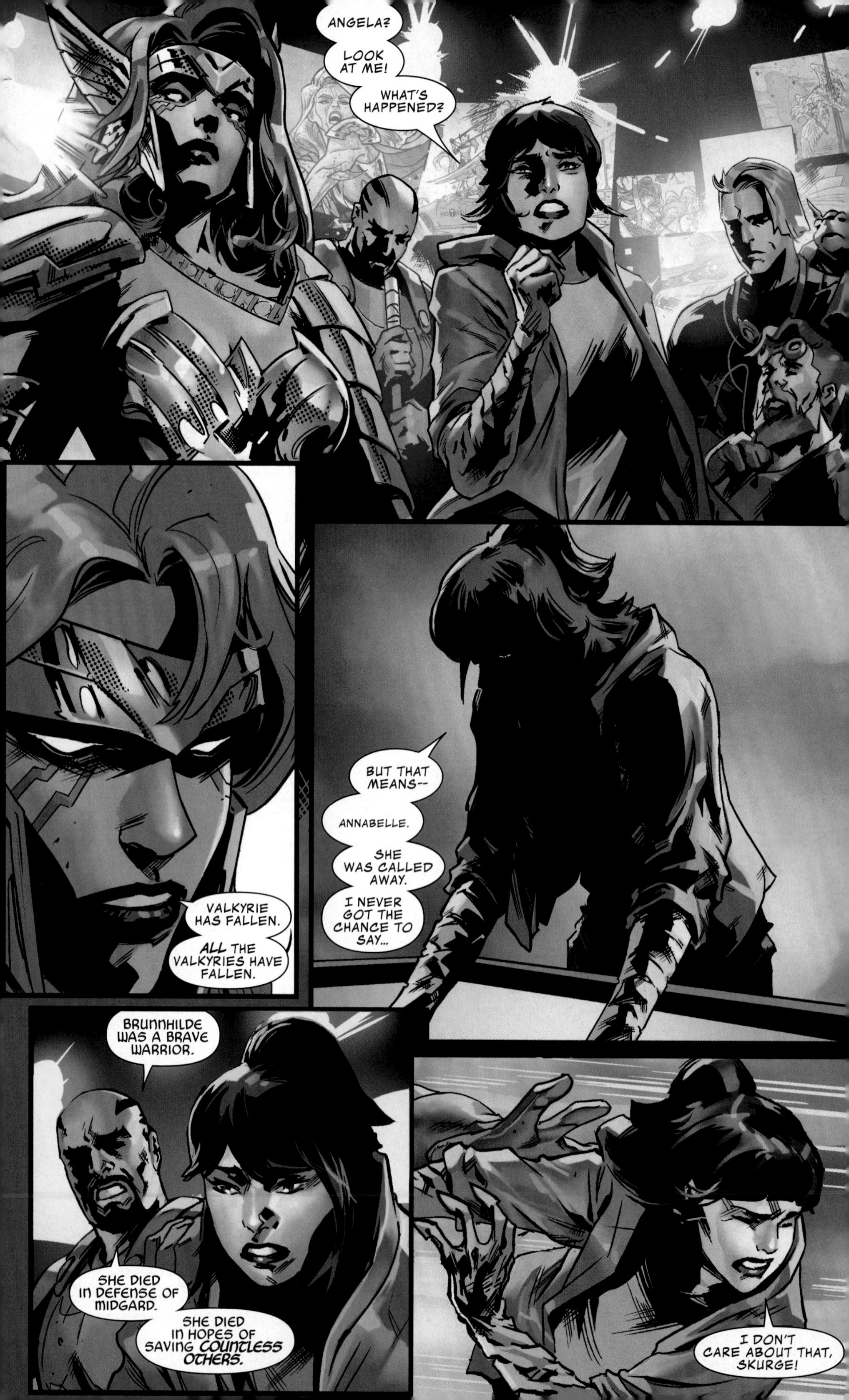
ANGELA?
LOOK AT ME!
WHAT'S HAPPENED?
VALKYRIE HAS FALLEN.
ALL THE VALKYRIES HAVE FALLEN.
BUT THAT MEANS--
ANNABELLE.
SHE WAS CALLED AWAY.
I NEVER GOT THE CHANCE TO SAY...
BRUNNHILDE WAS A BRAVE WARRIOR.
SHE DIED IN DEFENSE OF MIDGARD.
SHE DIED IN HOPES OF SAVING COUNTLESS OTHERS.
I DON'T CARE ABOUT THAT, SKURGE!

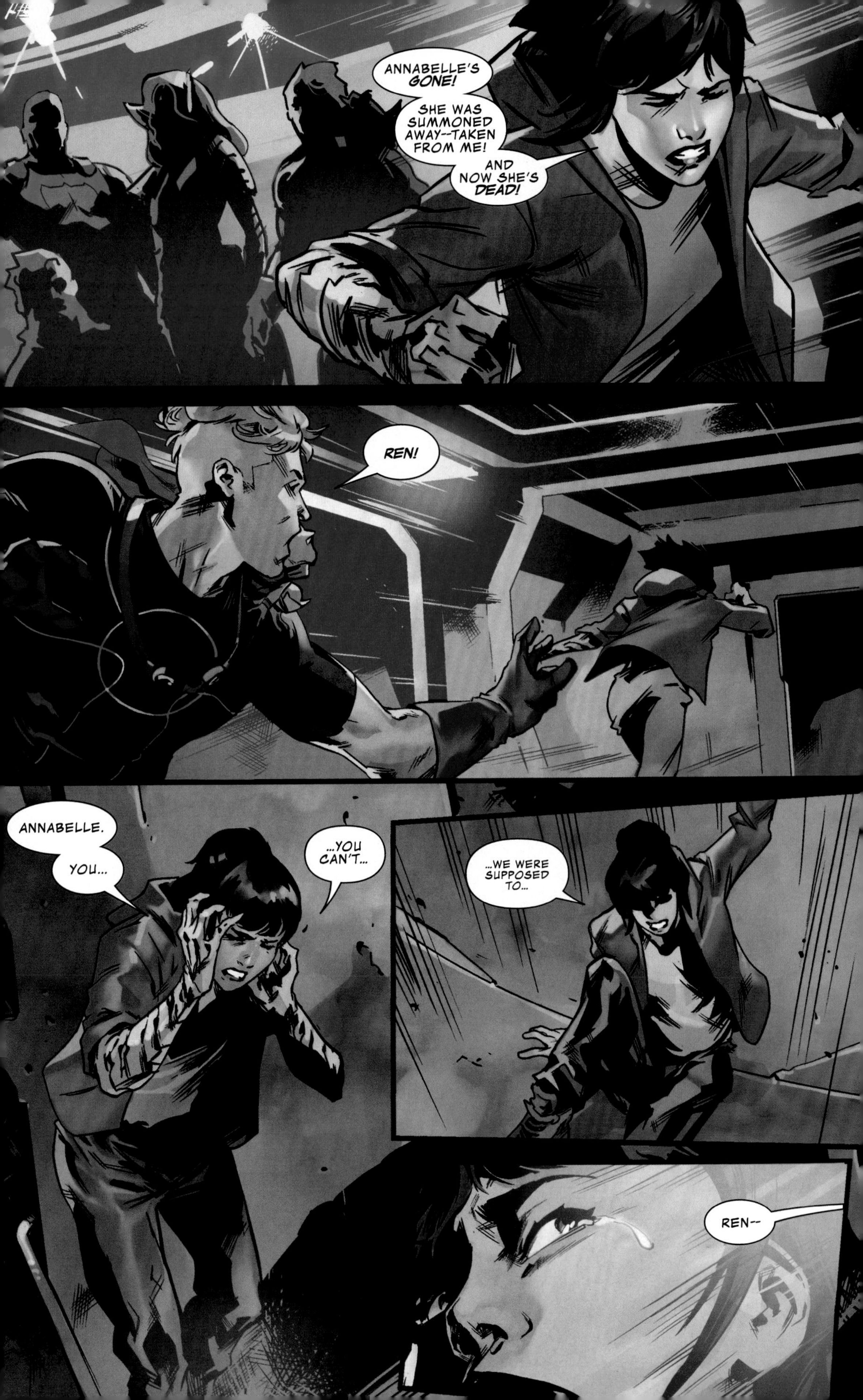
ANNABELLE'S GONE!
SHE WAS SUMMONED AWAY--TAKEN FROM ME!
AND NOW SHE'S DEAD!
REN!
ANNABELLE.
YOU...
...YOU CAN'T...
...WE WERE SUPPOSED TO...
REN--

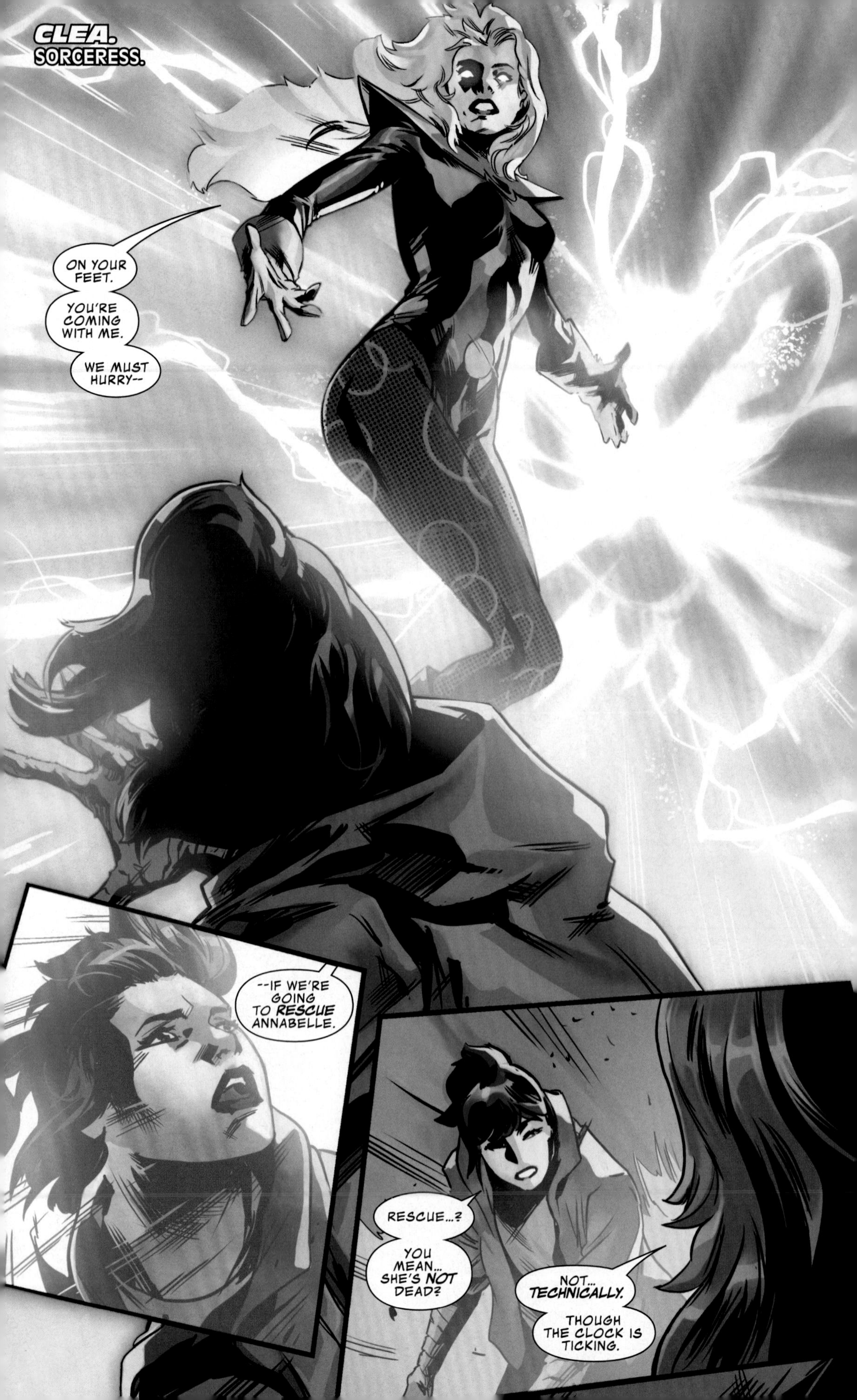
CLEA.
SORCERESS.
ON YOUR FEET.
YOU'RE COMING WITH ME.
WE MUST HURRY--
--IF WE'RE GOING TO RESCUE ANNABELLE.
RESCUE...?
YOU MEAN... SHE'S NOT DEAD?
NOT... TECHNICALLY.
THOUGH THE CLOCK IS TICKING.

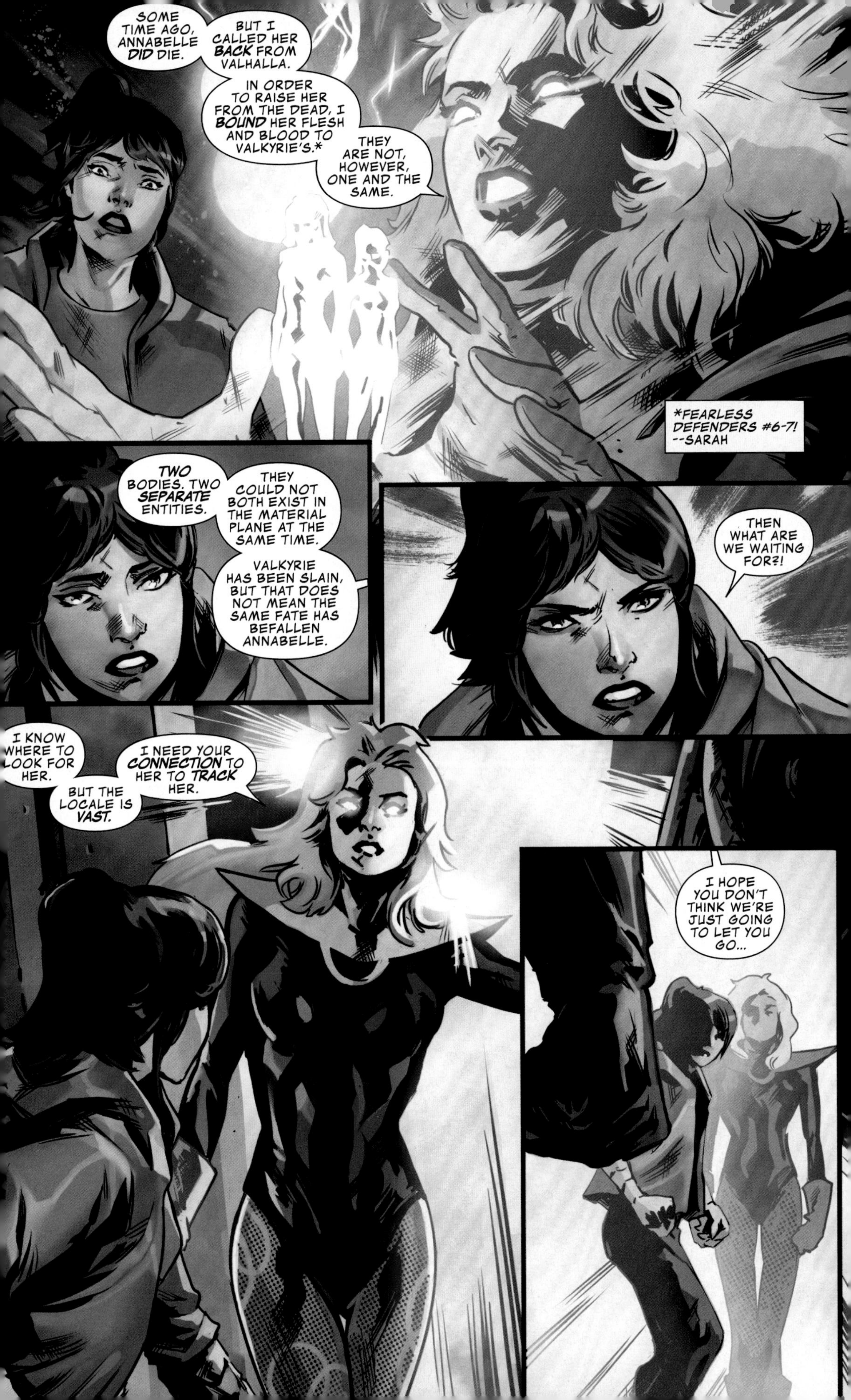
SOME TIME AGO, ANNABELLE DID DIE.
BUT I CALLED HER BACK FROM VALHALLA.
IN ORDER TO RAISE HER FROM THE DEAD, I BOUND HER FLESH AND BLOOD TO VALKYRIE'S.*
THEY ARE NOT, HOWEVER, ONE AND THE SAME.
*FEARLESS DEFENDERS #6-7! --SARAH
TWO BODIES. TWO SEPARATE ENTITIES.
THEY COULD NOT BOTH EXIST IN THE MATERIAL PLANE AT THE SAME TIME.
VALKYRIE HAS BEEN SLAIN, BUT THAT DOES NOT MEAN THE SAME FATE HAS BEFALLEN ANNABELLE.
THEN WHAT ARE WE WAITING FOR?!
I KNOW WHERE TO LOOK FOR HER.
BUT THE LOCALE IS VAST.
I NEED YOUR CONNECTION TO HER TO TRACK HER.
I HOPE YOU DON'T THINK WE'RE JUST GOING TO LET YOU GO...

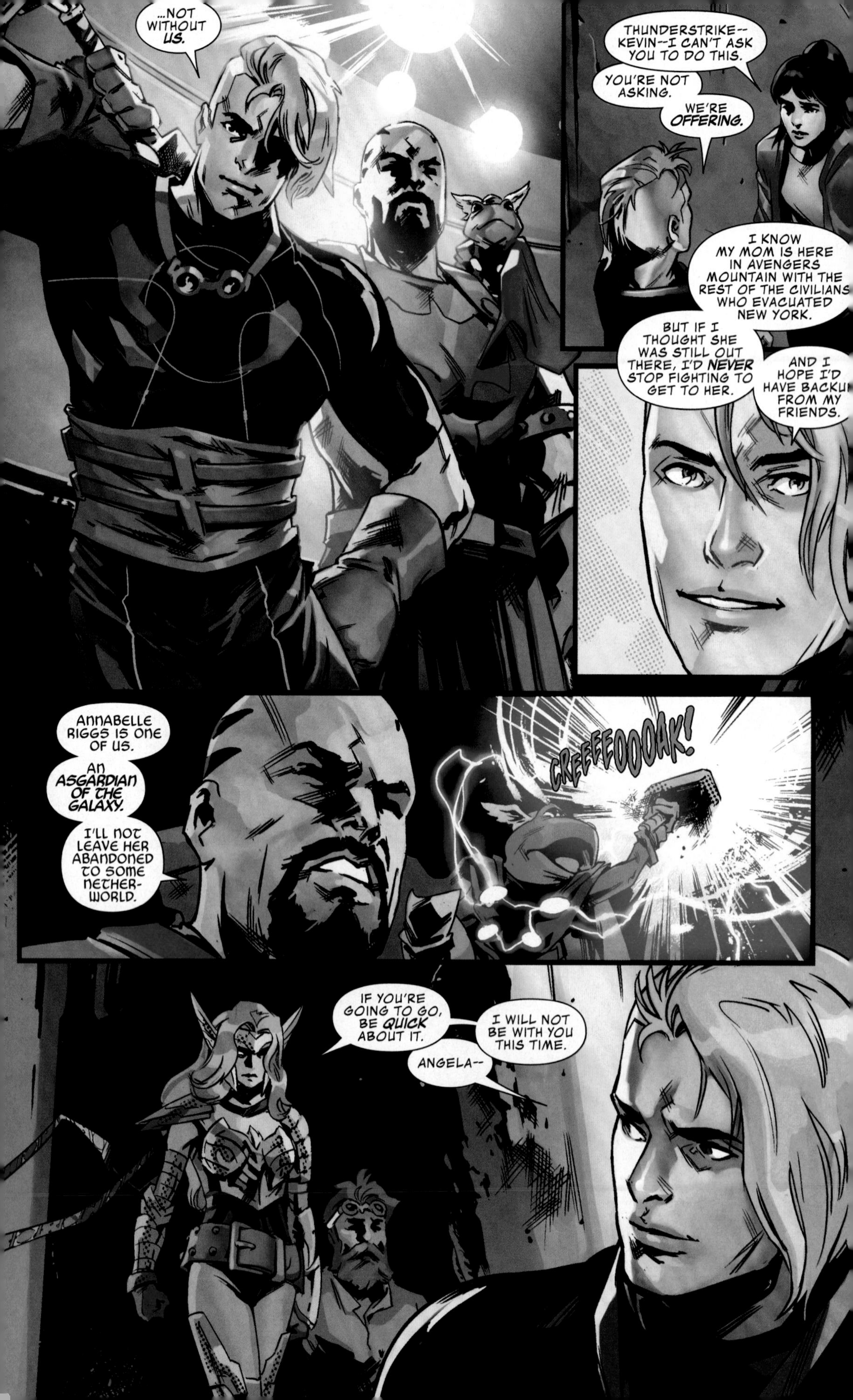
...NOT WITHOUT US.
THUNDERSTRIKE-- KEVIN--I CAN'T ASK YOU TO DO THIS.
YOU'RE NOT ASKING.
WE'RE OFFERING.
I KNOW MY MOM IS HERE IN AVENGERS MOUNTAIN WITH THE REST OF THE CIVILIANS WHO EVACUATED NEW YORK.
BUT IF I THOUGHT SHE WAS STILL OUT THERE, I'D NEVER STOP FIGHTING TO GET TO HER.
AND I HOPE I'D HAVE BACKUP FROM MY FRIENDS.
ANNABELLE RIGGS IS ONE OF US.
AN ASGARDIAN OF THE GALAXY.
I'LL NOT LEAVE HER ABANDONED TO SOME NETHER-WORLD.
CREEEEOOOAK!
IF YOU'RE GOING TO GO, BE QUICK ABOUT IT.
I WILL NOT BE WITH YOU THIS TIME.
ANGELA--

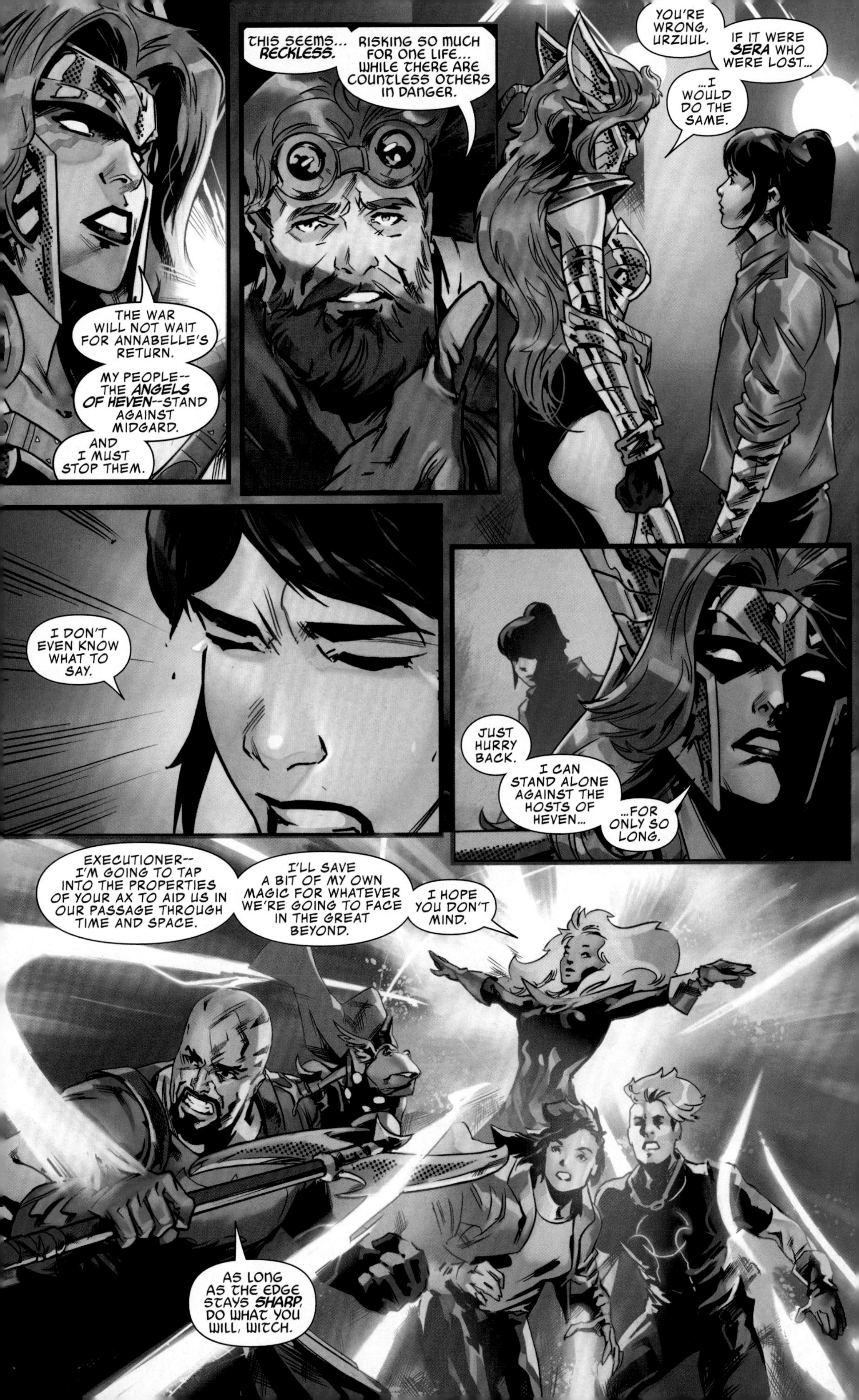
THE WAR WILL NOT WAIT FOR ANNABELLE'S RETURN.
MY PEOPLE-- THE ANGELS OF HEVEN--STAND AGAINST MIDGARD.
AND I MUST STOP THEM.
THIS SEEMS... RECKLESS.
RISKING SO MUCH FOR ONE LIFE... WHILE THERE ARE COUNTLESS OTHERS IN DANGER.
YOU'RE WRONG, URZUUL.
IF IT WERE SERA WHO WERE LOST...
...I WOULD DO THE SAME.
I DON'T EVEN KNOW WHAT TO SAY.
JUST HURRY BACK.
I CAN STAND ALONE AGAINST THE HOSTS OF HEVEN...
...FOR ONLY SO LONG.
EXECUTIONER-- I'M GOING TO TAP INTO THE PROPERTIES OF YOUR AX TO AID US IN OUR PASSAGE THROUGH TIME AND SPACE.
I'LL SAVE A BIT OF MY OWN MAGIC FOR WHATEVER WE'RE GOING TO FACE IN THE GREAT BEYOND.
I HOPE YOU DON'T MIND.
AS LONG AS THE EDGE STAYS SHARP, DO WHAT YOU WILL, WITCH.

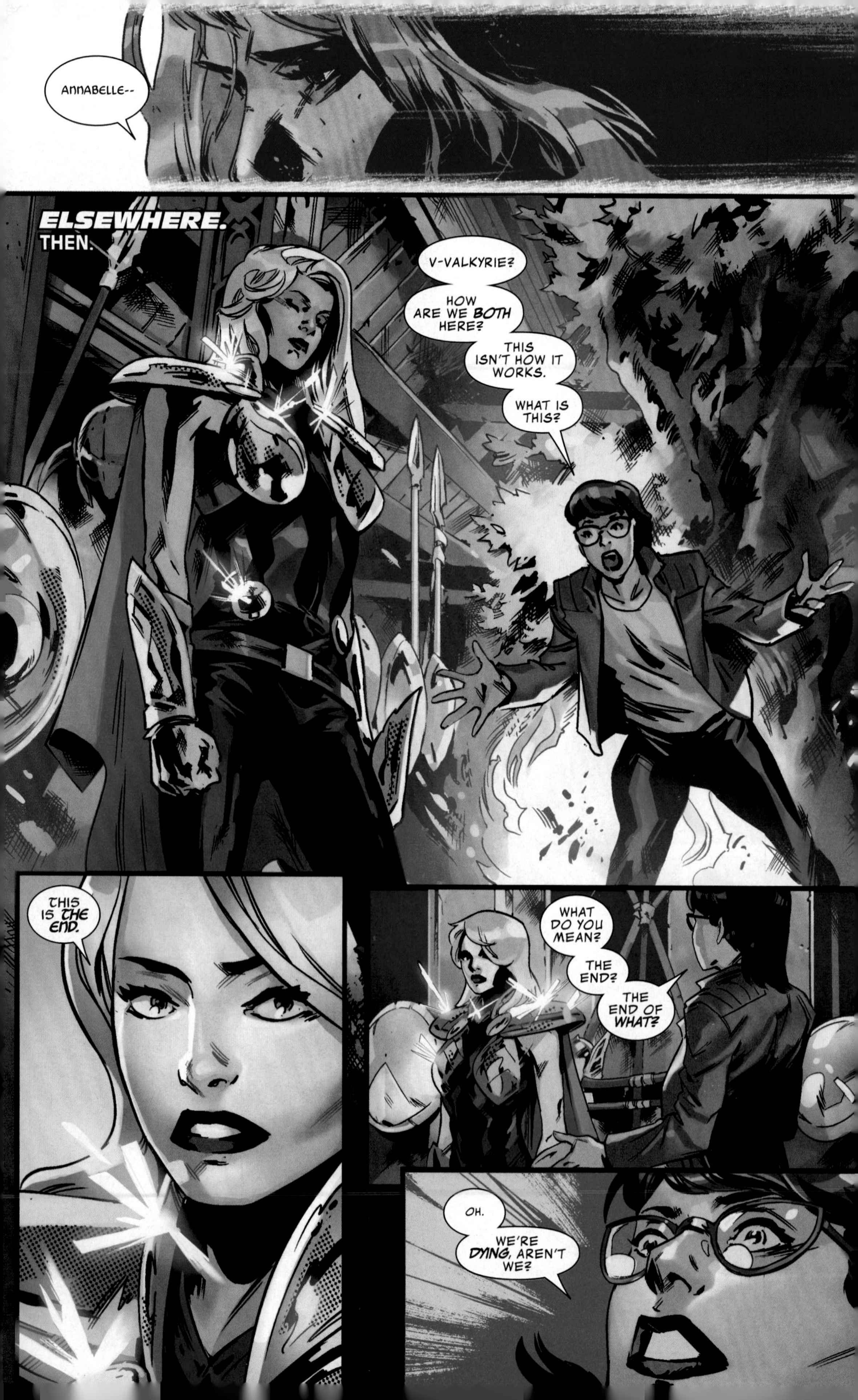
ANNABELLE--
ELSEWHERE.
THEN.
V-VALKYRIE?
HOW ARE WE BOTH HERE?
THIS ISN'T HOW IT WORKS.
WHAT IS THIS?
THIS IS THE END.
WHAT DO YOU MEAN?
THE END?
THE END OF WHAT?
OH.
WE'RE DYING, AREN'T WE?

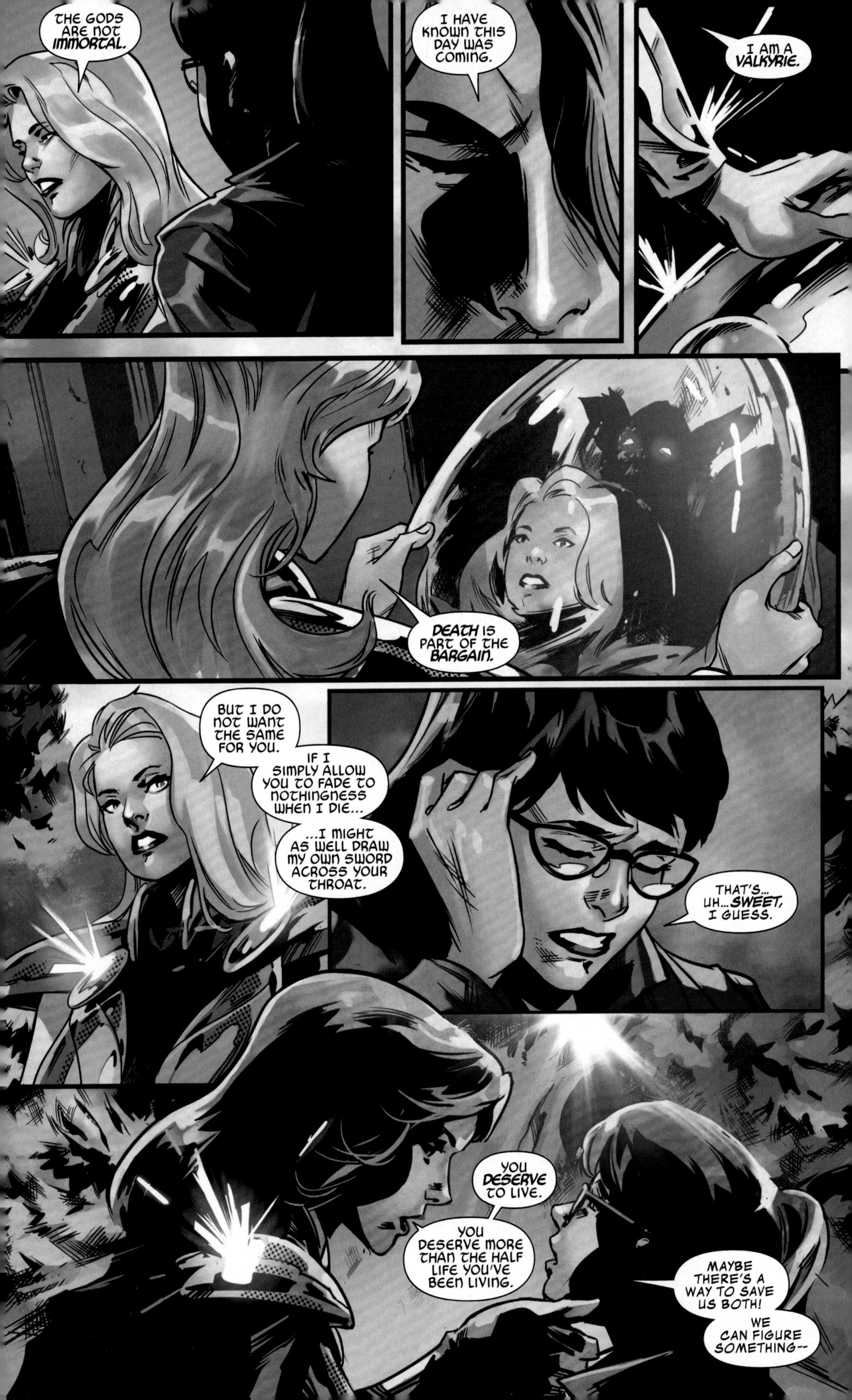
THE GODS ARE NOT IMMORTAL.
I HAVE KNOWN THIS DAY WAS COMING.
I AM A VALKYRIE.
DEATH IS PART OF THE BARGAIN.
BUT I DO NOT WANT THE SAME FOR YOU.
IF I SIMPLY ALLOW YOU TO FADE TO NOTHINGNESS WHEN I DIE...
...I MIGHT AS WELL DRAW MY OWN SWORD ACROSS YOUR THROAT.
THAT'S... UH...SWEET, I GUESS.
YOU DESERVE TO LIVE.
YOU DESERVE MORE THAN THE HALF LIFE YOU'VE BEEN LIVING.
MAYBE THERE'S A WAY TO SAVE US BOTH!
WE CAN FIGURE SOMETHING--

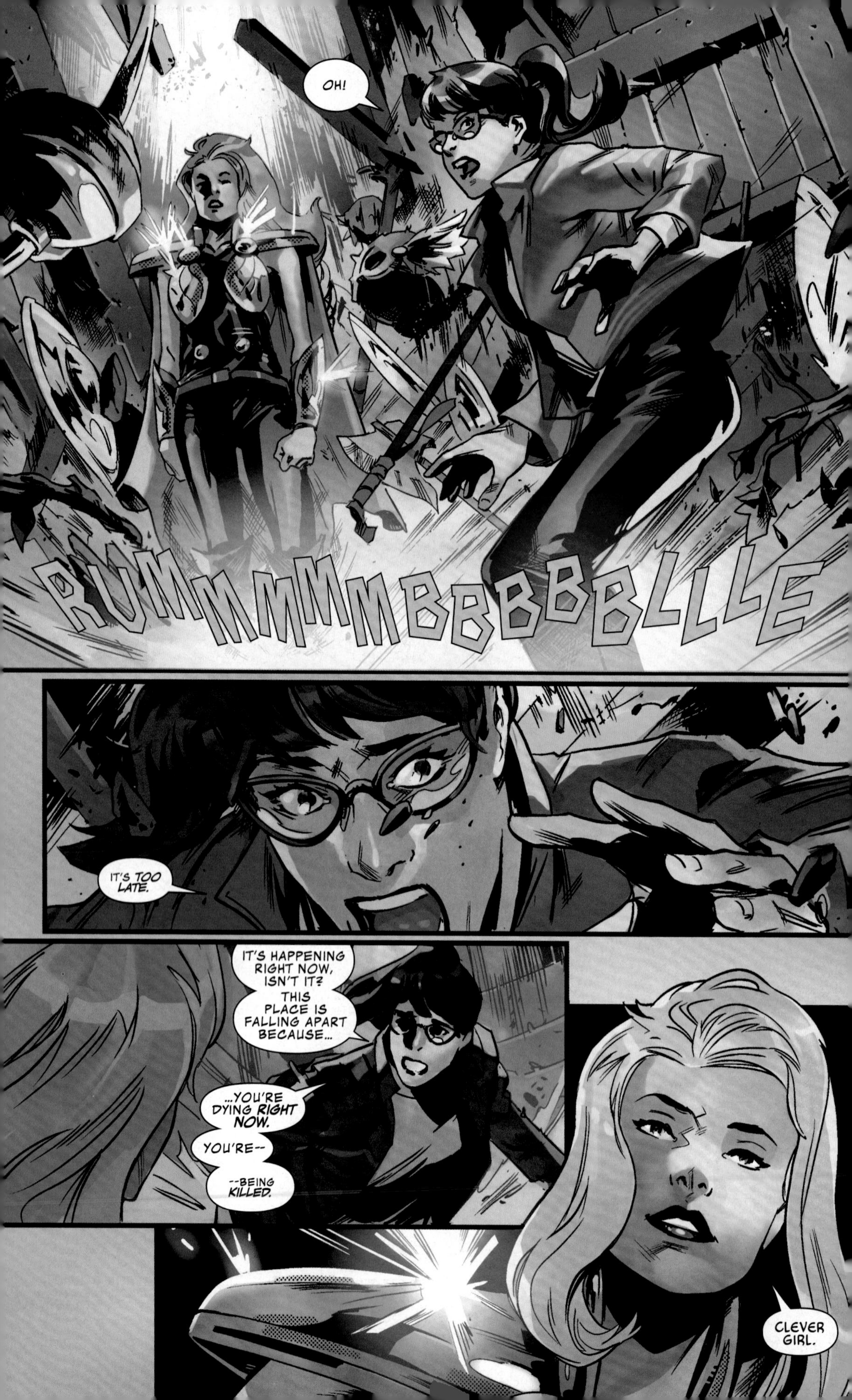
OH!
RUMMMMMMMBBBBBLLLE
IT'S *TOO* *LATE.*
IT'S HAPPENING RIGHT NOW, ISN'T IT?
THIS PLACE IS FALLING APART BECAUSE...
...YOU'RE DYING **RIGHT NOW.**
YOU'RE--
--BEING *KILLED.*
CLEVER GIRL.

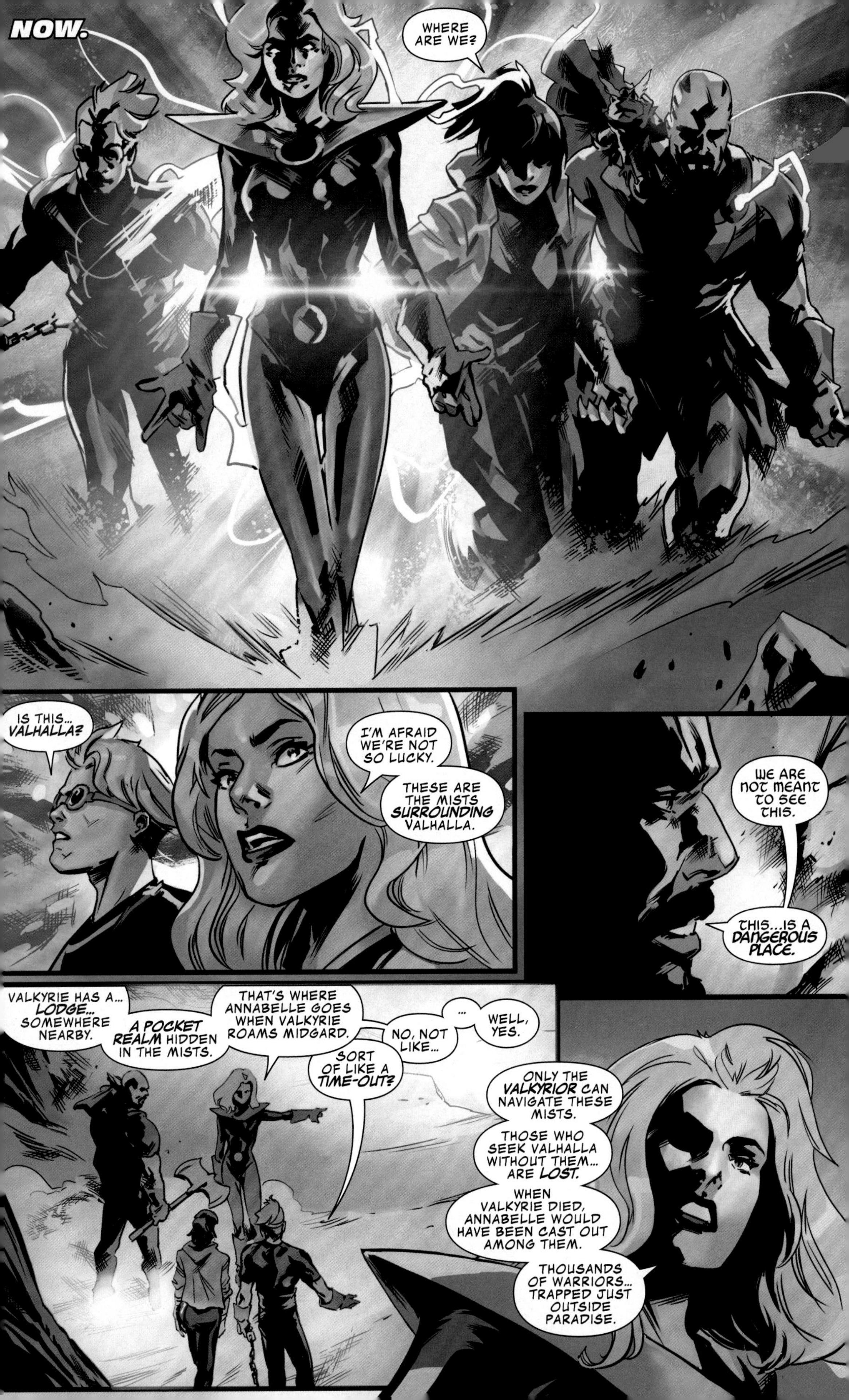
NOW.
WHERE ARE WE?
IS THIS... VALHALLA?
I'M AFRAID WE'RE NOT SO LUCKY.
THESE ARE THE MISTS SURROUNDING VALHALLA.
WE ARE NOT MEANT TO SEE THIS.
THIS...IS A DANGEROUS PLACE.
VALKYRIE HAS A... LODGE... SOMEWHERE NEARBY.
A POCKET REALM HIDDEN IN THE MISTS.
THAT'S WHERE ANNABELLE GOES WHEN VALKYRIE ROAMS MIDGARD.
SORT OF LIKE A TIME-OUT?
NO, NOT LIKE...
...
WELL, YES.
ONLY THE VALKYRIOR CAN NAVIGATE THESE MISTS.
THOSE WHO SEEK VALHALLA WITHOUT THEM... ARE LOST.
WHEN VALKYRIE DIED, ANNABELLE WOULD HAVE BEEN CAST OUT AMONG THEM.
THOUSANDS OF WARRIORS... TRAPPED JUST OUTSIDE PARADISE.

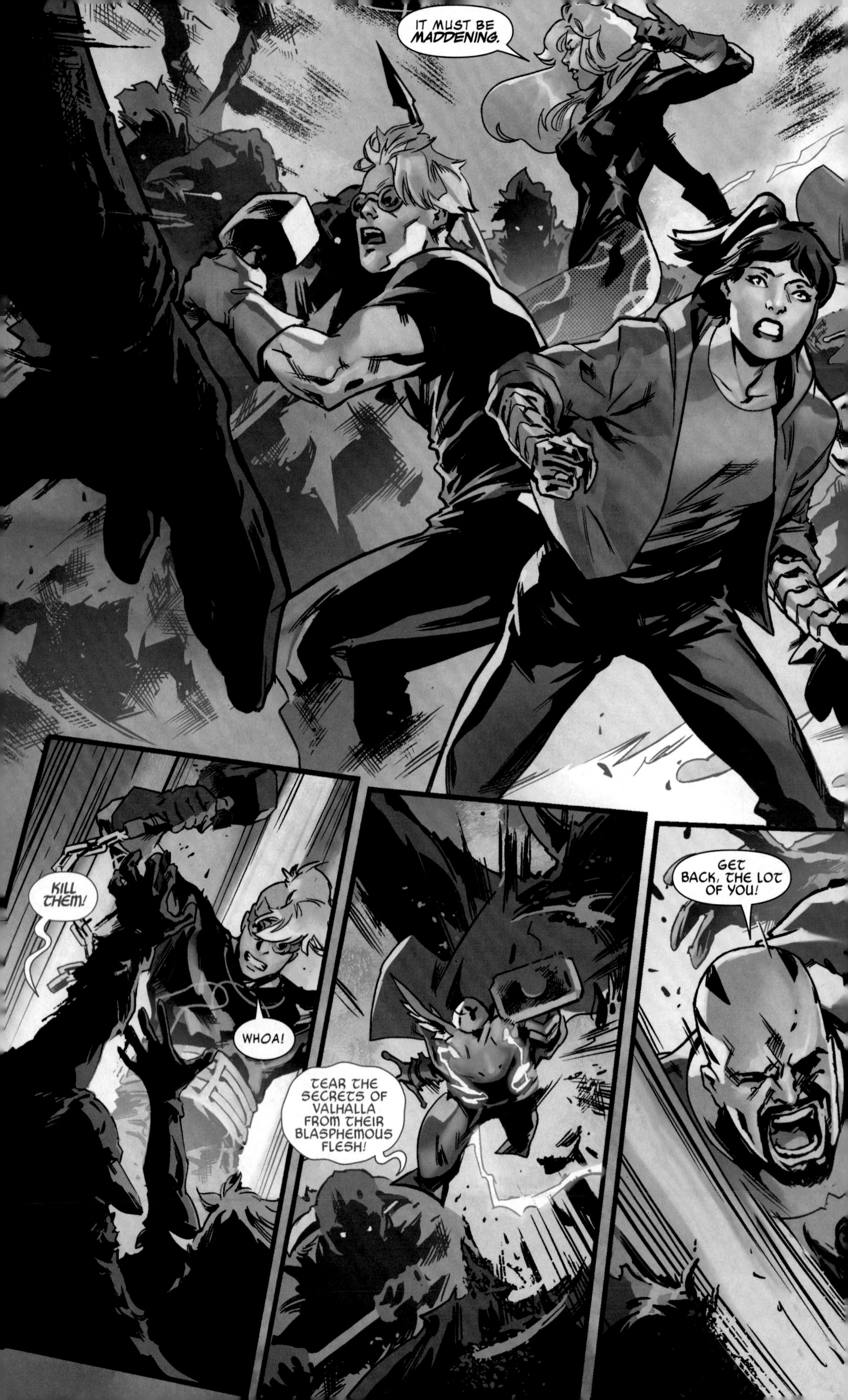
IT MUST BE MADDENING.
KILL THEM!
WHOA!
TEAR THE SECRETS OF VALHALLA FROM THEIR BLASPHEMOUS FLESH!
GET BACK, THE LOT OF YOU!

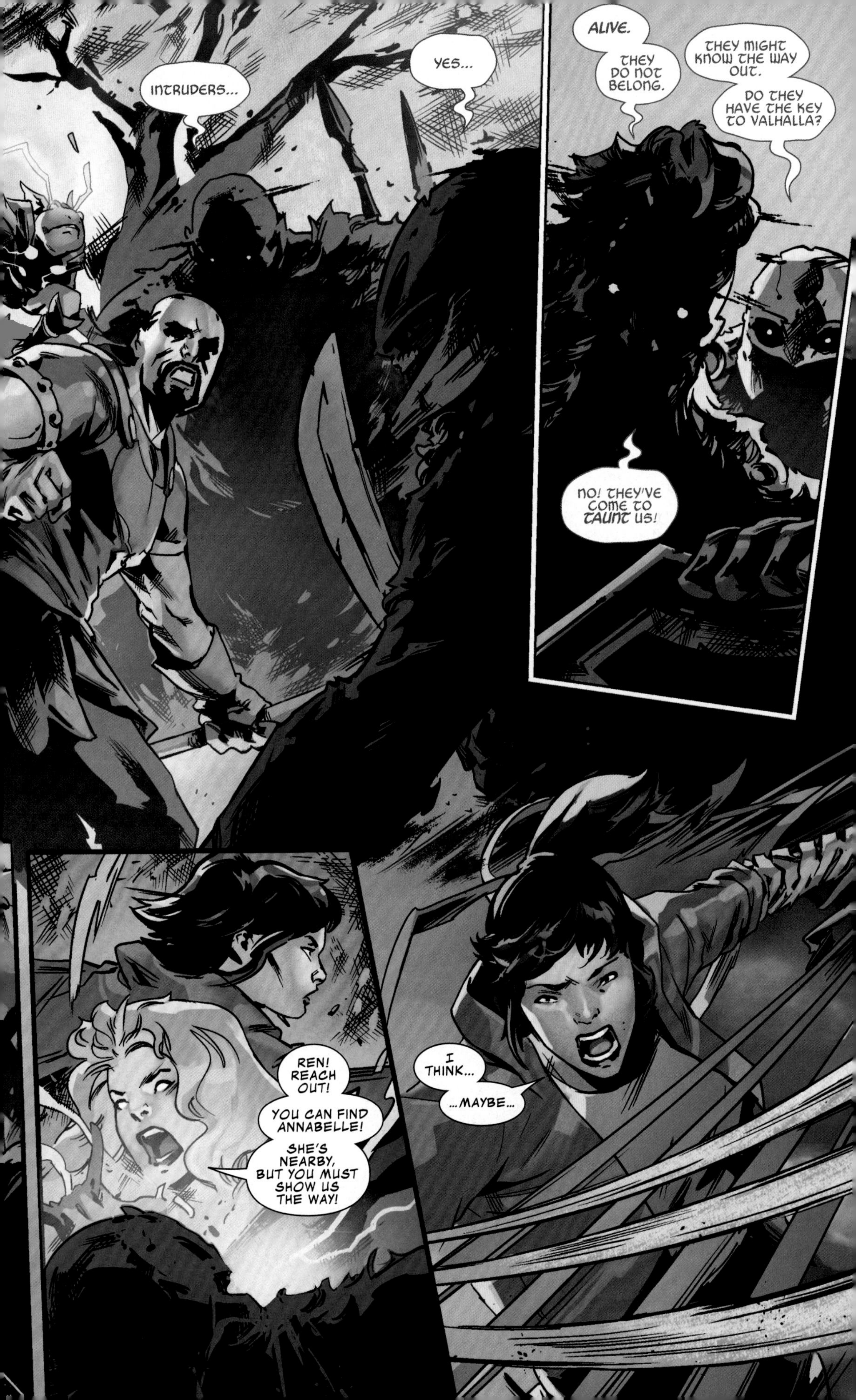
INTRUDERS...
YES...
ALIVE.
THEY DO NOT BELONG.
THEY MIGHT KNOW THE WAY OUT.
DO THEY HAVE THE KEY TO VALHALLA?
NO! THEY'VE COME TO TAUNT US!
REN! REACH OUT!
YOU CAN FIND ANNABELLE!
SHE'S NEARBY, BUT YOU MUST SHOW US THE WAY!
I THINK...
...MAYBE...

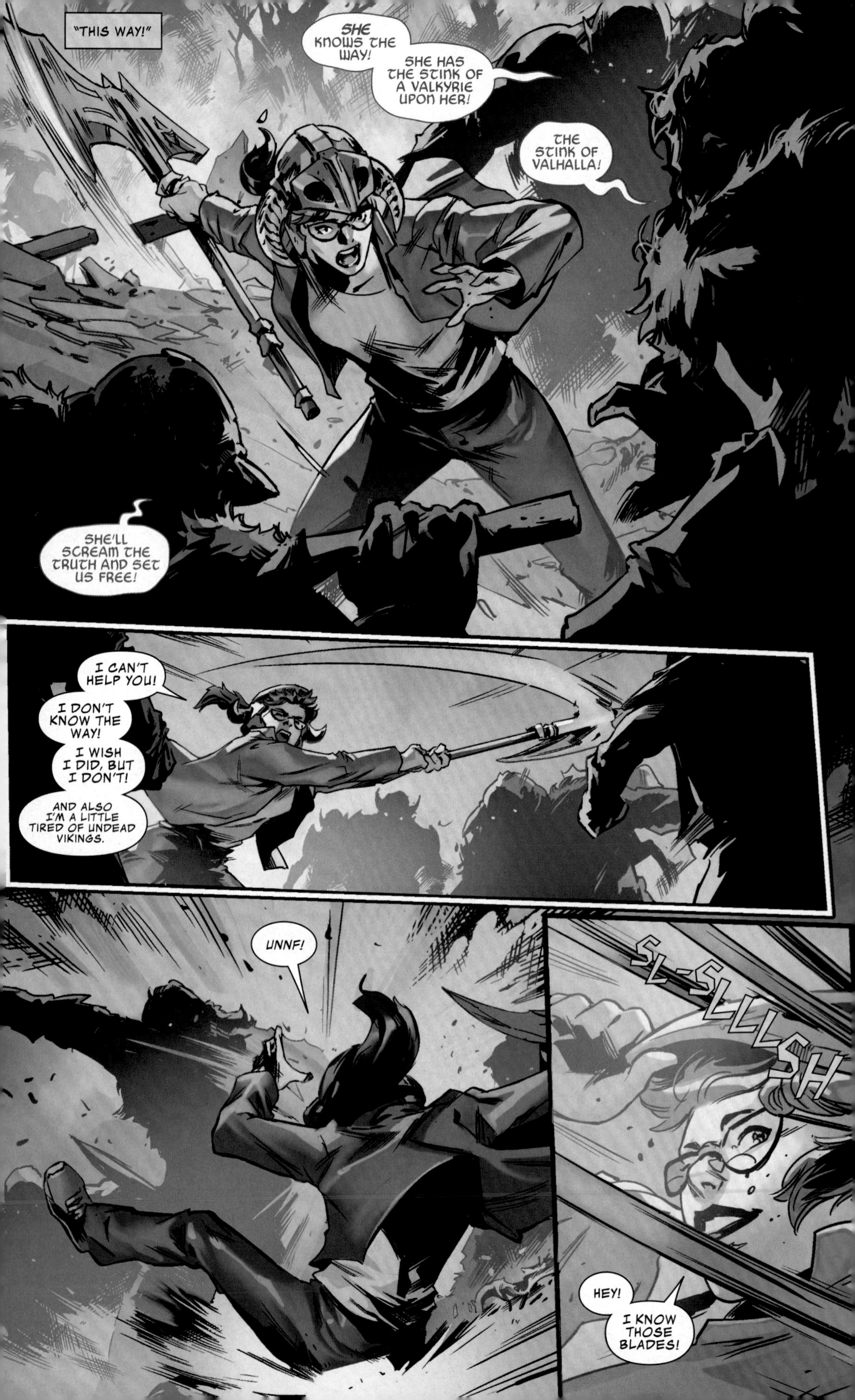
"THIS WAY!"
SHE KNOWS THE WAY!
SHE HAS THE STINK OF A VALKYRIE UPON HER!
THE STINK OF VALHALLA!
SHE'LL SCREAM THE TRUTH AND SET US FREE!
I CAN'T HELP YOU!
I DON'T KNOW THE WAY!
I WISH I DID, BUT I DON'T!
AND ALSO I'M A LITTLE TIRED OF UNDEAD VIKINGS.
UNNF!
SL-SLLLSH
HEY!
I KNOW THOSE BLADES!

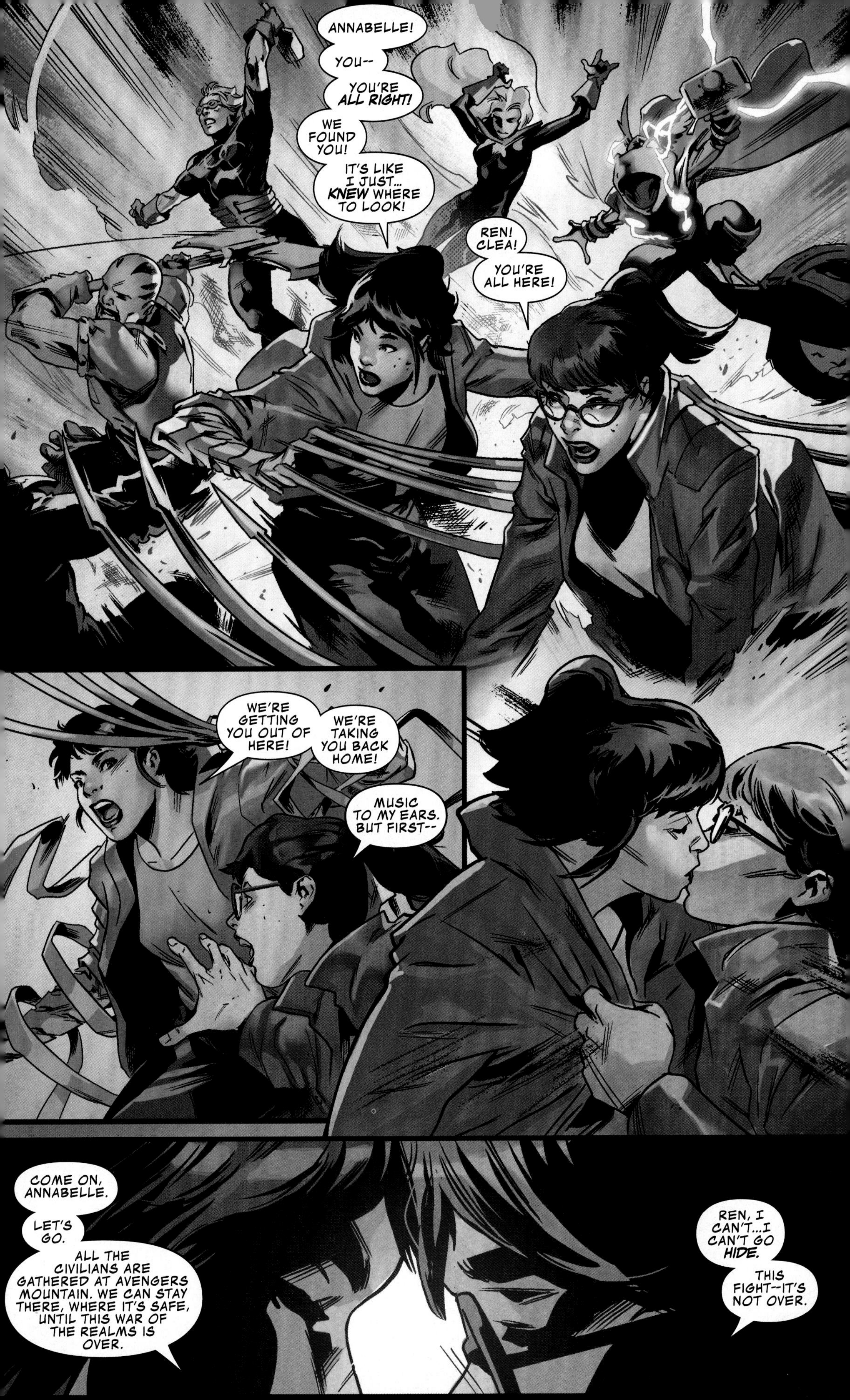

ANNABELLE!
YOU--
YOU'RE ALL RIGHT!
WE FOUND YOU!
IT'S LIKE I JUST... KNEW WHERE TO LOOK!
REN! CLEA!
YOU'RE ALL HERE!
WE'RE GETTING YOU OUT OF HERE!
WE'RE TAKING YOU BACK HOME!
MUSIC TO MY EARS. BUT FIRST--
COME ON, ANNABELLE.
LET'S GO.
ALL THE CIVILIANS ARE GATHERED AT AVENGERS MOUNTAIN. WE CAN STAY THERE, WHERE IT'S SAFE, UNTIL THIS WAR OF THE REALMS IS OVER.
REN, I CAN'T...I CAN'T GO HIDE.
THIS FIGHT--IT'S NOT OVER.

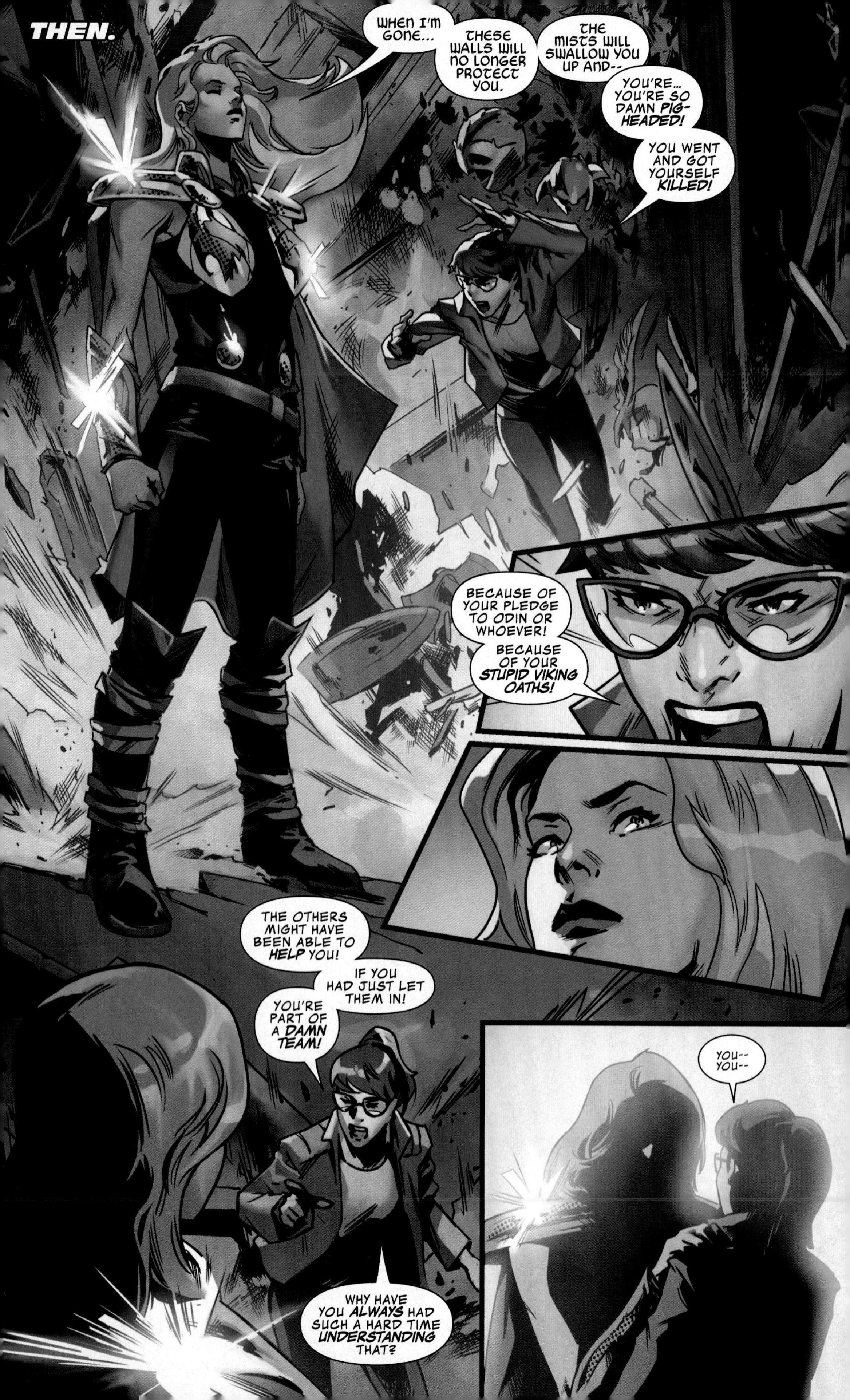
THEN.
WHEN I'M GONE...
THESE WALLS WILL NO LONGER PROTECT YOU.
THE MISTS WILL SWALLOW YOU UP AND--
YOU'RE... YOU'RE SO DAMN PIG-HEADED!
YOU WENT AND GOT YOURSELF KILLED!
BECAUSE OF YOUR PLEDGE TO ODIN OR WHOEVER!
BECAUSE OF YOUR STUPID VIKING OATHS!
THE OTHERS MIGHT HAVE BEEN ABLE TO HELP YOU!
IF YOU HAD JUST LET THEM IN!
YOU'RE PART OF A DAMN TEAM!
WHY HAVE YOU ALWAYS HAD SUCH A HARD TIME UNDERSTANDING THAT?
YOU-- YOU--

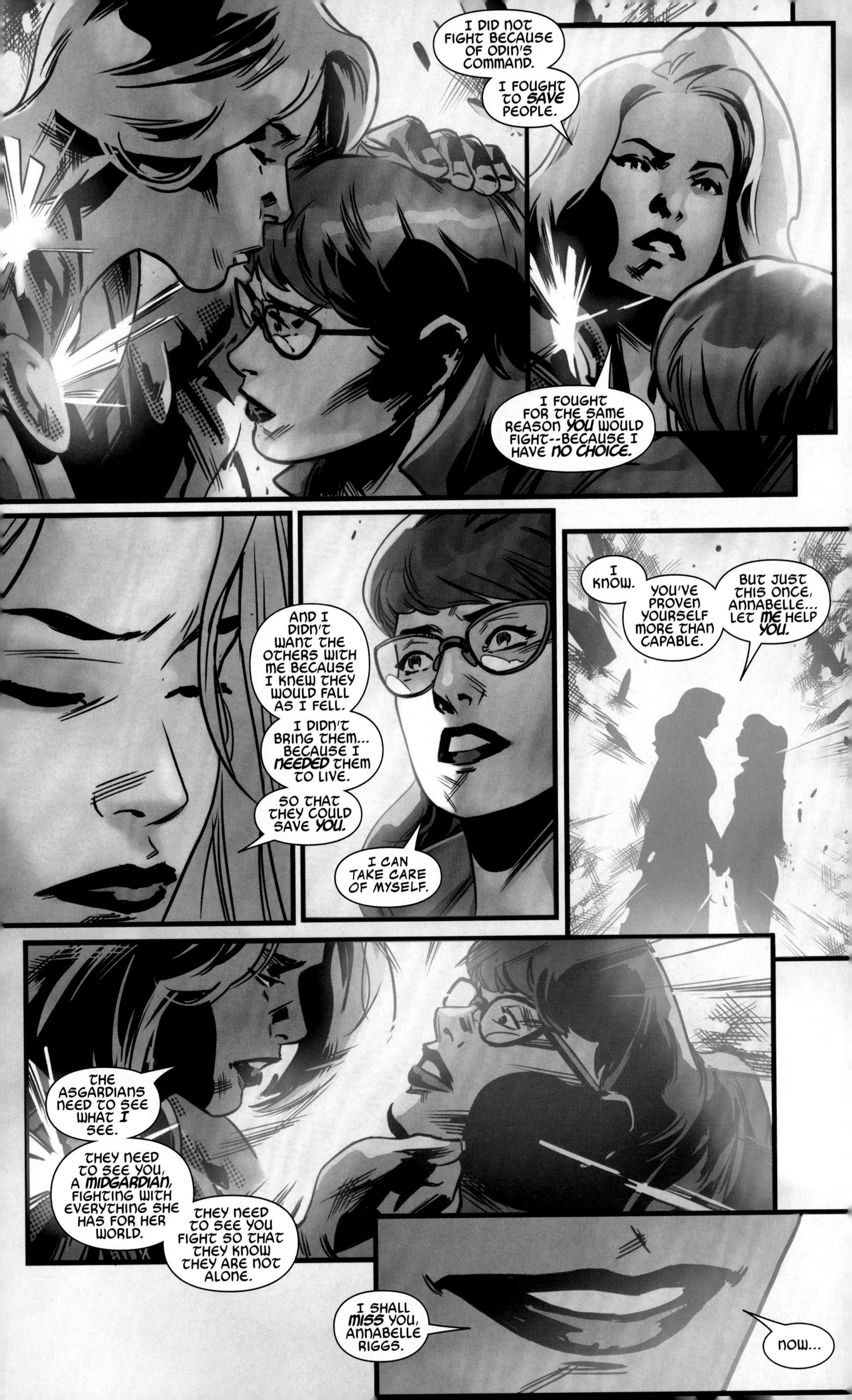

I DID NOT FIGHT BECAUSE OF ODIN'S COMMAND.
I FOUGHT TO SAVE PEOPLE.
I FOUGHT FOR THE SAME REASON YOU WOULD FIGHT--BECAUSE I HAVE NO CHOICE.
AND I DIDN'T WANT THE OTHERS WITH ME BECAUSE I KNEW THEY WOULD FALL AS I FELL.
I DIDN'T BRING THEM... BECAUSE I NEEDED THEM TO LIVE.
SO THAT THEY COULD SAVE YOU.
I CAN TAKE CARE OF MYSELF.
I KNOW.
YOU'VE PROVEN YOURSELF MORE THAN CAPABLE.
BUT JUST THIS ONCE, ANNABELLE... LET ME HELP YOU.
THE ASGARDIANS NEED TO SEE WHAT I SEE.
THEY NEED TO SEE YOU, A MIDGARDIAN, FIGHTING WITH EVERYTHING SHE HAS FOR HER WORLD.
THEY NEED TO SEE YOU FIGHT SO THAT THEY KNOW THEY ARE NOT ALONE.
I SHALL MISS YOU, ANNABELLE RIGGS.
NOW...

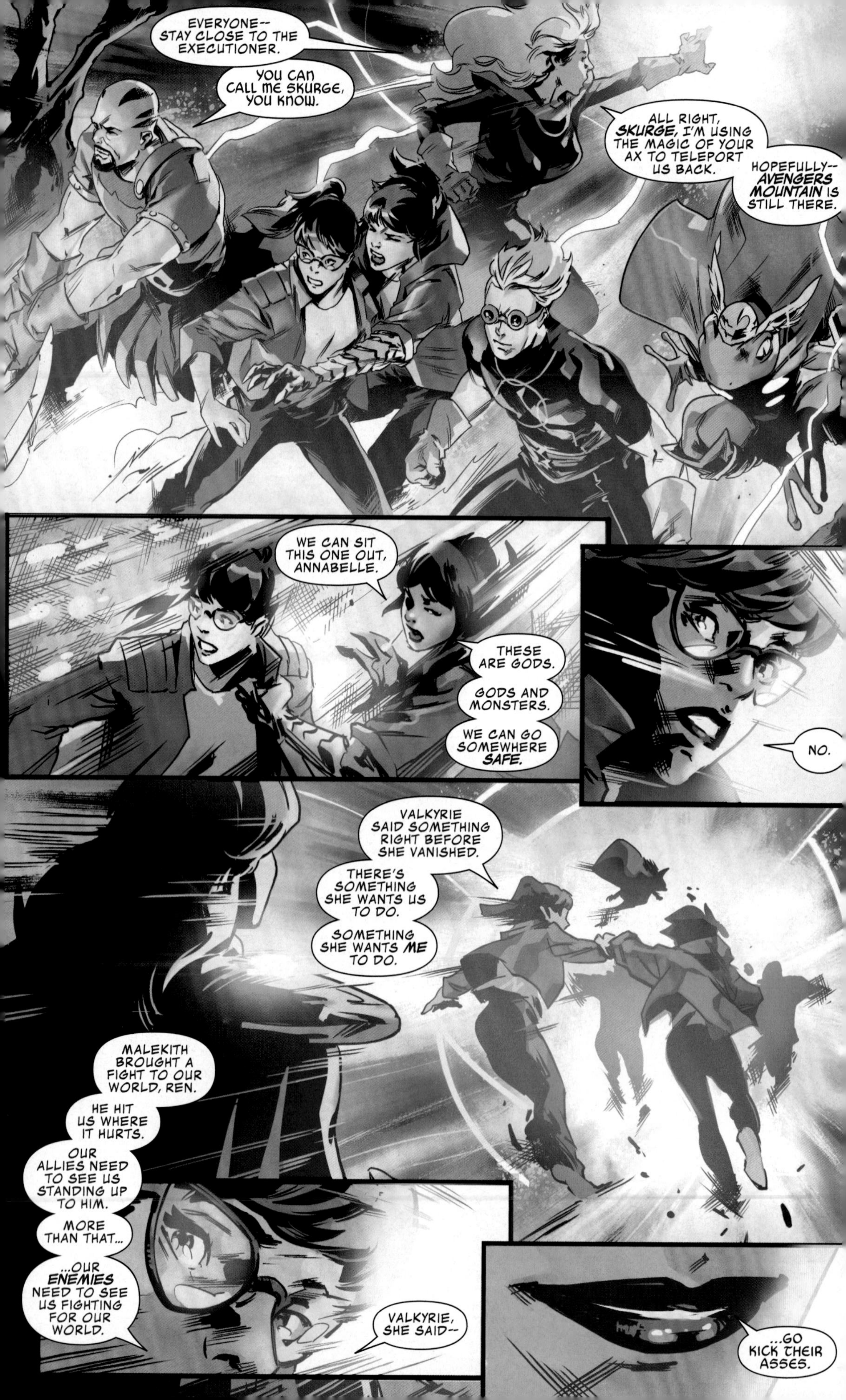
EVERYONE--
STAY CLOSE TO THE EXECUTIONER.
YOU CAN CALL ME SKURGE, YOU KNOW.
ALL RIGHT, SKURGE, I'M USING THE MAGIC OF YOUR AX TO TELEPORT US BACK.
HOPEFULLY-- AVENGERS MOUNTAIN IS STILL THERE.
WE CAN SIT THIS ONE OUT, ANNABELLE.
THESE ARE GODS.
GODS AND MONSTERS.
WE CAN GO SOMEWHERE SAFE.
NO.
VALKYRIE SAID SOMETHING RIGHT BEFORE SHE VANISHED.
THERE'S SOMETHING SHE WANTS US TO DO.
SOMETHING SHE WANTS ME TO DO.
MALEKITH BROUGHT A FIGHT TO OUR WORLD, REN.
HE HIT US WHERE IT HURTS.
OUR ALLIES NEED TO SEE US STANDING UP TO HIM.
MORE THAN THAT...
...OUR ENEMIES NEED TO SEE US FIGHTING FOR OUR WORLD.
VALKYRIE, SHE SAID--
...GO KICK THEIR ASSES.

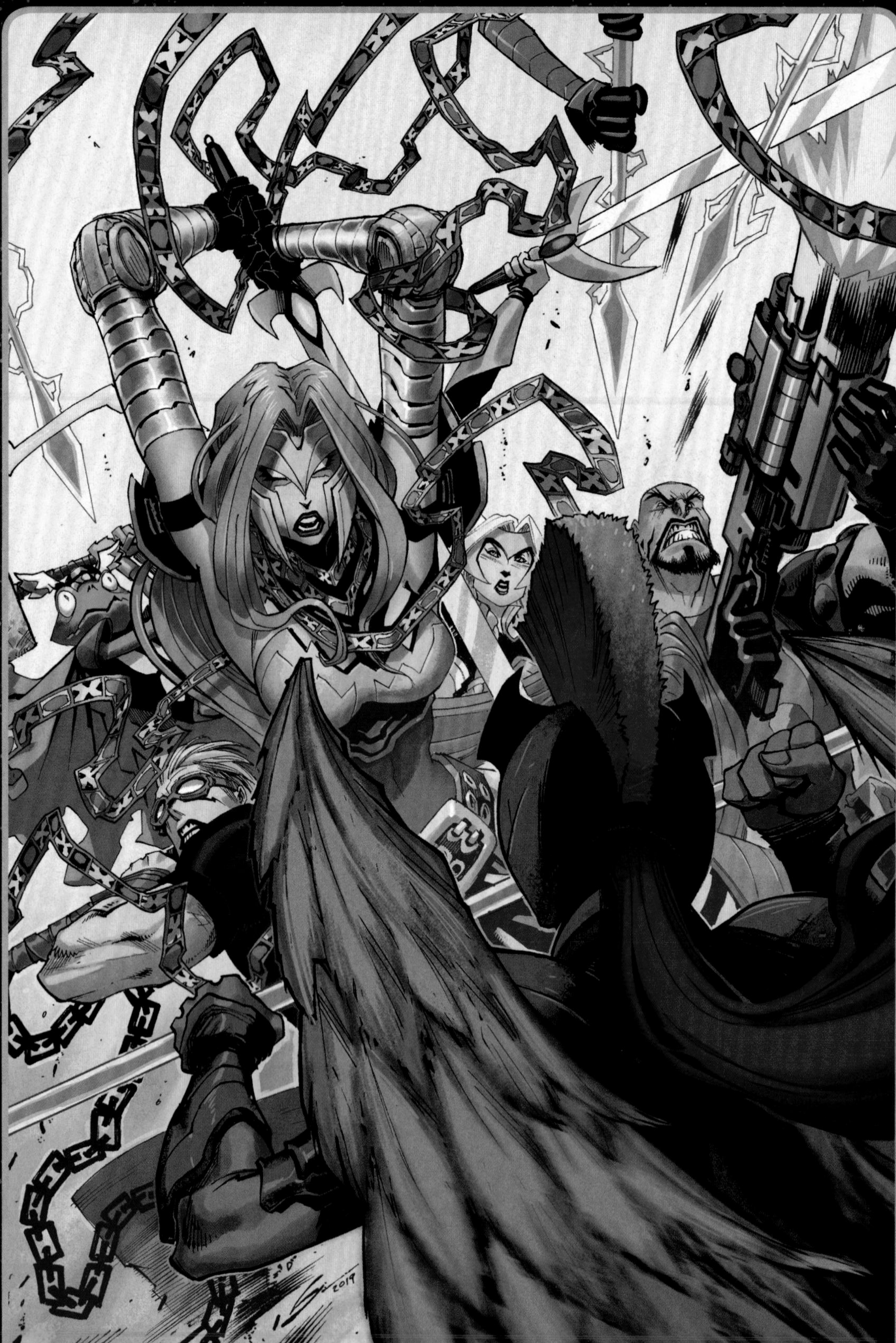

10

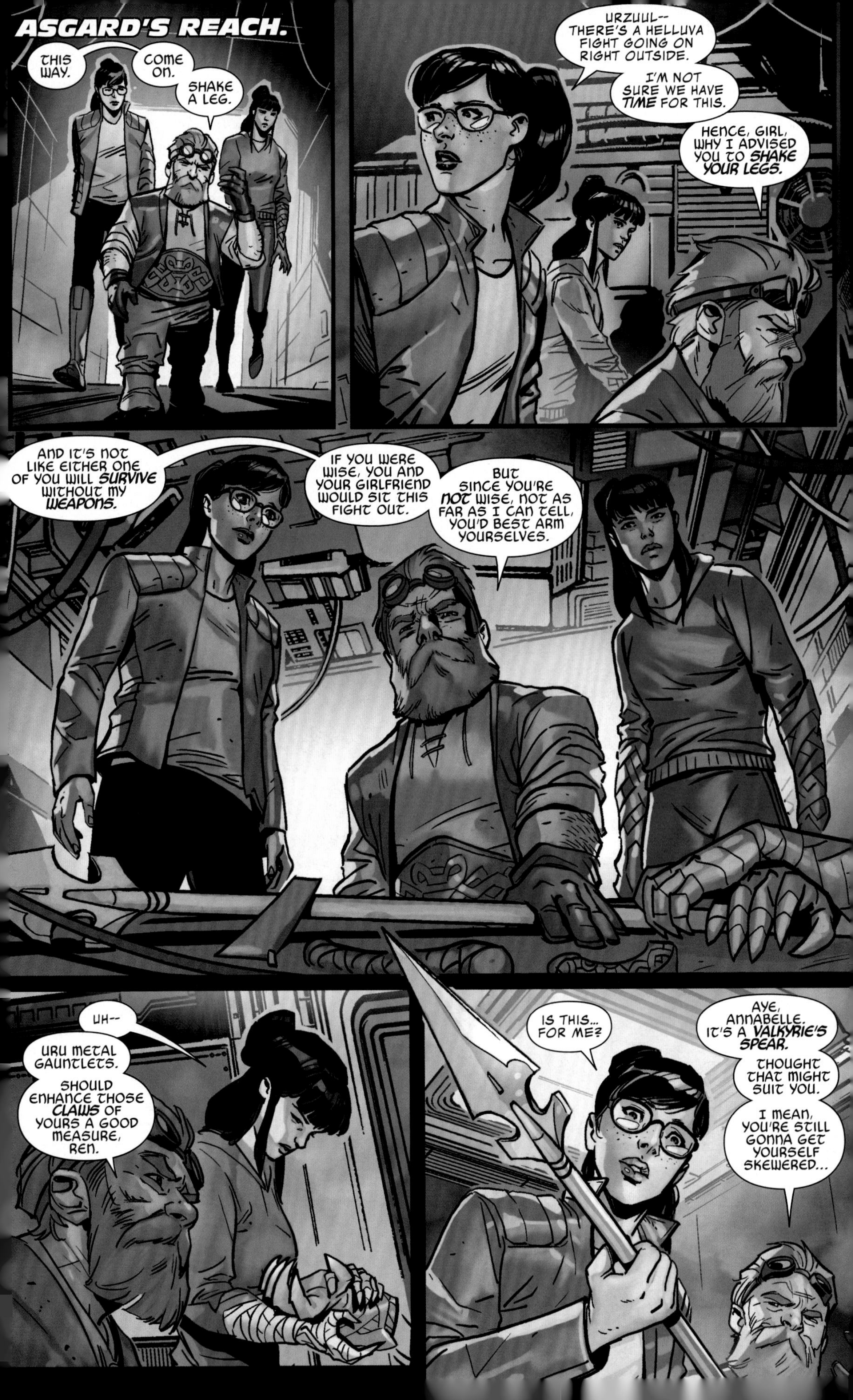
ASGARD'S REACH.
THIS WAY.
COME ON.
SHAKE A LEG.
URZUUL-- THERE'S A HELLUVA FIGHT GOING ON RIGHT OUTSIDE.
I'M NOT SURE WE HAVE TIME FOR THIS.
HENCE, GIRL, WHY I ADVISED YOU TO SHAKE YOUR LEGS.
AND IT'S NOT LIKE EITHER ONE OF YOU WILL SURVIVE WITHOUT MY WEAPONS.
IF YOU WERE WISE, YOU AND YOUR GIRLFRIEND WOULD SIT THIS FIGHT OUT.
BUT SINCE YOU'RE NOT WISE, NOT AS FAR AS I CAN TELL, YOU'D BEST ARM YOURSELVES.
UH--
URU METAL GAUNTLETS.
SHOULD ENHANCE THOSE CLAWS OF YOURS A GOOD MEASURE, REN.
IS THIS... FOR ME?
AYE, ANNABELLE. IT'S A VALKYRIE'S SPEAR.
THOUGHT THAT MIGHT SUIT YOU.
I MEAN, YOU'RE STILL GONNA GET YOURSELF SKEWERED...

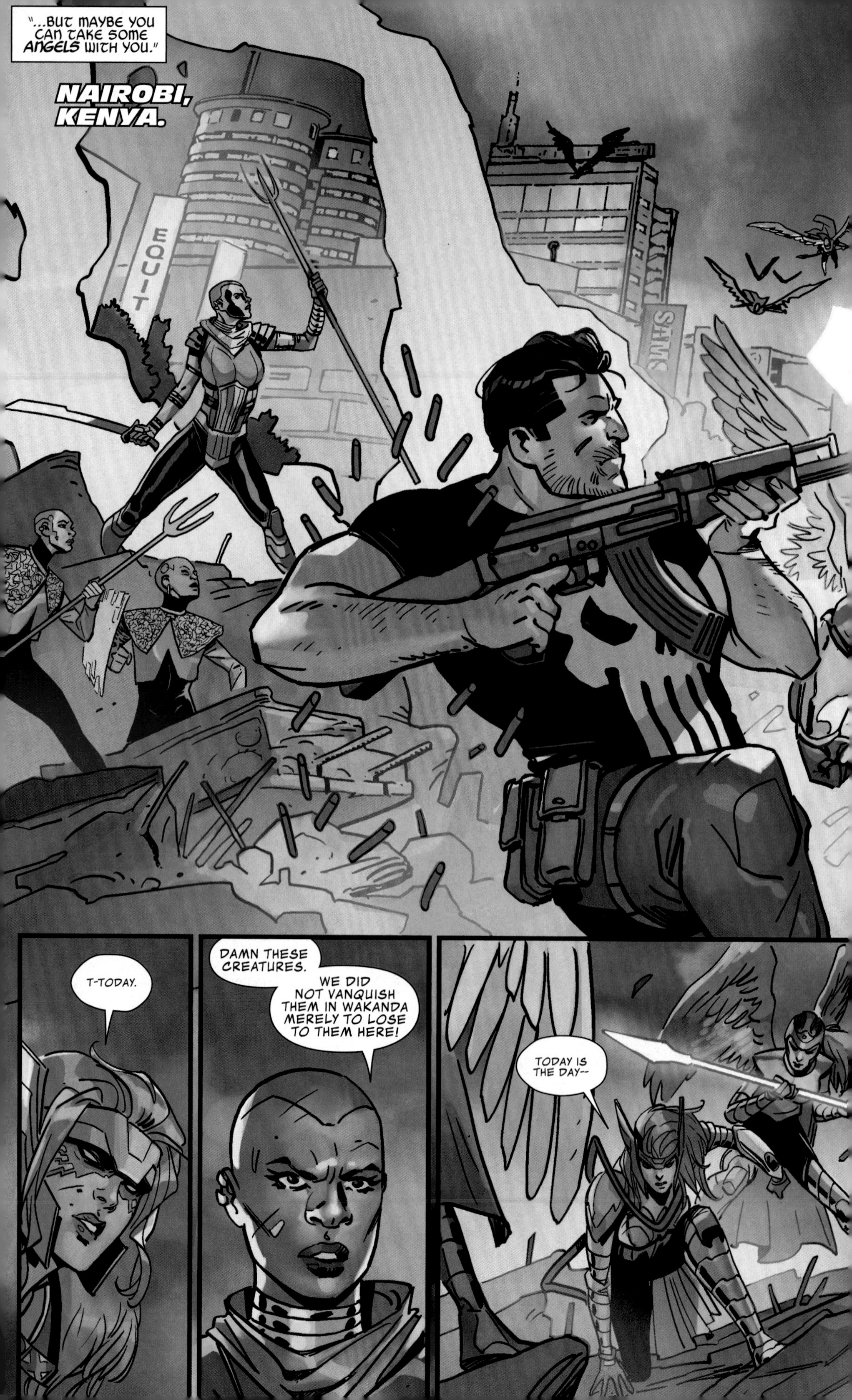
"...BUT MAYBE YOU CAN TAKE SOME ANGELS WITH YOU."
NAIROBI, KENYA.
EQUIT
T-TODAY.
DAMN THESE CREATURES.
WE DID NOT VANQUISH THEM IN WAKANDA MERELY TO LOSE TO THEM HERE!
TODAY IS THE DAY--

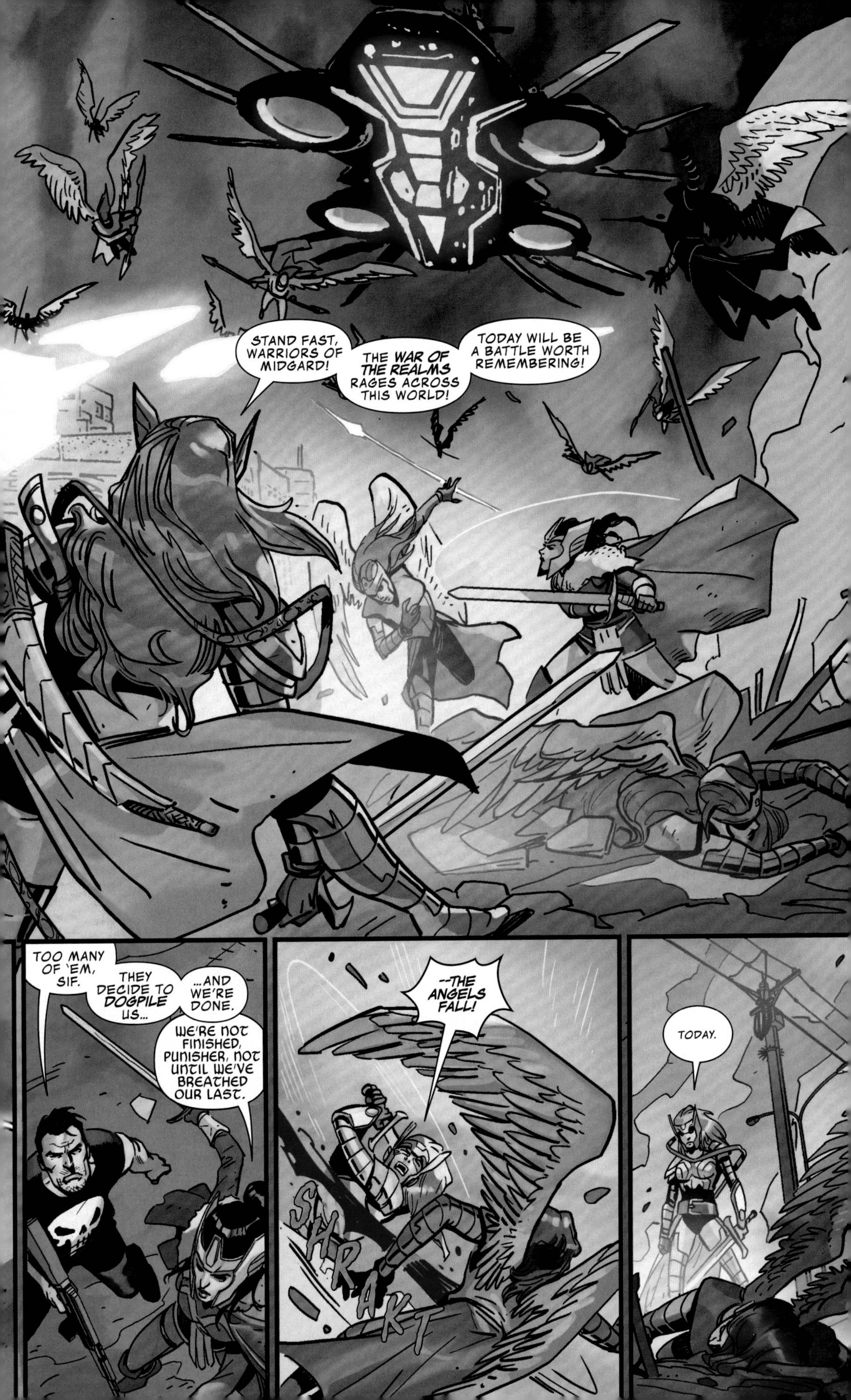
STAND FAST, WARRIORS OF MIDGARD!
THE WAR OF THE REALMS RAGES ACROSS THIS WORLD!
TODAY WILL BE A BATTLE WORTH REMEMBERING!
TOO MANY OF 'EM, SIF.
THEY DECIDE TO DOGPILE US...
...AND WE'RE DONE.
WE'RE NOT FINISHED, PUNISHER, NOT UNTIL WE'VE BREATHED OUR LAST.
--THE ANGELS FALL!
SHRAKT
TODAY.

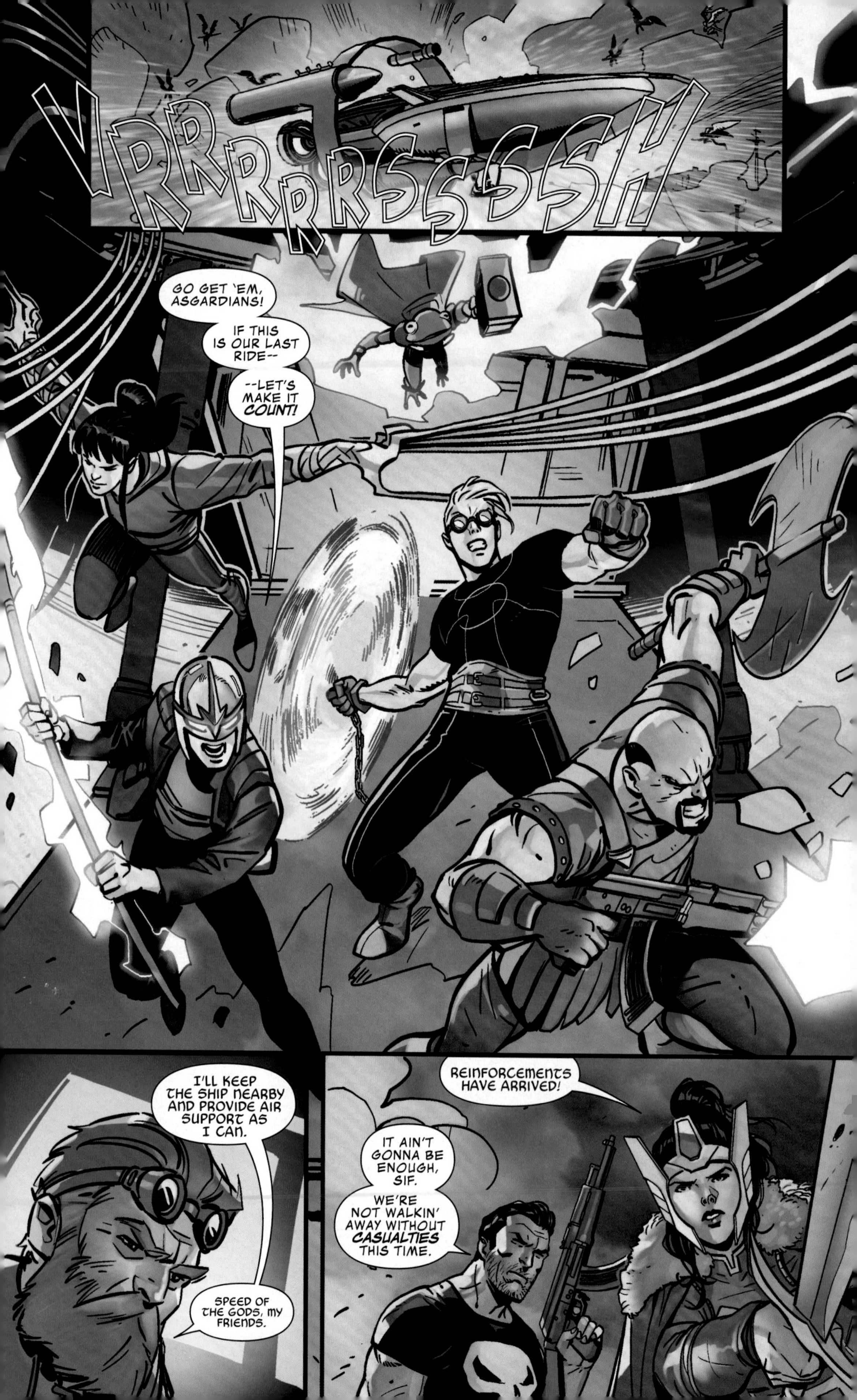
VRRRRRSSSSH
GO GET 'EM, ASGARDIANS!
IF THIS IS OUR LAST RIDE--
--LET'S MAKE IT COUNT!
I'LL KEEP THE SHIP NEARBY AND PROVIDE AIR SUPPORT AS I CAN.
SPEED OF THE GODS, MY FRIENDS.
REINFORCEMENTS HAVE ARRIVED!
IT AIN'T GONNA BE ENOUGH, SIF.
WE'RE NOT WALKIN' AWAY WITHOUT CASUALTIES THIS TIME.

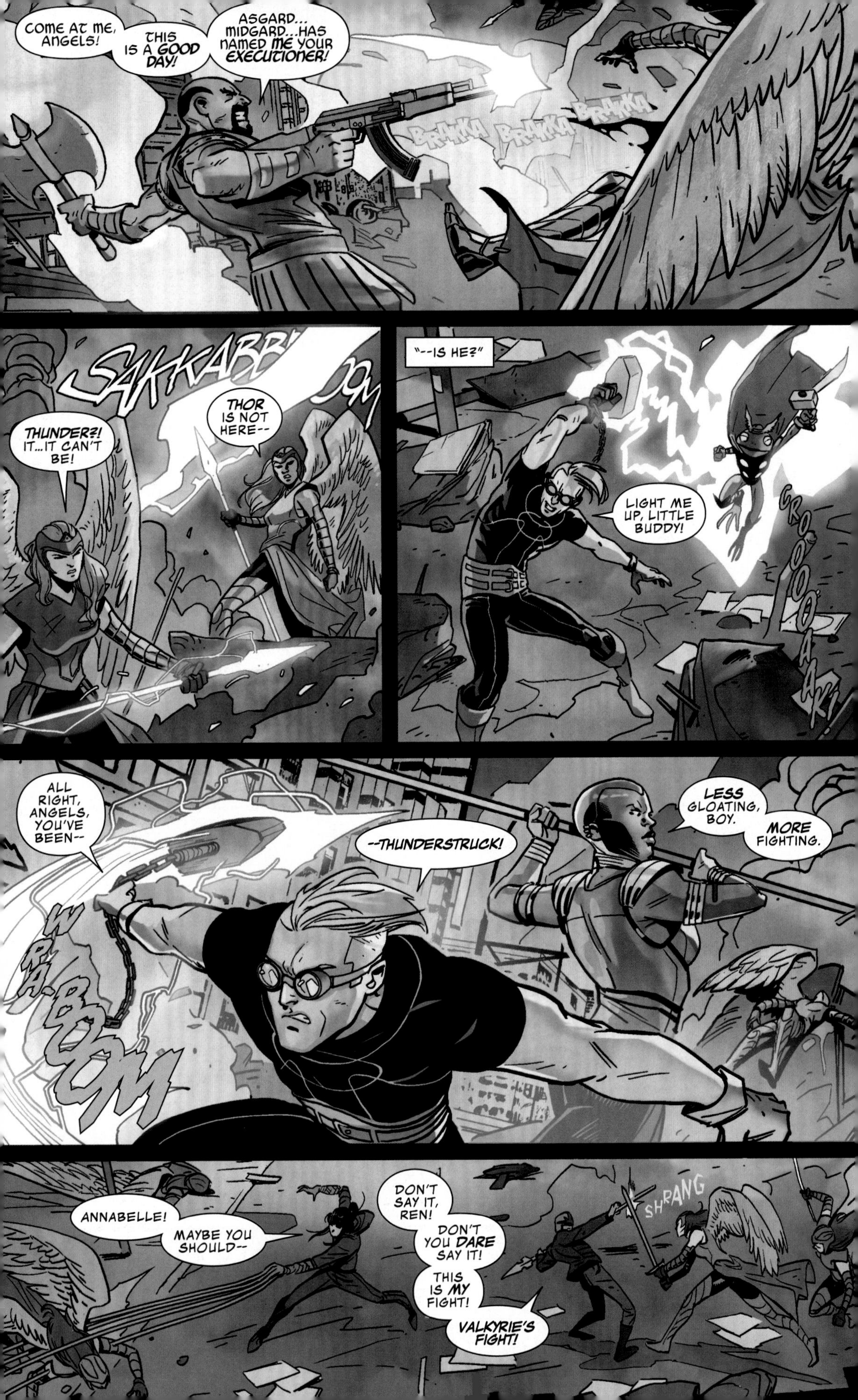
COME AT ME, ANGELS!
THIS IS A GOOD DAY!
ASGARD... MIDGARD...HAS NAMED ME YOUR EXECUTIONER!
BRAKKA BRAKKA BRAKKA
SAKKABB'OOM
THUNDER?! IT...IT CAN'T BE!
THOR IS NOT HERE--
"--IS HE?"
LIGHT ME UP, LITTLE BUDDY!
GROOOOAAAR
ALL RIGHT, ANGELS, YOU'VE BEEN--
--THUNDERSTRUCK!
LESS GLOATING, BOY. MORE FIGHTING.
WRA-BOOM
ANNABELLE!
MAYBE YOU SHOULD--
DON'T SAY IT, REN!
DON'T YOU DARE SAY IT!
THIS IS MY FIGHT!
VALKYRIE'S FIGHT!
SHRANG

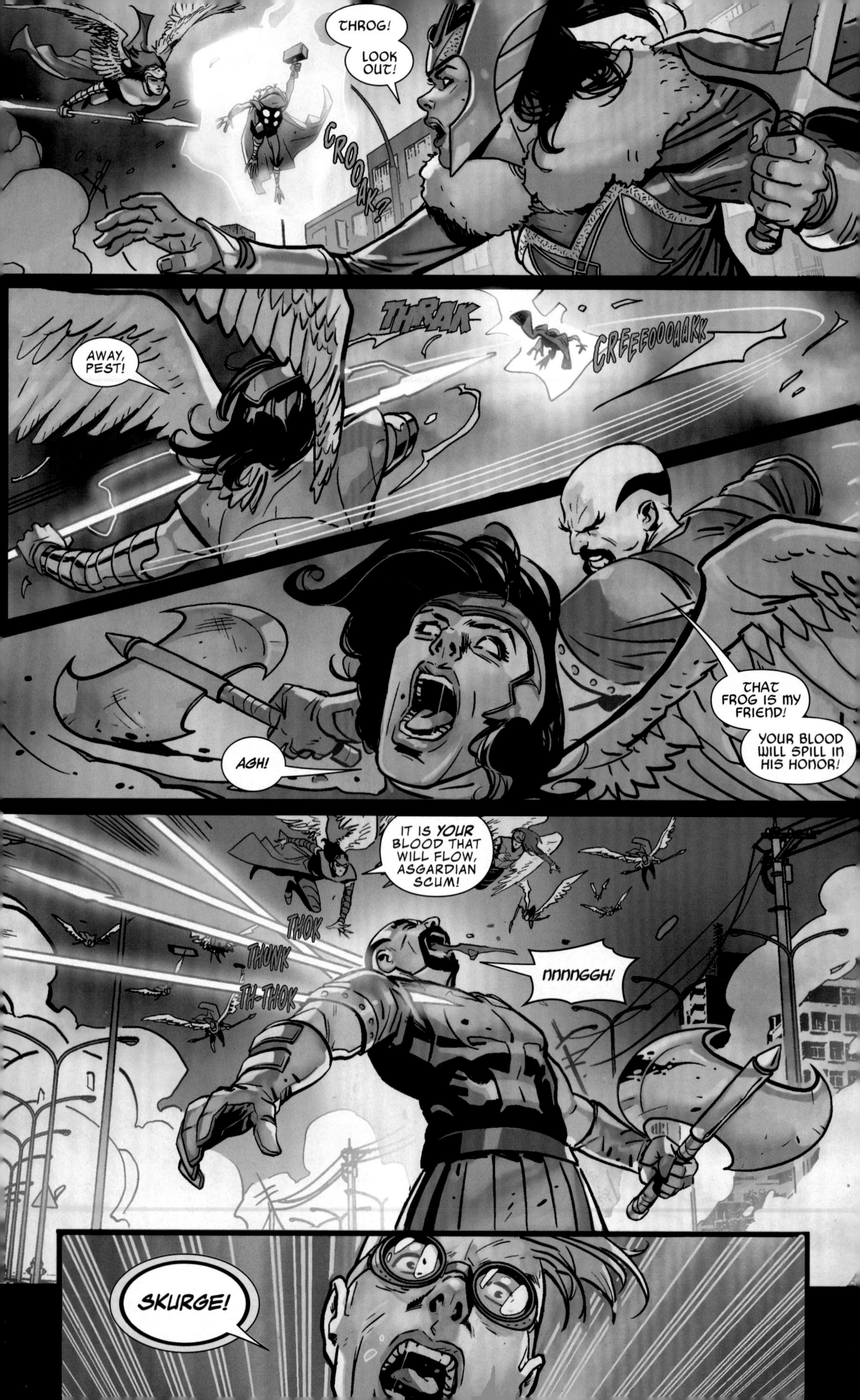
THROG!
LOOK OUT!
CROOOAK?!
THRAK
CREEEOOOAAKK
AWAY, PEST!
THAT FROG IS MY FRIEND!
YOUR BLOOD WILL SPILL IN HIS HONOR!
AGH!
IT IS YOUR BLOOD THAT WILL FLOW, ASGARDIAN SCUM!
THOK
THUNK
TH-THOK
NNNNGGH!
SKURGE!

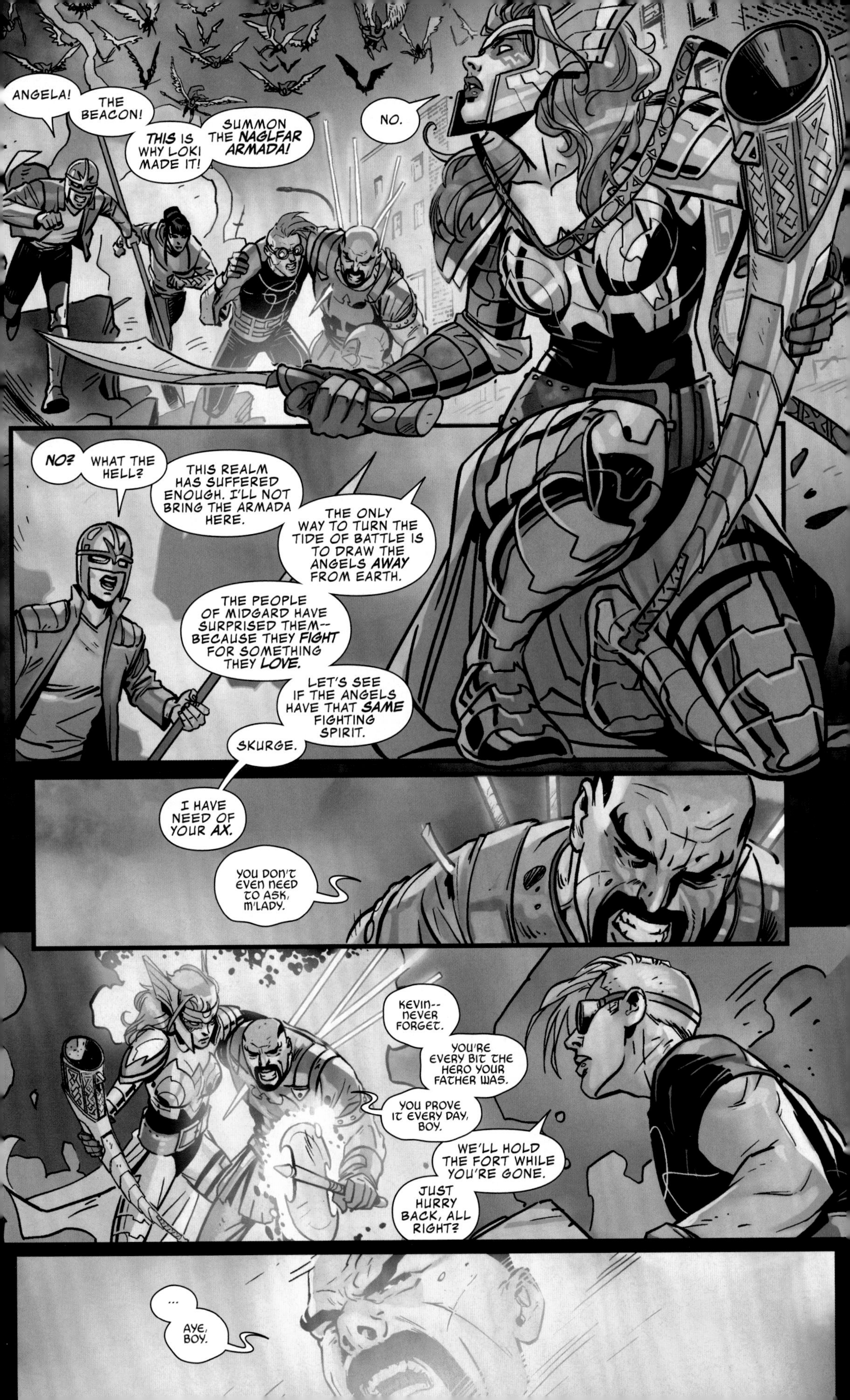

ANGELA!
THE BEACON!
THIS IS WHY LOKI MADE IT!
SUMMON THE NAGLFAR ARMADA!
NO.
NO? WHAT THE HELL?
THIS REALM HAS SUFFERED ENOUGH. I'LL NOT BRING THE ARMADA HERE.
THE ONLY WAY TO TURN THE TIDE OF BATTLE IS TO DRAW THE ANGELS AWAY FROM EARTH.
THE PEOPLE OF MIDGARD HAVE SURPRISED THEM-- BECAUSE THEY FIGHT FOR SOMETHING THEY LOVE.
LET'S SEE IF THE ANGELS HAVE THAT SAME FIGHTING SPIRIT.
SKURGE.
I HAVE NEED OF YOUR AX.
YOU DON'T EVEN NEED TO ASK, M'LADY.
KEVIN-- NEVER FORGET.
YOU'RE EVERY BIT THE HERO YOUR FATHER WAS.
YOU PROVE IT EVERY DAY, BOY.
WE'LL HOLD THE FORT WHILE YOU'RE GONE.
JUST HURRY BACK, ALL RIGHT?
...
AYE, BOY.

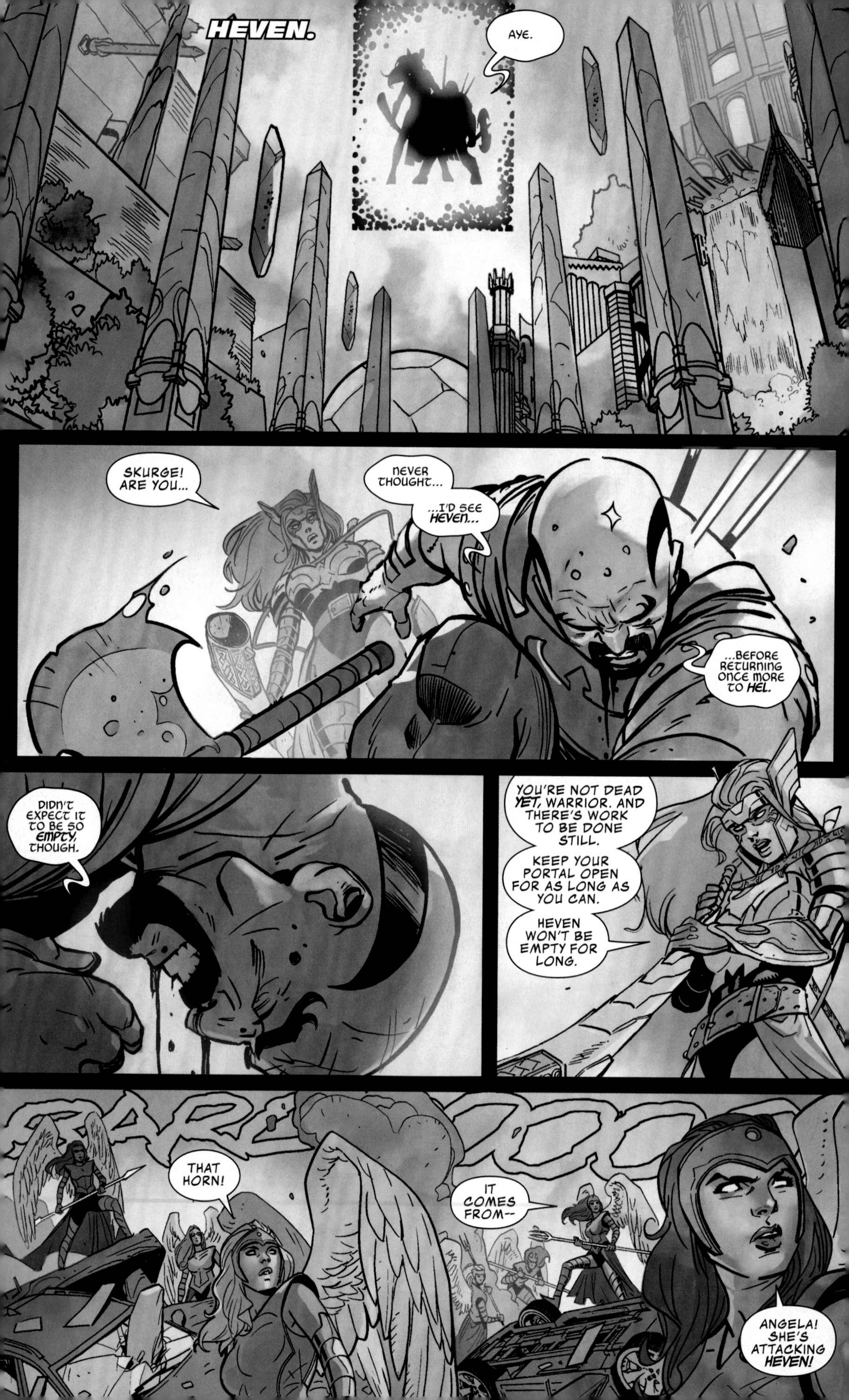
HEVEN.
AYE.
SKURGE! ARE YOU...
NEVER THOUGHT...
...I'D SEE HEVEN...
...BEFORE RETURNING ONCE MORE TO HEL.
DIDN'T EXPECT IT TO BE SO EMPTY, THOUGH.
YOU'RE NOT DEAD YET, WARRIOR. AND THERE'S WORK TO BE DONE STILL.
KEEP YOUR PORTAL OPEN FOR AS LONG AS YOU CAN.
HEVEN WON'T BE EMPTY FOR LONG.
THAT HORN!
IT COMES FROM--
ANGELA! SHE'S ATTACKING HEVEN!

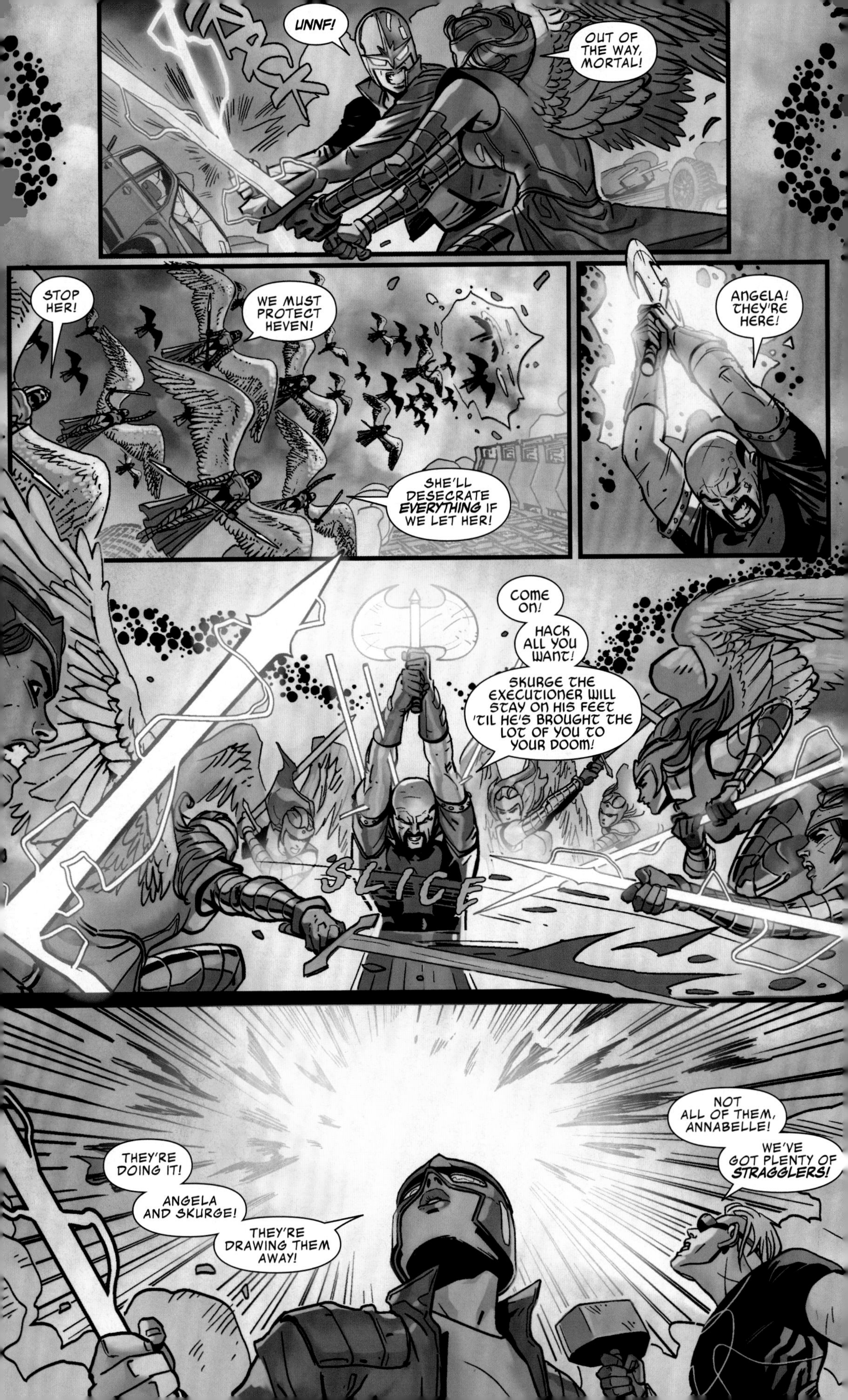
KRACK
UNNF!
OUT OF THE WAY, MORTAL!
STOP HER!
WE MUST PROTECT HEVEN!
SHE'LL DESECRATE EVERYTHING IF WE LET HER!
ANGELA! THEY'RE HERE!
COME ON!
HACK ALL YOU WANT!
SKURGE THE EXECUTIONER WILL STAY ON HIS FEET 'TIL HE'S BROUGHT THE LOT OF YOU TO YOUR DOOM!
SLICE
THEY'RE DOING IT!
ANGELA AND SKURGE!
THEY'RE DRAWING THEM AWAY!
NOT ALL OF THEM, ANNABELLE!
WE'VE GOT PLENTY OF STRAGGLERS!

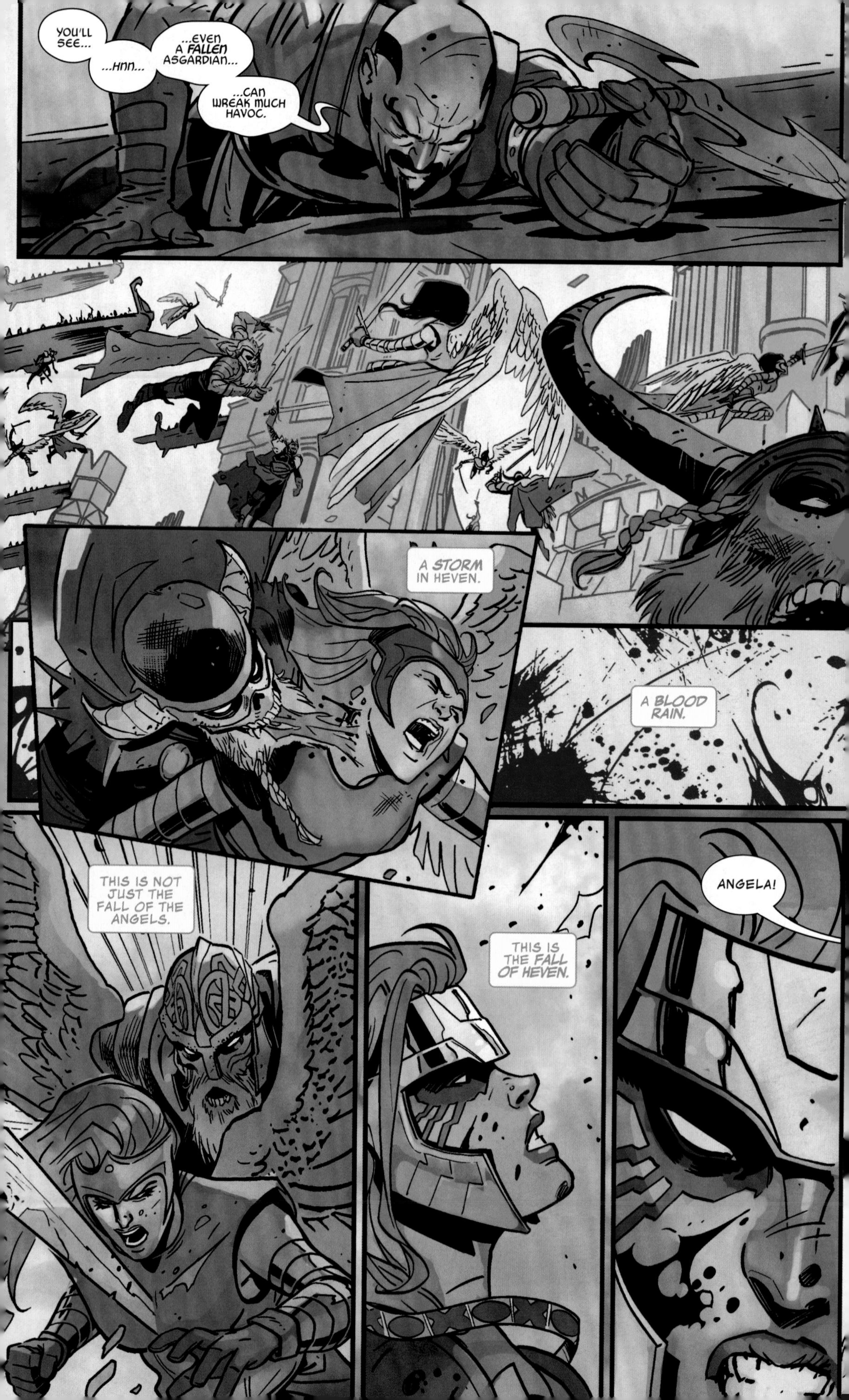
YOU'LL SEE...
...HNN...
...EVEN A FALLEN ASGARDIAN...
...CAN WREAK MUCH HAVOC.
A STORM IN HEVEN.
A BLOOD RAIN.
THIS IS NOT JUST THE FALL OF THE ANGELS.
THIS IS THE FALL OF HEVEN.
ANGELA!

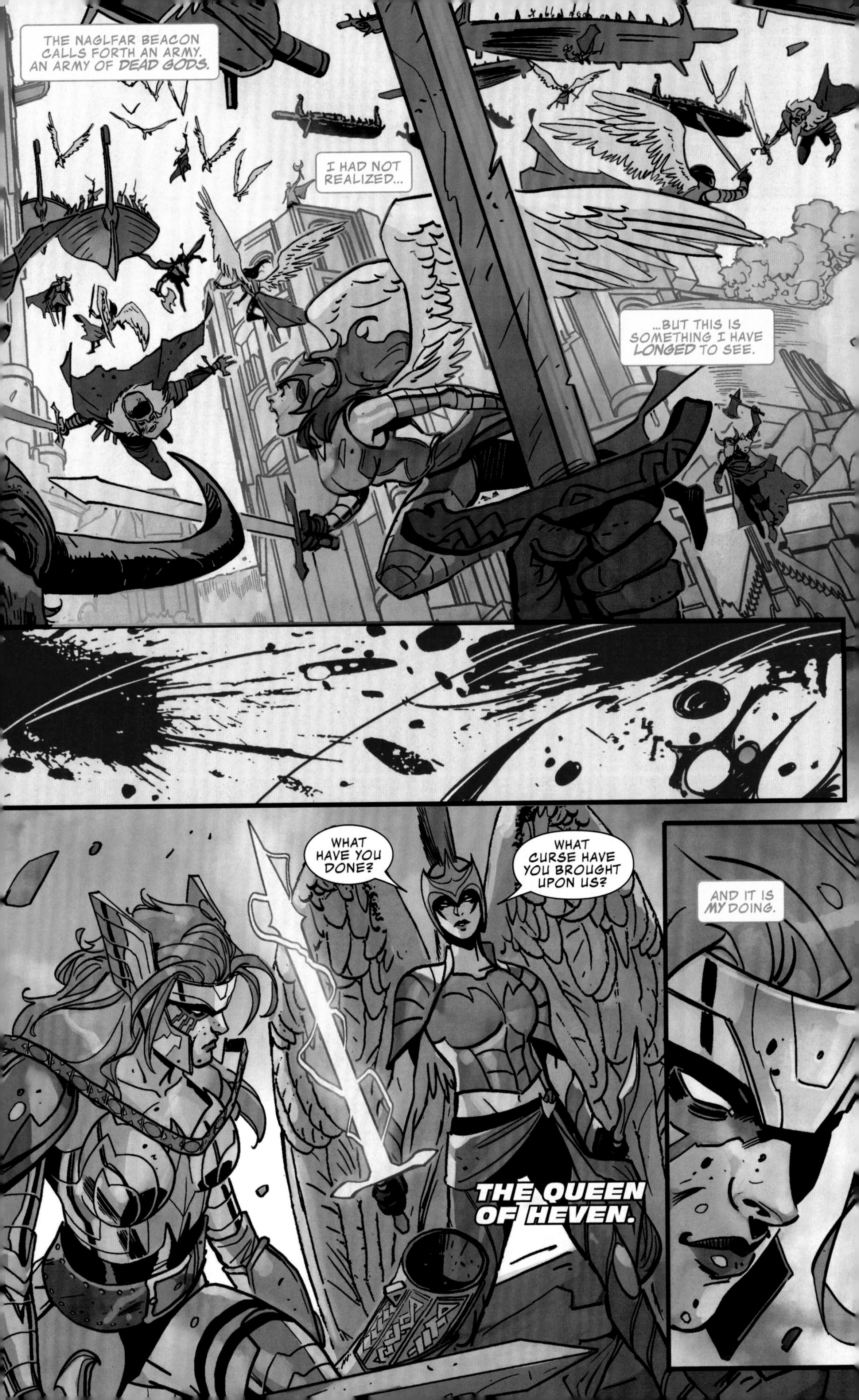

THE NAGLFAR BEACON CALLS FORTH AN ARMY. AN ARMY OF DEAD GODS.
I HAD NOT REALIZED...
...BUT THIS IS SOMETHING I HAVE LONGED TO SEE.
WHAT HAVE YOU DONE?
WHAT CURSE HAVE YOU BROUGHT UPON US?
AND IT IS MY DOING.
THE QUEEN OF HEVEN.

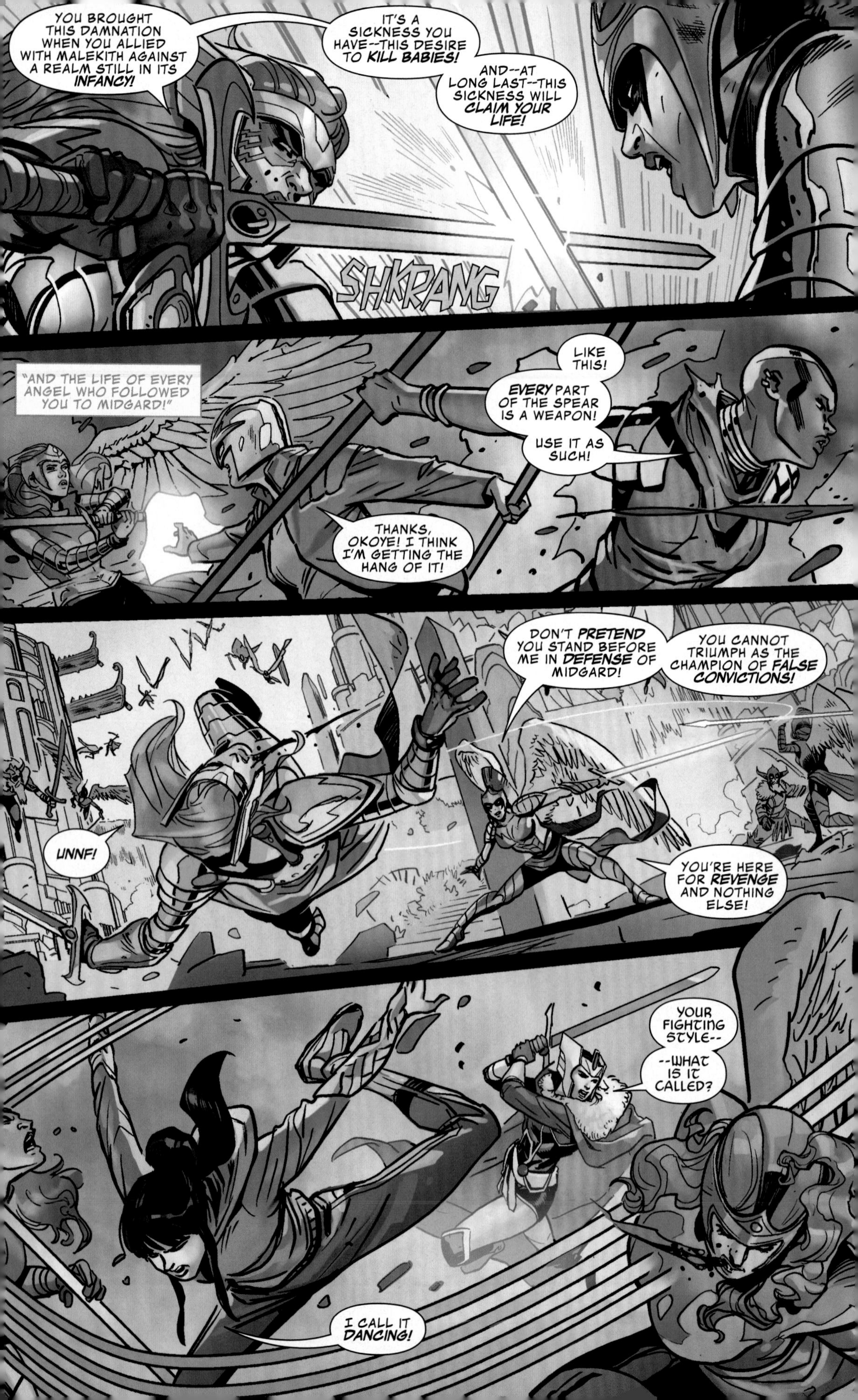
YOU BROUGHT THIS DAMNATION WHEN YOU ALLIED WITH MALEKITH AGAINST A REALM STILL IN ITS INFANCY!
IT'S A SICKNESS YOU HAVE--THIS DESIRE TO KILL BABIES!
AND--AT LONG LAST--THIS SICKNESS WILL CLAIM YOUR LIFE!
SHKRANG
"AND THE LIFE OF EVERY ANGEL WHO FOLLOWED YOU TO MIDGARD!"
LIKE THIS!
EVERY PART OF THE SPEAR IS A WEAPON!
USE IT AS SUCH!
THANKS, OKOYE! I THINK I'M GETTING THE HANG OF IT!
DON'T PRETEND YOU STAND BEFORE ME IN DEFENSE OF MIDGARD!
YOU CANNOT TRIUMPH AS THE CHAMPION OF FALSE CONVICTIONS!
UNNF!
YOU'RE HERE FOR REVENGE AND NOTHING ELSE!
YOUR FIGHTING STYLE--
--WHAT IS IT CALLED?
I CALL IT DANCING!

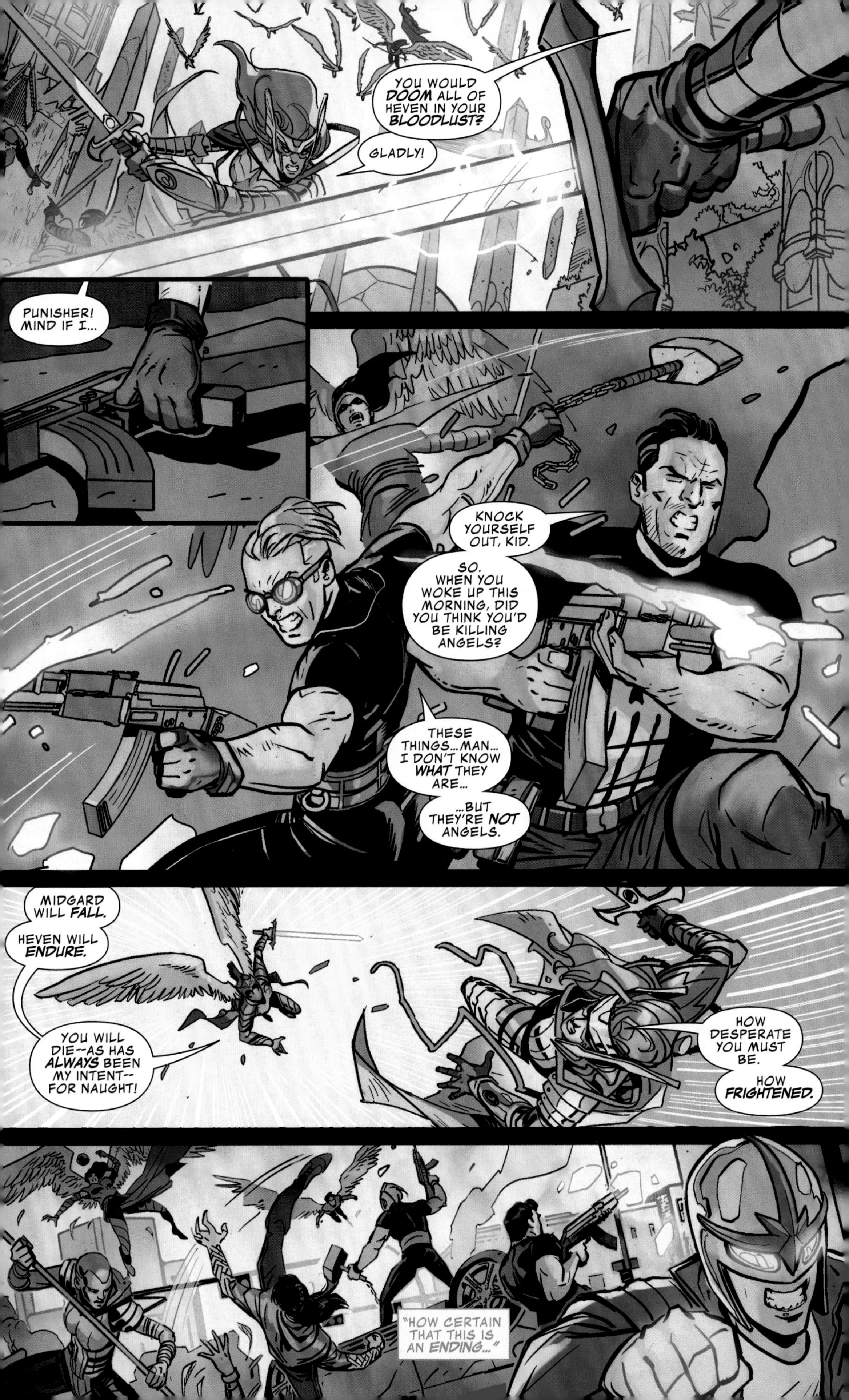
YOU WOULD DOOM ALL OF HEVEN IN YOUR BLOODLUST?
GLADLY!
PUNISHER! MIND IF I...
KNOCK YOURSELF OUT, KID.
SO. WHEN YOU WOKE UP THIS MORNING, DID YOU THINK YOU'D BE KILLING ANGELS?
THESE THINGS...MAN... I DON'T KNOW WHAT THEY ARE...
...BUT THEY'RE NOT ANGELS.
MIDGARD WILL FALL.
HEVEN WILL ENDURE.
YOU WILL DIE--AS HAS ALWAYS BEEN MY INTENT--FOR NAUGHT!
HOW DESPERATE YOU MUST BE.
HOW FRIGHTENED.
"HOW CERTAIN THAT THIS IS AN ENDING..."

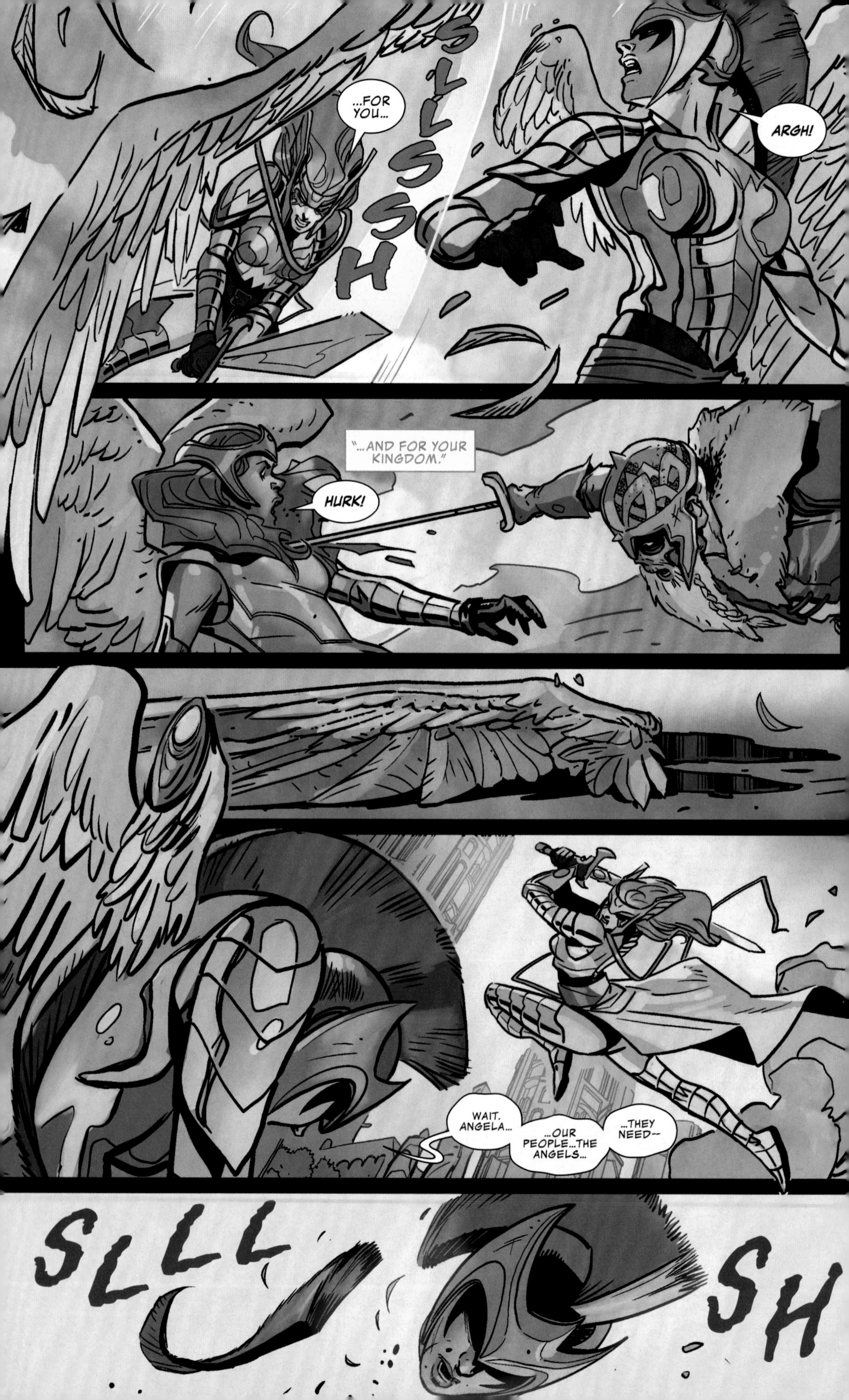
...FOR YOU...
SLLSSH
ARGH!
"...AND FOR YOUR KINGDOM."
HURK!
WAIT. ANGELA...
...OUR PEOPLE...THE ANGELS...
...THEY NEED--
SLLLSH

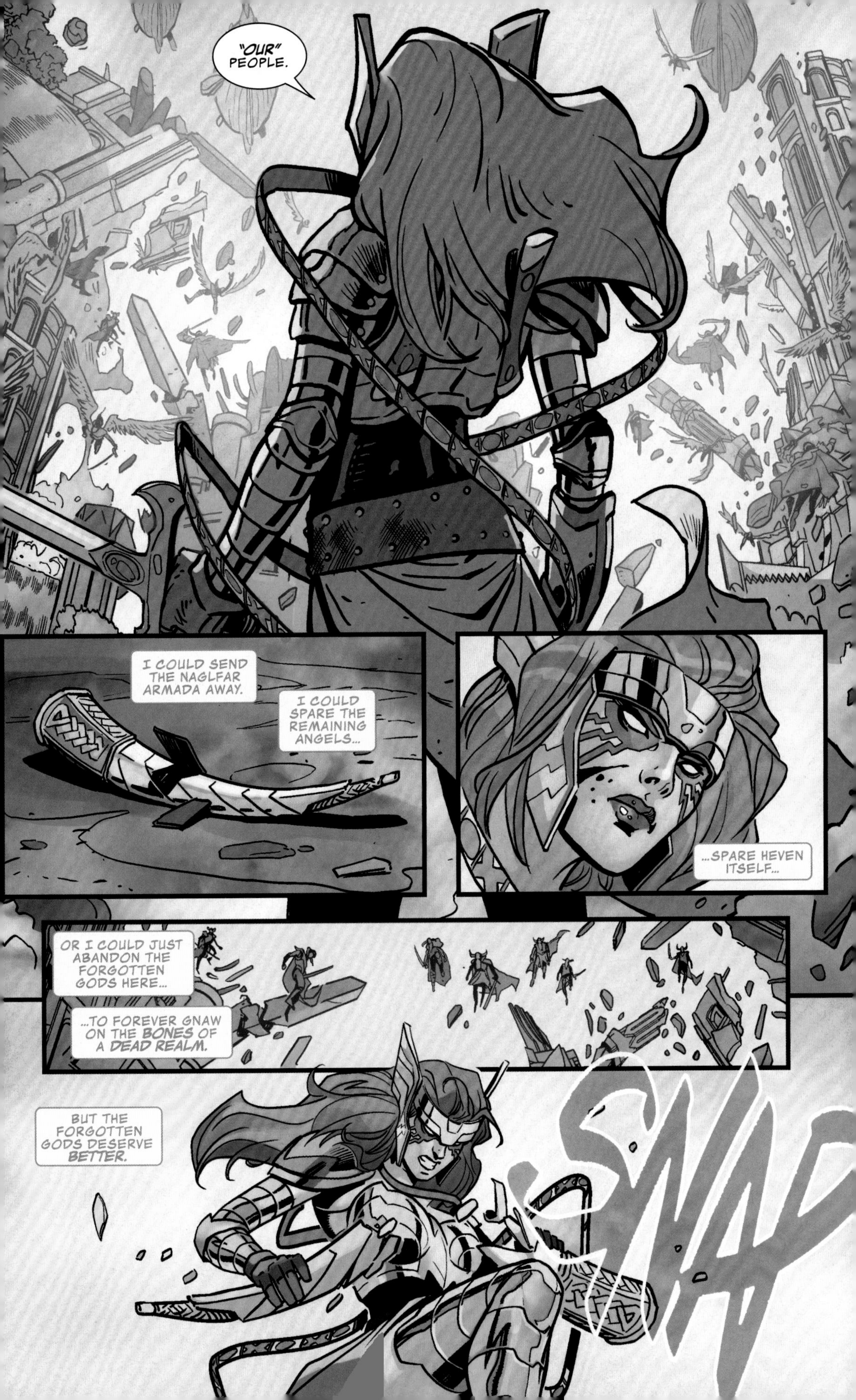
"OUR" PEOPLE.
I COULD SEND THE NAGLFAR ARMADA AWAY.
I COULD SPARE THE REMAINING ANGELS...
...SPARE HEVEN ITSELF...
OR I COULD JUST ABANDON THE FORGOTTEN GODS HERE...
...TO FOREVER GNAW ON THE BONES OF A DEAD REALM.
BUT THE FORGOTTEN GODS DESERVE BETTER.

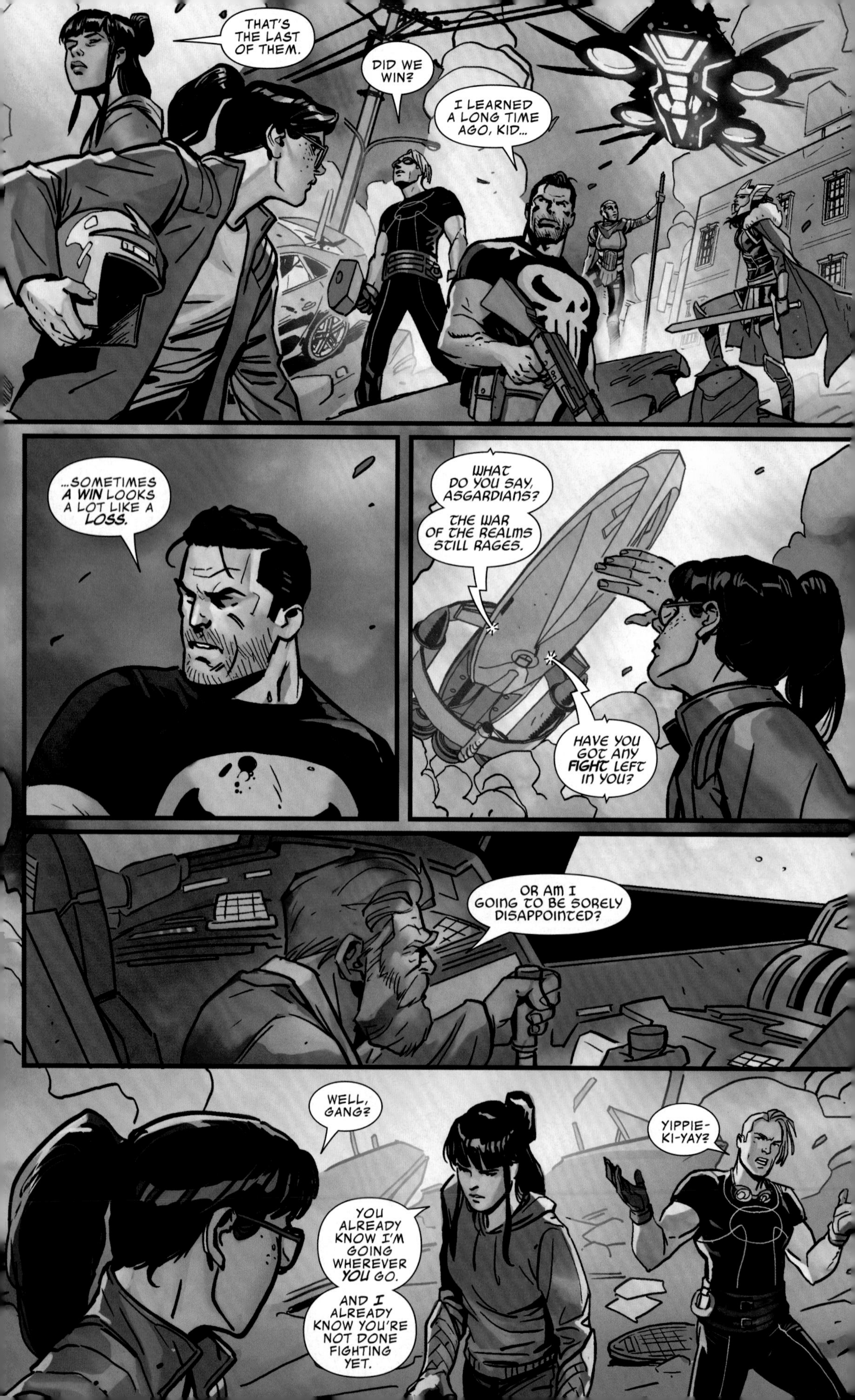
THAT'S THE LAST OF THEM.
DID WE WIN?
I LEARNED A LONG TIME AGO, KID...
...SOMETIMES A WIN LOOKS A LOT LIKE A LOSS.
WHAT DO YOU SAY, ASGARDIANS?
THE WAR OF THE REALMS STILL RAGES.
HAVE YOU GOT ANY FIGHT LEFT IN YOU?
OR AM I GOING TO BE SORELY DISAPPOINTED?
WELL, GANG?
YIPPIE-KI-YAY?
YOU ALREADY KNOW I'M GOING WHEREVER YOU GO.
AND I ALREADY KNOW YOU'RE NOT DONE FIGHTING YET.

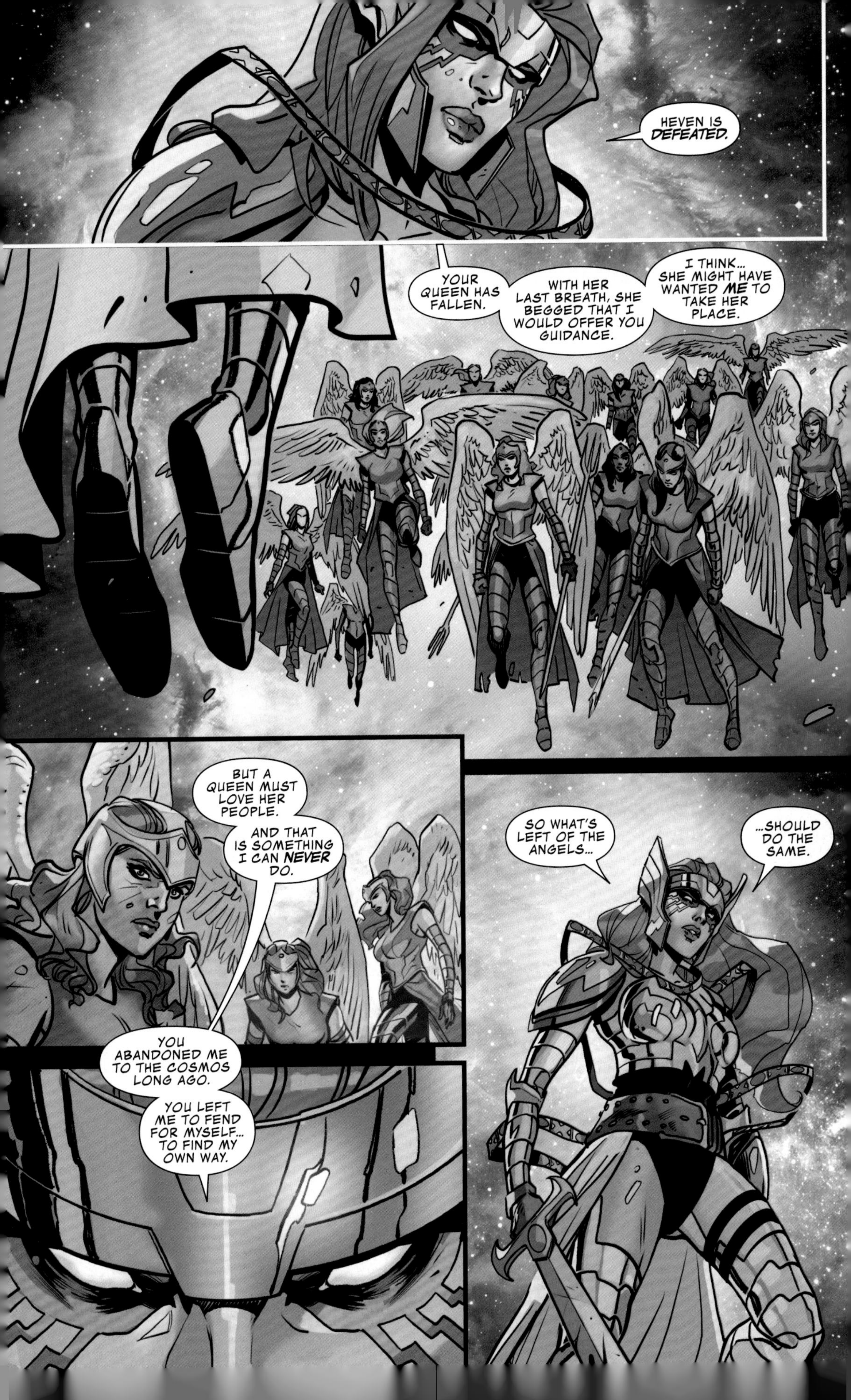
HEVEN IS DEFEATED.
YOUR QUEEN HAS FALLEN.
WITH HER LAST BREATH, SHE BEGGED THAT I WOULD OFFER YOU GUIDANCE.
I THINK... SHE MIGHT HAVE WANTED ME TO TAKE HER PLACE.
BUT A QUEEN MUST LOVE HER PEOPLE.
AND THAT IS SOMETHING I CAN NEVER DO.
YOU ABANDONED ME TO THE COSMOS LONG AGO.
YOU LEFT ME TO FEND FOR MYSELF... TO FIND MY OWN WAY.
SO WHAT'S LEFT OF THE ANGELS...
...SHOULD DO THE SAME.

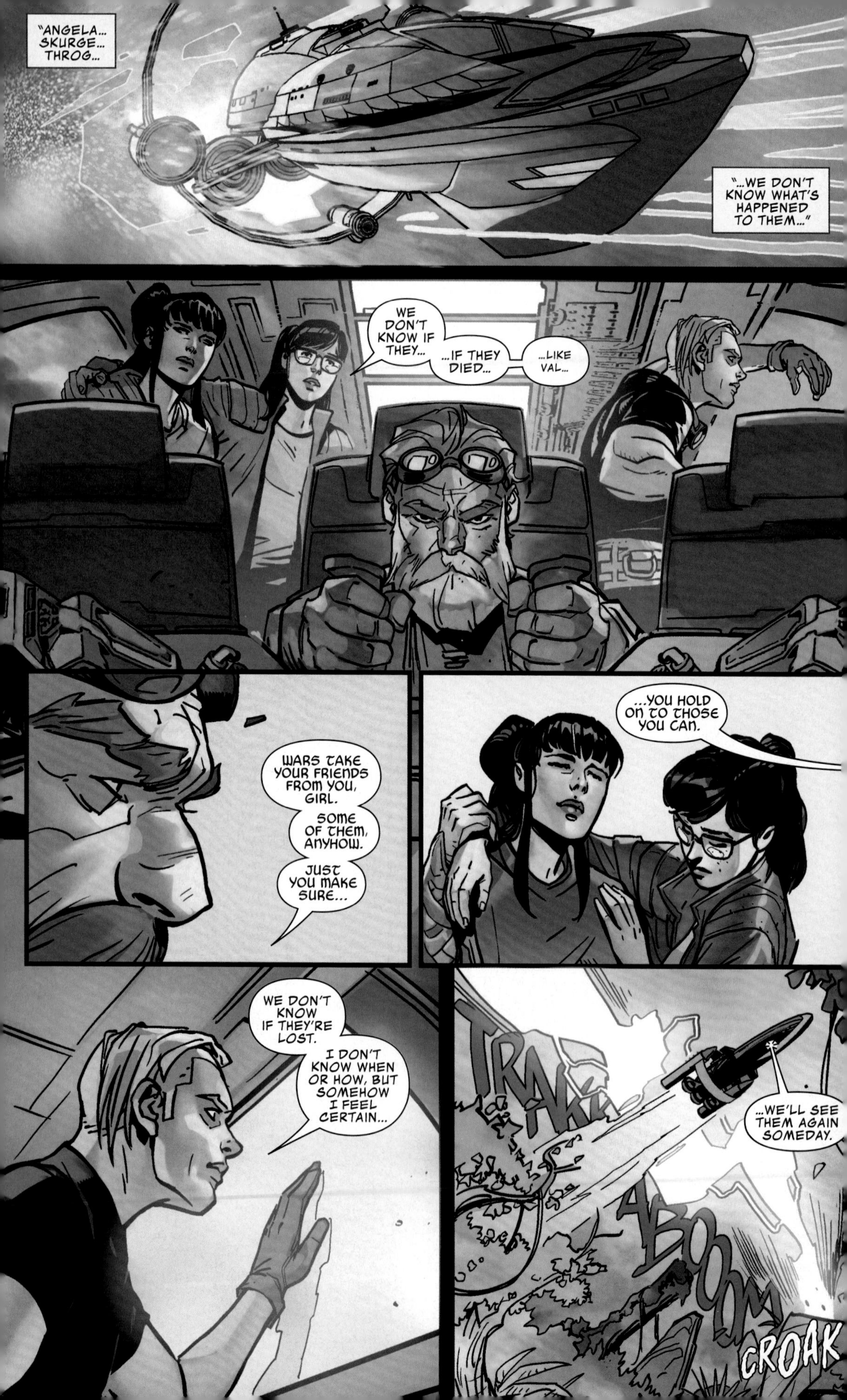
"ANGELA... SKURGE... THROG...
"...WE DON'T KNOW WHAT'S HAPPENED TO THEM..."
WE DON'T KNOW IF THEY...
...IF THEY DIED...
...LIKE VAL...
WARS TAKE YOUR FRIENDS FROM YOU, GIRL.
SOME OF THEM, ANYHOW.
JUST YOU MAKE SURE...
...YOU HOLD ON TO THOSE YOU CAN.
WE DON'T KNOW IF THEY'RE LOST.
I DON'T KNOW WHEN OR HOW, BUT SOMEHOW I FEEL CERTAIN...
...WE'LL SEE THEM AGAIN SOMEDAY.
KABOOM
CROAK

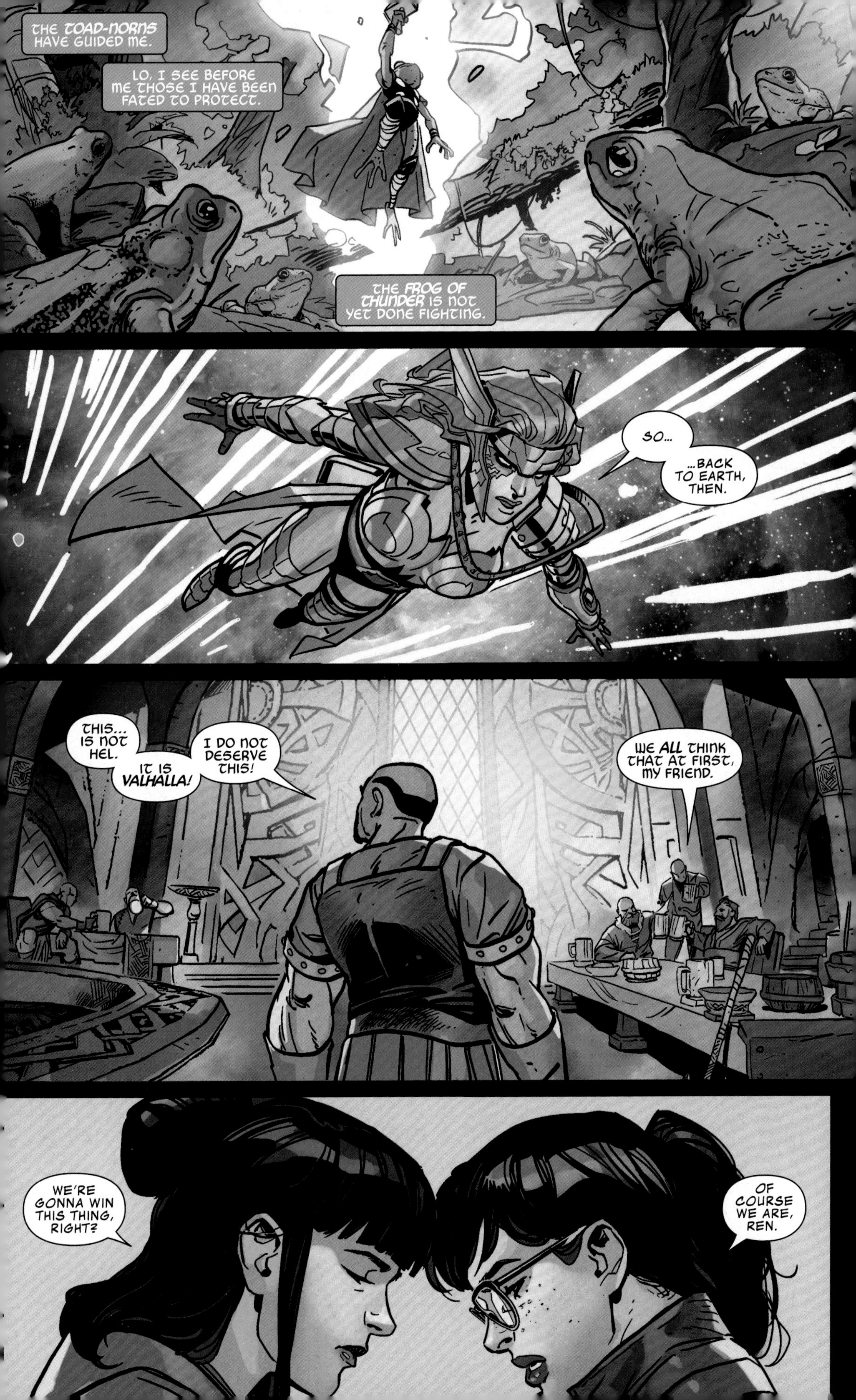
THE TOAD-NORNS HAVE GUIDED ME.
LO, I SEE BEFORE ME THOSE I HAVE BEEN FATED TO PROTECT.
THE FROG OF THUNDER IS NOT YET DONE FIGHTING.
SO...
...BACK TO EARTH, THEN.
THIS... IS NOT HEL.
IT IS VALHALLA!
I DO NOT DESERVE THIS!
WE ALL THINK THAT AT FIRST, MY FRIEND.
WE'RE GONNA WIN THIS THING, RIGHT?
OF COURSE WE ARE, REN.

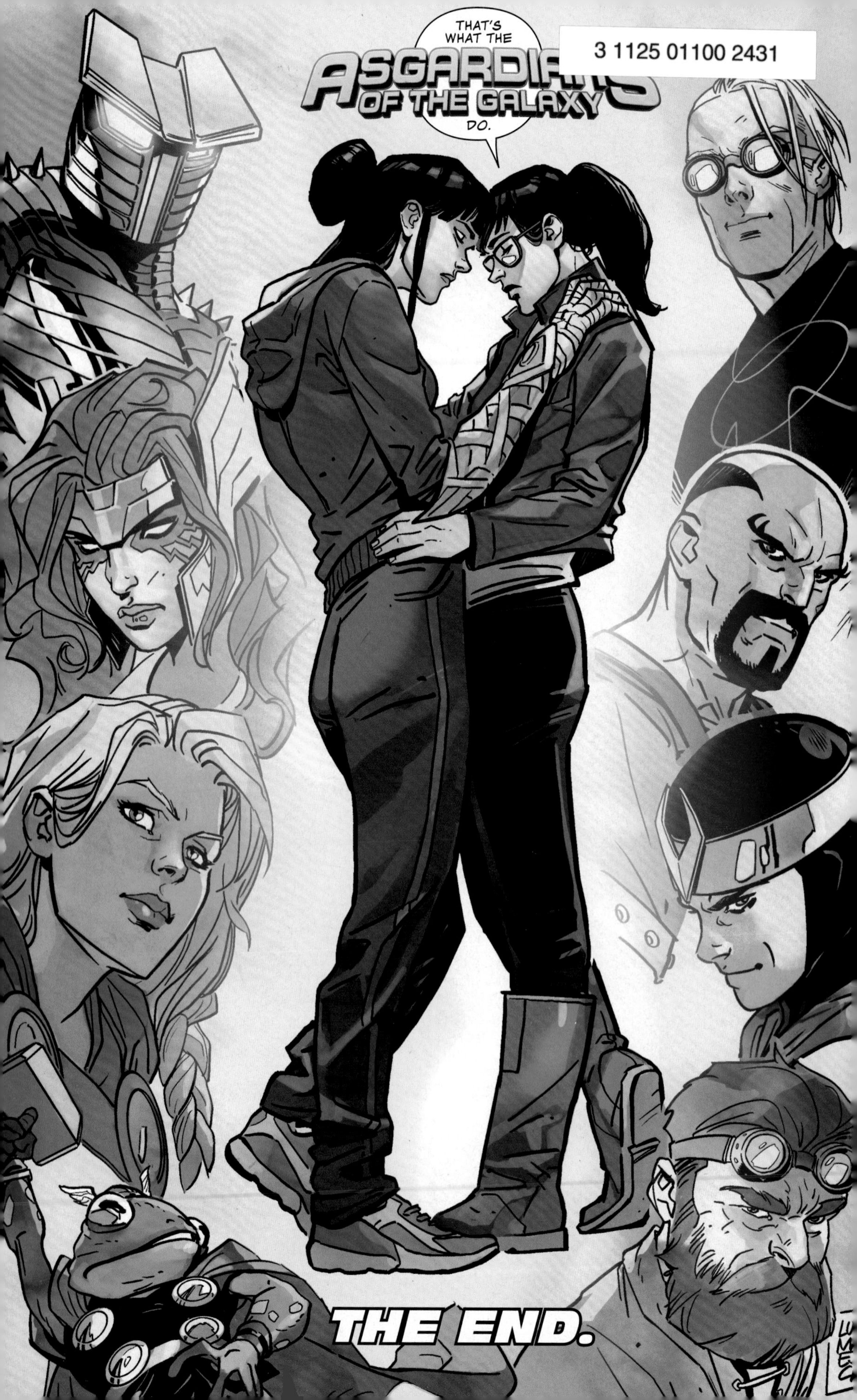
THAT'S WHAT THE
ASGARDIANS OF THE GALAXY
DO.
THE END.